In Search of Gender Justice

Ideas about gender and human rights have exerted considerable influence over African policymakers and civil society organisations in recent years, and Malawi is no exception. There, concerted efforts at civic education have made the concepts of human and women's rights widely accessible to the rural poor, albeit in modified form. In this book, Jessica Johnson listens to the voices of ordinary Malawian citizens as they strive to resolve disputes and achieve successful gender and marital relations. Through nuanced ethnographic descriptions of aspirations for gender and marital relationships, extended analysis of dispute resolution processes, and an examination of the ways in which the approaches of chiefs, police officers, and magistrates intersect, this study puts relationships between law, custom, rights, and justice under the spotlight.

JESSICA JOHNSON is a lecturer in the Department of African Studies and Anthropology at the University of Birmingham. Her research has been published in the journals *Africa*, *Journal of the Royal Anthropological Institute*, and *Review of African Political Economy*. She is an editor of the Journal of Southern African Studies, and co-editor of Pursuing Justice in Africa: competing imaginaries and contested practices with George Karekwaivanane (Ohio University Press, 2018).

THE INTERNATIONAL AFRICAN LIBRARY

General Editors

LESLIE BANK, *Human Sciences Research Council, South Africa*
HARRI ENGLUND, *University of Cambridge*
ADELINE MASQUELIER, *Tulane University, Louisiana*
BENJAMIN SOARES, *University of Florida, Gainesville*

The International African Library is a major monograph series from the International African Institute. Theoretically informed ethnographies, and studies of social relations 'on the ground' which are sensitive to local cultural forms, have long been central to the Institute's publications programme. The IAL maintains this strength and extends it into new areas of contemporary concern, both practical and intellectual. It includes works focused on the linkages between local, national and global levels of society; writings on political economy and power; studies at the interface of the socio-cultural and the environmental; analyses of the roles of religion, cosmology, and ritual in social organisation; and historical studies, especially those of a social, cultural or interdisciplinary character.

For a list of titles published in the series, please see the end of the book.

In Search of Gender Justice

Rights and Relationships in Matrilineal Malawi

Jessica Johnson

University of Birmingham

International African Institute, London

and

CAMBRIDGE
UNIVERSITY PRESS

CAMBRIDGE
UNIVERSITY PRESS

University Printing House, Cambridge CB2 8BS, United Kingdom

One Liberty Plaza, 20th Floor, New York, NY 10006, USA

477 Williamstown Road, Port Melbourne, VIC 3207, Australia

314–321, 3rd Floor, Plot 3, Splendor Forum, Jasola District Centre,
New Delhi – 110025, India

79 Anson Road, #06–04/06, Singapore 079906

Cambridge University Press is part of the University of Cambridge.

It furthers the University's mission by disseminating knowledge in the pursuit of
education, learning, and research at the highest international levels of excellence.

www.cambridge.org
Information on this title: www.cambridge.org/9781108473705
DOI: 10.1017/9781108563031

First published 2018

Printed and bound in Great Britain by Clays Ltd, Elcograf S.p.A.

A catalogue record for this publication is available from the British Library.

Library of Congress Cataloging-in-Publication Data
Names: Johnson, Jessica, 1984-, author.
Title: In search of gender justice : rights and relationships in matrilineal Malawi /
    Jessica Johnson, University of Birmingham.
Description: New York : Cambridge University Press, 2018. |
    Includes bibliographical references and index.
Identifiers: LCCN 2018021299 | ISBN 9781108473705 (hardback : alk. paper)
    | ISBN 9781108462471 (pbk. : alk. paper)
Subjects: LCSH: Sex discrimination against women–Law and
    legislation–Malawi. | Equality before the law–Malawi. |
    Matriarchy–Malawi. | Women's rights–Malawi.
Classification: LCC KSS210.8 .J64 2018 | DDC 342.689708/78–dc23
    LC record available at https://lccn.loc.gov/2018021299

ISBN 978-1-108-47370-5 Hardback

For my two Janes

Contents

Figures

Maps

Tables

Acknowledgements

Ndingathokoze bwanji anthu onse amene anandilandira kuMalawiko? Poyambirira, Tiffany Banda eased me into the language and culture of Malawi, opening up her home to me in the year before I began fieldwork and offering expert Chichewa tuition. It was through Tiffany that I met Lynda and Talumba Chilinkhwambe, who went out of their way to welcome me upon my arrival in Malawi. *Zikomo kwambiri!*

During fieldwork, I was affiliated to the Centre for Social Research at the University of Malawi, where Annie Sigere and Alistair Munthali provided crucial advice and administrative support. I also enjoyed many hours of Chichewa tuition with Mario Thodi at the Centre for Language Studies. My thanks also to the History Department for allowing me to live in the Mulunguzi house while I found my feet. At the house, Andrew was invaluable company and I thank him for all that he did to make my stay comfortable and secure. Ngeyi Kanyongolo was instrumental in helping me secure my retreat from the comforts of Zomba to village life in Chiradzulu. She acted instinctively, helping a foreign researcher simply because she could. I suspect she did not realise how much she was doing for me, or how grateful I was. I could never thank her enough for facilitating my transition, all the more so because the village she helped me locate became such a happy home.

Soon after my arrival in the village, my thinly disguised favouritism towards a four-year-old boy living in the same compound was quickly recognised and he became known as my 'husband'. Through him, I acquired ramifying relationships of affinity with a great many of my fellow villagers; it is to my many *alamu* and *apongozi* that I owe the largest debt of gratitude. I also thank all the villagers who welcomed me into their homes and compounds, their committees, meetings, celebrations, and conversations. In addition, I am profoundly grateful to the local traditional authorities who gave their consent to my unusual project and offered their protection. My thanks also to the *alangizi* (initiators), NGO workers, the sheikh, police officers, magistrates, and court staff who were similarly accommodating as they carried out their important work. Sadly, I cannot name them here, but I hope that my commitment to these ongoing relationships expresses at least some of my immense appreciation. My closest companion in my village home knows who she is. More than anyone else, she made my life and research in Malawi possible.

This book would have been much improved by the contributions of two women who tragically passed away during my fieldwork. The first had become a valued friend, the second died before I had the opportunity to get to know her as well as I would have liked. I hope that my presentation of their work in the initiation camps and magistrates' courts of rural Chiradzulu does some justice to their memory.

In the end, my efforts to work with a research assistant were not successful, but I am extremely grateful to Diana for persevering with me, and I hope that I will have the chance to thank her again in person.

Harri Englund helped nurture this project from its earliest inception. An inspirational teacher, writer, and researcher, I am sure that I will always be guided by the example he has set. Perveez Mody and Deborah James also provided valuable feedback. I am grateful to Marilyn Strathern, who was a tremendous faculty adviser, generous with her time and her comments on my work. Barbara Bodenhorn first introduced me to social anthropology as an undergraduate student, and if it weren't for her personal warmth and guidance, it is highly unlikely that I would have followed this path. Pauline Peters listened to my excited and rambling early accounts of my field experience and encouraged me to think anthropologically, while Megan Vaughan reminded me of the importance of history. George Karekwaivanane shared my interest in justice in Africa, and our collaboration has doubtless strengthened my research. I cannot thank Dorothy Hodgson enough for her hospitality and her attentive engagement with my work during a three-month research visit to Rutgers University in late 2011. My thanks also go to my hosts at the Institute for Research on Women and the members of their weekly seminar group. Faculty, staff, and students in the Rutgers Anthropology Department also made me feel welcome on campus, for which I am grateful. I imagine that all those mentioned here would want to push me further than I have so far managed to go; I can only hope that our conversations will extend into the future.

A number of lasting friendships blossomed in the Cambridge anthropology basement as this project was taking shape. In particular, the camaraderie of Ela Drazkiewicz, Jialing Luo, Chloe Nahum-Claudel, and Alice Wilson was much appreciated. Above ground, participants in the writing-up seminar offered constructive and provocative feedback on drafts of several chapters, and the friendship of Liana Chua Zoë Groves, Chris Kaplonski, Nayanika Mathur, and Anthony Pickles kept me going through my postdoctoral research and beyond. This book would not have come to fruition without the support of Ron, who has long awaited the sound of it dropping through his letterbox.

Since leaving Cambridge I have had the good fortune of joining a community of Africanists in Birmingham who have engaged thoughtfully with my work. My thanks to Karin Barber, Maxim Bolt, Reginald Cline-Cole, Juliet Gilbert, Rebecca Jones, Insa Nolte, Benedetta Rossi, Keith Shear, and Kate Skinner.

For financial support, I gratefully acknowledge the Economic and Social Research Council; Pembroke College, Cambridge; the Cambridge Department of Social Anthropology; the Gibbs Travelling Research Fund at Newnham College, Cambridge; and the William Wyse Fund at Trinity College, Cambridge.

Sections of Chapter 1 appear in an article published by *Journal of the Royal Anthropological Institute* (Johnson 2018). Earlier versions of Chapter 3 and Chapter 6 appear in *Personal Autonomy in Plural Societies: a principle and its paradoxes* (Johnson 2018), and the journal *Africa* (Johnson 2012), respectively.

Throughout this project, I have relied on my family for all kinds of material and immaterial support. My thanks to Len and Tina Miller for opening up their homes to me and providing a refuge in South Africa. Their care and concern were much appreciated, as was their patience in listening to my unstoppable tales of Malawi. I am also grateful to Amanda Schoua, who saw me at my worst, hobbled by mysterious bacteria and poor company for my worried aunt and mother who were supposed to be on holiday. Sheelah Wilson was gloriously unconcerned by the practicalities of this project; her instinctive pride and steadfast love have been the greatest gifts. My mother, Jane, and late father, Bill, were ever supportive. Their unconditional love is a constant source of inspiration. As this project comes to an end, I am entering a future quite different from anything I could have imagined when I first set out for Malawi. To Tom, and to our future, with love.

Glossary of Chichewa terms

akamwini	in-marrying husbands (singular: *mkamwini*)
alamu	brothers-/sisters-in-law (singular: *mlamu*)
Amayi angathe	women are able (women's radio listening group)
ambuye	grandmother or senior maternal uncle
amfumu	chiefs (singular: *mfumu*)
amuna	men, husbands (singular: *mwamuna*)
ankhoswe	marriage guardians, advocates (singular: *nkhoswe*)
apongozi	mothers-/fathers-/sons-/daughters-in-law (singular: *mpongozi*)
banja	marriage, family, household (plural: *mabanja*)
boma	government, district, administrative centre of a district
bwalo	chief's court, village meeting place
chibwenzi	boy-/girlfriend, sexual partner (plural: *zibwenzi*)
chikamwini	uxorilocal marriage, bride-service
chikhalidwe	culture, behaviour
chikondi	love
chilungamo	justice, truth, righteousness
chinamwali	initiation rites
chinkhoswe	customary marriage formalities and ceremony during which *ankhoswe* are appointed, sometimes translated as 'engagement ceremony'
chitukuko	development
ganyu	piecework
jenda	gender
kachasu	locally distilled spirit
kufunsira	to propose
kukonda	to love
kutsala	to leave behind

kutsalidwa	to be left behind
kuyang'anitsa	to be vigilant
kwawo	his/her/their home
mabanja	marriages, families, households (singular: *banja*)
maufulu	rights, freedoms (singular: *ufulu*)
mbeta	unmarried woman
mbumba	minimal matrilineage, matrilineal extended family
mfumu	chief (plural: *amfumu*)
mfundo	clan name, inherited from one's father
mitala	polygamy
miyambo	customs, traditions, rites (singular: *mwambo*)
mkamwini	in-marrying husband (plural: *akamwini*)
mlamu	brother-/sister-in-law (plural: *alamu*)
mpongozi	mother-/father-/son-/daughter-in-law (plural: *apongozi*)
mtendere	peace, harmony, freedom
mtundu	tribe, kind, type
mwambo	custom, tradition, rite (plural: *miyambo*)
mwamuna	man, husband (plural: *amuna*)
mwini	owner
ndiwo	relish, accompaniment to *nsima*
ndondomeko	programme, procedure, structure, plan
nkhanza	cruelty, violence, commonly used to refer to gender-based violence
nkhokwe	granary for the storage of dried maize
nkhoswe	marriage guardian, advocate (plural: *ankhoswe*)
nsima	staple food, a stiff porridge made from maize flour
ubale	kinship
udindo	responsibility
ufulu	right, freedom (plural: *maufulu*)
ufulu wachibadwidwe	human rights (the freedom one is born with)
ufumu	chieftaincy
ukwati	marriage, wedding
ulemu	respect
unkhoswe	the institution of *chinkhoswe*, including the assignment of *ankhoswe* (marriage guardians)
zibwenzi	boy-/girlfriends, sexual partners (singular: *chibwenzi*)

Abbreviations and acronyms

AIDS	acquired immune deficiency syndrome
ARV	antiretroviral (medication)
CBO	community-based organisation
CPSB	Community Policing Services Branch
CVSU	community victim support unit
DFID	Department for International Development (UK)
FGM	first-grade magistrate
GVH	group village head
HIV	human immunodeficiency virus
NGO	non-governmental organisation
SGM	second-grade magistrate
Sub-T/A	Sub-Traditional Authority
T/A	Traditional Authority
TGM	third-grade magistrate
UK	United Kingdom
UNICEF	United Nations Children's Fund
VH	village head
VSU	victim support unit
WLSA	Women and Law in Southern Africa

Introduction

> My husband was a drinker and he would disappear on his days off. He would go to the market and buy meat for me to cook, and then he would just disappear for hours and hours, even days. When I questioned him, he would become violent and we had huge fights. I didn't know then that that was *nkhanza* [cruelty, gender violence]; we didn't know about *ufulu* [rights, freedom] then.

These were the words of a woman in Chiradzulu District, spoken on the veranda of my rented village home as we relaxed one cool evening in 2009. As Anachisale reflected on her marriage to her late husband, she was struck by how much had changed in Malawi since the coming of 'democracy' (*demokalase*).[1] Growing up during the dictatorship of Dr Hastings Kamuzu Banda (1964–94), she had experienced the violent excesses of earlier decades, both within and beyond the household, and she compared the contemporary period favourably with those years. These days, she said, women have rights, and there are non-governmental organisations (NGOs) and institutions such as police victim support units that have been set up to educate and protect Malawian citizens. On this occasion, Anachisale's urge to stress the degree to which the country had changed meant that she underplayed her personal scepticism towards formal authorities and NGOs, a scepticism that she would reveal in other conversations and muttered remarks. Welcome as the political transition of 1993–4 had been, she and her fellow villagers were by no means uncritical of the new dispensation and the proliferation of human rights talk and projects it had brought in its wake. As I was to learn over the course of my fieldwork, the fact that rights could be both cherished and ridiculed by the same individuals is revealing not only of deep-seated ambivalence about the ability of wealthy politicians and professional rights advocates to live up to their lofty promises, but also of the potential polysemy of rights themselves.

Indeed, ideas about human and women's rights have had a profound impact in Malawi in recent years, as they have in much of the Global

---

[1] Unless otherwise stated, all informants' names are pseudonyms.

South. Their influence on policymakers and civil society has been considerable, and concerted efforts at civic education have made the discourses and concepts of rights widely accessible, albeit in modified form, to the rural poor. An examination of the effects of these international notions of justice lies at the heart of this book, and my analysis lays bare the tensions between powerful global formulations and alternative understandings of justice that are at once part of a longer historical tradition of justice in Malawi and responsive to new ideas. Drawing on field research conducted between January 2009 and September 2010, as well as subsequent visits in September 2013 and April–October 2015, this book challenges the universality of a model of gender justice that is rooted in the logic of equality as sameness, arguing for greater sensitivity to local concepts and for openness to the possibility that liberal tenets, so deeply naturalised in Euro-American understandings of the world, provide shaky foundations for global comparison.

This is a study of gender justice in postcolonial Africa. But the pages of this book do not recount events in the High Court or the work of professional legal practitioners. Instead, the focus is on the institutions of law that were accessible to ordinary Malawian citizens in Chiradzulu District as they pursued gendered disputes, and the forms of justice administered and aspired to in these settings (see Maps 1 and 2). Much of my research was carried out in two rural magistrates' courts, in a police victim support unit, and at the chiefs' court (*bwalo*) in the village in which I resided. These forums were interconnected, and disputants often consulted them sequentially, carrying referral letters from one to another and sometimes back again (see Chapter 2). I observed case hearings in each of these venues, particularly of marital disputes, and I came to focus on their form and texture in order to understand what 'gender justice' might look like in Malawi. My argument hinges on the importance of the broader matrilineal context for the forms of justice that men and women sought when they turned to family members, traditional authorities, police officers, and magistrates for assistance.

What follows is thus not simply a study of legal arenas and dispute hearings; it is also a study of gender and marital relations more broadly, building on rural ethnography that offers an insight into the ebb and flow of daily life, quotidian obligations, and aspirations for just relationships. The point is not to provide a backdrop of 'healthy' sociality against which 'pathological' disputes might be better understood, but rather to demonstrate the mundanity of gendered contestation. It is by understanding gender relations as they are lived and contested in the course of routine exchanges that a sense of what justice might look like for men and women in matrilineal Malawi can be developed. For this reason, the following sections of this Introduction, and Chapter 1, focus on marriage and

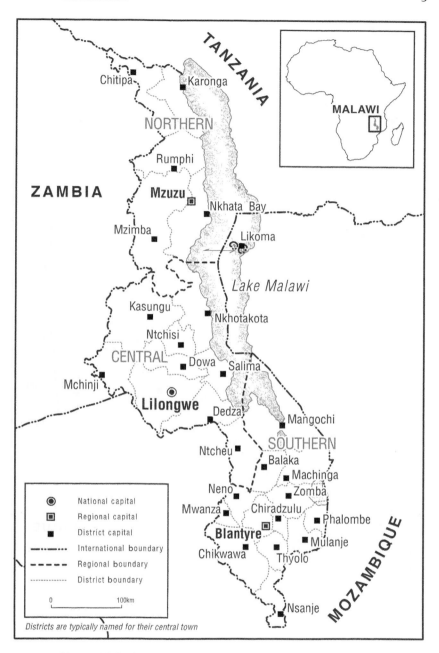

Map 1 Malawi

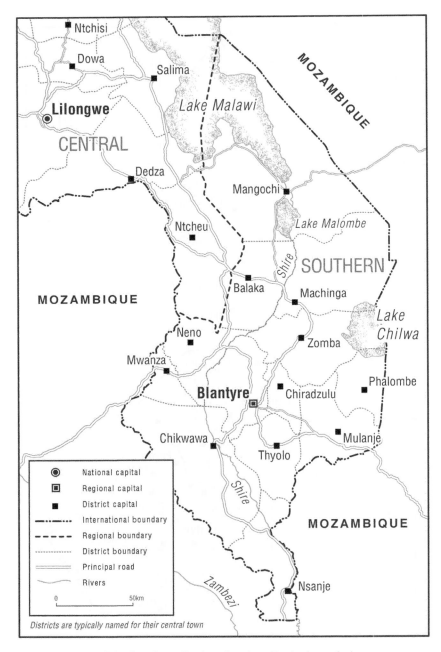

Map 2 The Southern Region showing district boundaries

matriliny beyond the legal forums on which the subsequent chapters concentrate, while Chapter 6 introduces a dispute between cross-sex siblings in the matrilineal context. I seek to convey the contours of matrilineal norms and practices, their historical contingency, and the ways in which they have been (mis)understood by anthropologists and other observers since the late nineteenth century. While matriliny might have a certain appeal for feminist analysts, my ethnographic argument, which posits that the kind of gender justice sought in the disputes I studied was rooted in a desire for 'complementarity', challenges the liberal feminist emphasis on the fundamental equality (or sameness) of men and women. Later in this Introduction, and again in the Conclusion, I address the tension between liberal feminism, with its emphasis on autonomy and equality, and ethnographic findings that equate justice with interdependence. Crucially, interdependence and complementarity are not a gloss for female subordination or a justification for gender-based violence. They do, however, entail making space in feminist analysis, and feminist politics, for difference.

Southern Malawi: matriliny and gender relations

In contrast with much of northern Malawi and the country's southern tip, Chiradzulu lies within what has been called South-Central Africa's 'matrilineal belt', which extends across northern Zambia, central and southern Malawi, and northern Mozambique. Historically and into the present day, social life in this part of the country has been profoundly shaped by uxorilocal marriage and matrilineal norms of descent and inheritance. The area, like much of the country, is also rural and residents are highly reliant on subsistence agriculture. In this context, conjugal households, consisting of a woman and her husband and children, maintain a significant degree of autonomy, despite their location within clusters of houses (compounds) belonging to groups of categorical sisters and their descendants. Each adult woman has her own granary (*nkhokwe*) in which she stores the maize produced in the fields allocated to her by her mother, and she has exclusive control over its disposal. Men and women (and children) work together in the fields, although women tend to provide the bulk of the labour, with men most involved during planting and harvesting. Megan Vaughan has written about how this seeming independence at the level of the household is often underpinned by a considerable degree of inter-household sharing and exchange among matrilineal kin (1987: 135–6). However, she argues that 'never in the accessible past had villages, let alone households, provided all their needs from their own labour on their own plots of land' (1987: 60), thus signalling the long history behind the current practice of supplementing agricultural production with cash income generated through male-dominated formal employment, men's and women's agricultural piecework (*ganyu*) and small-scale trading, and women's beer (*mowa*) and liquor (*kachasu*) brewing activities.

My analysis of marriage in rural Malawi suggests a contrast with a dominant strand in the regional literature, which posits a significant decline in the institution in recent decades (see, e.g., Griffiths 1997; Gulbrandsen 1986; Hunter 2010). I argue that marriage remains an important institution in Malawi but that marital strategies shift over the life course and in response to changing personal circumstances (see Chapters 1 and 6). First marriage and associated childbearing are widely desired, but divorced or widowed mothers often seek greater independence from men at the level of the household, while remaining embedded within the networks of matrilineal kin through which they gain access to material and immaterial resources and support.

Marriage in this context is almost always 'customary' marriage, as opposed to marriage under the Marriage Act, but both forms have constitutional recognition.[2] Customary marriage is easily contracted, with little ceremony marking either its commencement or its dissolution. The principal distinguishing feature of a marital relationship (*banja*), as opposed to a 'friendship' (*chibwenzi*), is the designation of *ankhoswe* or marriage guardians (Bruwer 1955). The matrilineal kin of the bride and groom each provide recognised *ankhoswe* who are to be the couple's first port of call in the event of marital difficulties, and whose testimony will be expected if disputes move on to other forums. Uxorilocal marriage is strongly favoured, and a great onus is placed on husbands to build houses in their wives' matrilineal compounds, close to those of their mothers- and sisters-in-law. Divorce rates in matrilineal societies are notoriously high, and although remarriage is common, single life can be relatively attractive to women given that their access to land and their belonging in their mothers' villages are assured, along with that of their children. For men, access to land and the right to be fed from a woman's maize store are usually gained through marriage. In the absence of a regular wage, a comfortable life for unmarried, divorced, or widowed men largely depends on the resources and patience of their mothers and sisters.

Not unlike missionaries and colonial officials, scholars have at times been baffled by the seeming contradictions of social arrangements that deny a man his 'natural' right of control over his wife and children. In the

---

[2] This contrasts with Griffiths' (1997) finding that marriages under the Marriage Act were relatively common in Botswana. The Malawian Divorce Act does not apply to customary marriages, and couples seeking divorce are thus not required to satisfy its restricted criteria or to seek divorce through the High Court. For the most part, I do not find it necessary to employ the term 'customary' to qualify my discussion of marriage, and neither did my informants.

words of Audrey Richards, 'women court men to give them children, but they do not allow them the full rights of a sociological father or *pater*' (1982 [1956]: 159). Having brought with them the lessons of their upbringing in Euro-American milieus, early observers were accustomed to assume patriarchal authority and nuclear families. In some cases, scholars seemed to accept the ethnocentric analyses of colonialists, repeating as fact, for example, the idea that if men lived uxorilocally, gained access to land through their wives, and could not pass that land on to their own sons, 'energetic male participation in agricultural improvements was unlikely' (Vail 1984: 22). As Paul Kishindo has observed, however, 'neither the government [colonial or postcolonial] nor the scholars who condemned uxorilocal marriages provided evidence directly linking them to lack of investment in agriculture' (2010: 90).[3] The concern with male commitment to agriculture as the primary requirement for agricultural 'development' rests on the androcentric assumption that 'farmers' are male and women are merely 'farmers' wives', which is and was 'completely at odds with the reality' of life in rural Malawi (Peters 2010: 186). Similar unexamined androcentricity can be detected in accounts of the inevitability of men's desire to avoid or reverse uxorilocal marriage, and in the assumed incompatibility between matrilineal kinship organisation and capitalist endeavour (Mair 1951; Mitchell 1956; Peters 1997b; Phiri 1983; Power 1995).

While many predicted matriliny's inevitable demise under conditions of 'modernity' (see, e.g., Douglas 2001 [1969]; Gough 1961; Poewe 1981), others set about explaining its institutions in such a way as to undermine claims of 'difference' in the status of women in matrilineal societies. Against the images of 'matriarchy' that had occupied nineteenth-century writers, contributors to the influential volume *Matrilineal Kinship*, dedicated to Richards (Schneider and Gough 1961), reassured their readers that women in such societies were neither authoritative nor autonomous; they were simply subject to the control of their brothers and uncles, rather than that of their fathers and husbands. As David Schneider explained: '[T]he role of men as men is defined as having authority over women and children ... Positions of highest authority within the matrilineal descent group will, therefore, ordinarily be vested in statuses occupied by men' (1961: 6).

These writers were principally concerned with what had become known as the 'matrilineal puzzle' (Richards 1950): the question of how to reconcile the seeming dislocation, or tension, between men's

[3] Kishindo's research found that uxorilocal residence by itself had no direct bearing on male investment in land, but that the stability of a man's marriage, and hence his perception of his 'security in the village', was a factor in decisions relating to long-term investments (2010: 96–7).

roles as fathers and as maternal uncles within a system of uxorilocal marriage and matrilineal descent.[4] The puzzle resided in a perceived 'fundamental structural difference' between matrilineal and patrilineal kinship: whereas in patrilineal descent groups, 'both authority and group placement are male functions', in matrilineal descent groups, 'on the other hand, although the line of authority also runs through men, group placement runs through the line of women' (Schneider 1961: 7). E. R. Leach (1961) launched an early attack on this kind of 'butterfly collecting' anthropology in which scholars discover what their chosen system of classification allows. More recently, anthropologists have rejected the premises of the puzzle, rightly identifying the patriarchal and Eurocentric assumptions that guide its very definition (Peters 1997b). As stated by Signe Arnfred, 'Schneider's discussion, developed in detail, deals with relations between men' (2011: 228).

Indeed, recent studies question the idea that matriliny has little impact on the authority or status of women, and several anthropologists have argued that, on the contrary, matrilineal practices provide 'greater social and political space to women' (Peters 1997b: 133). Having shed the spectre of nineteenth-century evolutionism and embraced the politics of feminism, Pauline Peters suggests that, from the 1970s onwards, scholars were finally able to attest to 'greater degrees of independence, autonomy, formal authority in local politics and ritual, control of income, decisions concerning child-bearing, family relations and so forth enjoyed by women' in matrilineal settings (ibid.: 134).

A desire to understand what difference being born into matrilineal extended families (*mbumba*) makes to the lives of men and women in Chiradzulu guided my decision to foreground matriliny in this study. My response to this question is somewhat one-sided, however, reflecting a greater theoretical and methodological focus on women, necessitated in part by my own gendered identity. Nevertheless, an important strand of analysis running through this book relates to the difficulties that men face in living up to the material expectations of their wives and in-laws, and the relative precarity of their access to land. The male bias of early research notwithstanding, the situations and perspectives of men in matrilineal societies have been even less well studied than those of women. There is significant scope for future research to take up the challenge of understanding men's roles and aspirations in matrilineal societies, beyond the purview of a 'matrilineal puzzle' that assumes their position to be necessarily 'galling' (Richards 1982 [1956]: 40).

---

[4] The fact that tensions between natal and marital ties might not be exclusive to matriliny, or to men, was not given much consideration (see, e.g., James 1999a; 1999b). See Apter (2012) for a recent example of the deployment of the concept of the 'matrilineal puzzle' for analytical purposes.

The significance of matriliny as a defining feature of social life in rural southern Malawi does not entirely negate the importance of patrilineal connections. A person's *mfundo* or clan name, for example, the use of which marks respect, is inherited from his or her father. Clan names constitute an enduring connection with paternal kin, allowing people, 'at least under favourable circumstances, to claim relationships' (Englund 2002: 56) beyond the matriline. Nevertheless, Chiradzulu villagers rarely inherit land or property through patrilateral connections, and, with few exceptions, men do not inherit gardens (*minda*). Even within the relatively land-rich chiefly lineage in the area of my fieldwork, my innocent question about the possibility of the resident grandson of the eldest surviving female member of the *mbumba*, the direct descendant of her late son, inheriting land was met with incredulity: 'Why? This is not his home; his place is in Ntcheu.' Valued as a nephew and grand-son, carrying the clan name of his father, reliable, industrious, and perhaps the best educated of his generation with the potential to bring home a regular wage, Adzimbiri was welcome to live alongside his father's kin, but his real home (*kwawo*), where he truly belonged, was among his mother's family in a distant district in the Central Region. For the same reason, Adzimbiri would not be considered a potential successor to his paternal uncle as chief (cf. Englund 2002: 57). Con-versely, a number of young kin who were considered eligible for suc-cession and inheritance were living with their respective fathers' relatives in neighbouring Thyolo and Zomba Districts at the time of my original fieldwork. These arrangements were convenient for the time being, but in the long term all of the children concerned were expected to return to Chiradzulu.[5]

By contrast, research conducted in matrilineal areas of central Malawi reveals more 'cognatic' kinship practices with less significant distinctions drawn between matrilineal and patrilineal kin, and individuals more likely to inherit land and titles through their fathers than they are in Chiradzulu (see, e.g., Englund 2002). Such differences in kinship norms may be related to the influence of patrilineal Ngoni migrants from Southern Africa, who settled in large numbers in central Malawi in the nineteenth century (Phiri 1983). The Central Region is thus character-ised by a different history of migration and ethnic interaction than that of the Shire Highlands, in which Chiradzulu is located and where villagers who recognise matrilineal Yao, Lomwe, Man'ganja, and Nyanja roots far outnumber those claiming Ngoni heritage (see, e.g., Chirwa 1994; Vail 1984; Vail and White 1991).

[5] By 2015 they had indeed returned.

Indeed, contemporary matriliny cannot be understood outside the flow of historical time. It is important to note, for example, that the forces of missionary Christianity and British colonial rule (1891–1964) were unsympathetic to matriliny (Phiri 1983). In the context of increasing cash-crop production, taxation, and estate tenancy, '[i]t was men who, by necessity, forged the stronger links with the new capitalist economy which gave them a powerful bargaining position within the household' (Vaughan 1985: 42). Men as husbands, rather than as matrilineal kinsmen, were the focus of colonial policy and mission teachings, and by placing 'responsibility for a woman firmly on the shoulders of her husband' (ibid.: 43), colonial authorities undermined inter-household linkages and altered patterns of dependence within marriage. Nevertheless, shifts in matrilineal practices have been uneven and fluctuating. It is impossible to provide an overarching and coherent narrative of a decline in women's status alongside a rise in patrilocal marriage and patrilineal inheritance, even if, at certain times and in certain places, predictions of matriliny's submission have proved irresistible (see, e.g., Mandala 1990; Read 1942; White 1987).[6]

Against the expectations of many, the resilience of matriliny in South-Central Africa has been among its most remarked features in recent scholarship (Arnfred 2011; Barber 2001; Brantley 1997; Kishindo 2010; Peters 1997a; Vaughan 1987). Given the multiple ways in which matriliny has interacted with alternative modes of inheritance and patterns of residence, and the various shifts that have occurred in response to historically and geographically contingent pressures, many of which served to favour men as household heads, the persistence of matriliny in the Shire Highlands is indeed remarkable. But changes come and go in ebbs and flows. The period during which I conducted fieldwork coincided with conditions conducive to matrilineal norms. Paltry prospects for villagers in the formal economy, for one thing, ensured the ongoing significance of agricultural production for household reproduction, and a national fertiliser subsidy programme combined with favourable rains enhanced the viability of small-scale agriculture on land allocated to women, while simultaneously decreasing demand for male sources of income. Matriliny may be resilient, but it is not ahistorical.

Peters' point – that it is more constructive to 'consider matriliny as a set of characteristics rather than a totality or "system"' (Peters 1997b: 137; see also Brantley 1997) – is pertinent to this discussion and we ought to remain mindful of the fact that matriliny takes many forms and

---

[6] See Christine Oppong's (1974) work on urban Ghanaian elites, or Saradamoni (1999) on matriliny in Travancore, south India, for interesting comparative perspectives.

is subject to considerable variation over time and space. As the preceding discussion suggests, this geographical and historical variability is well illustrated by contrasting accounts from different areas of Malawi, from the Central Region (Englund 2002; Phiri 1983) to the lower Shire Valley (Mandala 1990) and the Shire Highlands (Vaughan 1985; White 1987). Research in matrilineal contexts in West Africa also suggests considerable differences in terms of inheritance patterns and transformations over time (see, e.g., Allman and Tashjian 2000; Burrill 2015). Shifts in norms and practices need to be understood as aspects of historical processes rather than as endpoints.

Notwithstanding the foregoing caveats, however, it is possible to provide an overview of a dominant social pattern pertaining to the period during which this study was undertaken, the contours of which have already been indicated. Crucially, custodianship of land was vested in women through the *mbumba*, the minimal lineage, which contained male and female members related through the female line and was often overseen by a male *mwini* or 'owner'. Marriage tended to be uxorilocal, with exceptions for headmen and some 'lineage owners', particularly where their families had plentiful land, although their wives were still likely to maintain gardens in their own villages of origin. Inheritance of land was through the female line, devolving from mothers to daughters. With rare exceptions, sons did not inherit. Inheritance of title was also through the matriline, and where a man held a title – a chieftaincy, for example – the assumption was that he would be succeeded by a matrilineal heir. His heir could be male or female, but was often male, and was usually a classificatory sibling, nephew, or niece. In this context, relationships between brothers and sisters were often close, with men playing an important supporting role in the lives of their sisters' children.

Food, hunger, and the politics of agriculture

The impossibility of excluding agriculture, land, and maize from the above discussion of marriage and matriliny is indicative of their centrality to almost all aspects of life in Malawi, where, at the last count, 85 per cent of the population lived in rural areas (NSO 2008c: 8). This fact helps explain why his personal association with a policy of subsidised farm inputs all but guaranteed President Bingu wa Mutharika's landslide re-election in May 2009 (Chinsinga 2011; 2012; Chirwa and Dorward 2013; Englund 2012b). The majority of agricultural production in Malawi is rain-fed and hence extremely vulnerable to variations in rainfall. Indeed, periodic failures of the rains, combined with assorted political and economic factors, have led to a number of major famines (including in 1862–3, 1903, 1922, 1949, and 2002), so that memories of suffering and shortage cast a shadow even in years of relative plenty.[7] Nevertheless, for the most part, it is seasonal hunger rather than famine that characterises life in Malawi (Mandala 2005). Although my fieldwork coincided with a time of favourable rains and expanded access to affordable fertiliser, I observed seasonal variations in food supplies and demand for purchased maize that villagers and scholars recognise as typical (Mandala 2005; Moore and Vaughan 1994; Richards 1939: 35–7). When the harvest was collected in April, food was abundant, and perhaps the majority of households maintained plentiful resources throughout much of the dry season (May–November). But by the time the rains arrived, towards the end of the year, many families had begun to purchase maize from their better-off neighbours and at local markets. January was a notoriously difficult month, coming after the previous year's stocks had been exhausted and before the first cobs of the new season could be plucked. In the months that followed, pumpkins and their leaves lessened the need for maize, but, for many, the new harvest could not come quickly enough.

Implicit in this discussion is the fact that, across much of Malawi, maize (*chimanga*) is synonymous with 'food' (*chakudya*). Indeed, villagers who had feasted upon sweet potatoes, cassava, and groundnuts did not lie when they described themselves as having gone without food. 'Real' food is *nsima*, a stiff porridge made from maize flour and water, which is consumed with a relish (*ndiwo*) that can take many forms. Fish, meat, eggs, pumpkin leaves, beans, cabbage, peas, and many other foodstuffs can all be prepared as relish; where possible, they are fried or boiled with cooking oil, tomatoes, and plenty of salt.

Nsima and relish are eminently shareable, and were usually served on communal plates to be consumed by groups sitting together on the ground and eating with their fingers. Husbands and wives sometimes dined together, but often men and women ate in single-sex groupings, with children tending to eat with their mothers or grandmothers. For the most part, adults ate food prepared from the granary (*nkhokwe*) and cooking fire of their own household, centred around a particular adult woman. However, they often sat with, and shared food among, members of the other households within the cluster of homes joined by matrilineal kinship ties, which I refer to as a 'compound', despite the rarity of walls or fences. Entitlement to eat from a woman's *nkhokwe* was earned through agricultural labour in her gardens, and invitations to share a meal often included the legitimating phrase 'you farmed' (*munalima*), just as polite refusals referred to the would-be guest's status as someone who had not cultivated the host's land (*sindinalime*). Most people took

---

[7] See Vaughan (1987) for an account of the famine of 1949, and Devereux (2002) for an assessment of the 2002 famine.

two meals per day, with breakfast a rare indulgence, although primary school pupils whose parents could afford the small fee received *phala*, a liquid porridge made with soya flour, during the school morning.[8] When available, fruit, sugarcane, cassava, groundnuts, fried cakes, and dough-nuts were among the most popular snacks, alongside shop-bought bread and biscuits.

As suggested by Anachisale's reference to the meat her husband would purchase before disappearing, gender tensions were often discussed in relation to food – its cultivation, purchase, preparation, and consumption. Maize, the essential ingredient of every meal, was usually the property of women, in whose gardens it had ideally been grown and in whose granaries it was stored. Husbands assisted with the cultivation and harvesting of maize but they were accorded particular responsibility for the provision of relish. In these days of mechanised grinding mills, husbands are often also expected to provide the necessary cash to pay for the processing of dried maize into flour (*ufa*). Just as a wife would be condemned for neglecting to cook for her husband, husbands were roundly criticised if they repeatedly failed to provide relish for their families. In such instances, great scrutiny would be placed on men's other expenditures, since they revealed their priorities and affections. In Anachisale's case, her late husband's generosity when it came to relish was a key motif in an ambiguous and painful narrative about a sometimes violent man whom she nevertheless remembered fondly in certain respects. Despite the emphasis on the male provision of relish, men and women both engaged in the cultivation of relish crops, and vege-tables from the wife's gardens were expected to fill the relish plates for perhaps the majority of meals. Many families also raised chickens, which provided eggs and meat for special occasions, but purchased relish remained an essential source of protein and necessary to satisfy the intense cravings (*nkhwilu*) that villagers endured after extended periods without meat or fish.[9]

Given that relish tends to be more perishable than dried maize, a great deal of daily creativity and graft must be expended in ensuring its provi-sioning. *Nsima* may be synonymous with food, but it is said that it cannot be eaten without relish, and a lack of relish was a common explanation for why a family had gone to bed on empty stomachs. Although maize flour and relish items were frequently exchanged between friends, neigh-bours, and relatives, this could not be relied upon to entirely prevent

---

[8] The school feeding programme was sponsored by UNICEF. Free universal primary education was one of the most prominent policies introduced by the country's first democratically elected president, Bakili Muluzi (1994–2004). Sadly, the quality of education provided is often very poor (Kadzamira and Rose 2003).

[9] Some relish foods could also be caught, including small birds, insects, mice, and rabbits.

skipped meals. That said, children were somewhat cushioned from the effects of daily shortages by the fact that they would always be invited to partake in a meal at the houses of their kin should they happen to be present at mealtimes.

As mentioned above, husbands became subjects of criticism if they consistently failed to provide relish; men were also admonished in jokes and local legends for their perceived stinginess with the relish they did supply (see Chapter 1). Beyond the scrutiny and light-hearted banter, however, lay a general acceptance that husbands ought to be served generously from the relish pot. Indeed, the distribution of relish was a serious matter and could lead to disputes: in the words of Elias Mandala, it constitutes 'an unequal system of sharing' (2005: 223). Children were frequently admonished for scooping too greedily from the relish bowl, and they learned from an early age to eat with caution. Accusations of selfish greed (*umbombo*) were not taken lightly: on several occasions I observed children thus accused withdraw from a meal in tears, suggesting important connections between food and moral personhood.

Conversations about food in Malawi are inevitably also about land. As we have seen, in rural settings, the ideal is that the majority of the food consumed in each household has been produced in nearby fields. Influential voices in the regional literature have related growing pressure on land in Malawi to rising rural landlessness and resultant increases in inter- and intra-familial conflict (see especially Peters 2002; 2006; Peters and Kambewa 2007). Although Chiradzulu is particularly densely populated by African (and Malawian) standards, these were not problems I encountered beyond a few isolated incidents of boundary disputes or contests over the proposed sale of land (see, for example, Chapter 6).[10] Land was certainly rented and sold in a manner that might lead to increased differentiation in access, but I am inclined to agree with Jul-Larsen and Mvula (2009) that the ambiguities of customary land tenure tend to promote land security. Differences between my experience in Chiradzulu and Peters' assessment of land tenure in neighbouring Zomba District may also reflect the micro-particularities of agricultural practices, such as the relative importance

[10] Malawi is one of the most densely populated countries in Africa (139 persons per square kilometre), and nowhere more so than the Southern Region (185 per square kilometre). With the exception of Likoma Island on Lake Malawi, Chiradzulu is the most densely populated rural district in the country (379 persons per square kilometre) (NSO 2008a). The fact that I did not encounter significant conflict over land may have been a consequence in part of differences in the routes by which land disputes travel in the search for justice, as compared with the pathways that marital disputants tend to tread: land issues were most commonly referred to the apex of the traditional authority hierarchy and to the district commissioner's office, rather than to the police or magistrates.

of burley tobacco as a cash crop in Zomba, and local historical variations with respect to the rise and fall of estate agriculture.[11] My sense was also that the ravages of HIV in the years before my arrival had provided temporary relief from acute land pressure. Thankfully, antiretroviral therapies (ARVs) have radically altered the course of the epidemic (see Chapter 6); as a result, it is likely that competition for land will increase in the coming years.

Justice, morality, and love

As we have seen, matriliny gives a particular flavour to gender relations in this setting, and to the division of labour within marriage. An analysis of this division of labour, and of expectations for the behaviour of 'good' husbands and wives, underpins my approach to justice (*chilungamo*). I suggest that understandings of just relationships centre on a complementary gendered division of labour in which the contributions of men and women to household reproduction are clearly delineated, making visible the fundamental obligations that flow between them, and thus their mutual dependence. This is an argument about morality, and it builds on ideas about the 'materiality of morality' in rural Malawi, a formulation that incorporates the material and emotional exchanges that constitute persons (Englund 2008). I argue that it is in the light of material morality that we ought to understand the kinds of justice women seek when they bring legal cases against their husbands. Rather than a vision of formal gender equality, such as they are taught by local NGOs (see Chapter 4), what emerges in the course of case hearings is an understanding of justice that values the complementarity of men's and women's roles within the household and beyond. The fact that gender complementarity defines this particular ideal of gender justice does not mean that Chiradzulu is an idyll of harmonious gender relations; nor does it imply that men and women in rural Malawi conform to uniform, undifferentiated identity categories marked by their gender alone. As my ethnographic analysis underlines, gender justice, rights, and morals are highly contested. However, this contestation takes place in the context of

[11] The Shire Highlands, where Zomba and Chiradzulu are located, were subject to extensive land alienation during the colonial period (McCracken 2012: 75–83; Power 2010: 13). Although he was a vocal critic of the estate sector prior to his ascent to power, Kamuzu Banda himself, and a good number of his high-profile associates, became large landowners, employing tenant labour on terms that were not dissimilar to those of their European predecessors (Chinsinga 2002: 25–6; McCracken 2012: 253; Vail 1984: 26–8). However, Banda and his fellow postcolonial landlords concentrated most of their attention on the Central Region (Vail and White 1991: 181), and, with the exception of the Mulanje and Thyolo tea estates, the enormous Shire Highlands estates were largely dismantled from the 1950s onwards (McCracken 2012: 254; see also Marks 1999: 558).

broadly shared ideals and cultural mores in which recognisable values guide expectations and aspirations, without providing a template for action in particular circumstances.

Max Gluckman's studies of Barotse jurisprudence (1965; 1973 [1955]) led the way in exploring the co-implication of morality, personhood, and property in Africa. The entanglement of moral and material processes is perhaps most evident in analyses of bridewealth (see, e.g., Hunter 2010), but it is also apparent in more mundane discussions of the obligations that characterise quotidian relations, and the ways in which the failure to fulfil such obligations, including those of material provisioning, can lead to legal disputes and the dissolution of relationships (see, e.g., Bohannan 1957: 91–2). Ethnographically grounded perspectives on morality in Africa imply a form of relational personhood, a recognition of the ways in which men and women are constituted as persons through their efforts to fulfil and sustain moral and material obligations to one another. This approach to the study of morality is thus distinct from analyses of moral or ethical subjectivity in which the notion of the autonomous individual is conceived as central to aspirations for love, morality, and marriage (see, e.g., Zigon 2013).

For the present study, Gluckman's assessment of the relationship between law and morality provides further stimulus. Gluckman considered it imperative that law and morality be discussed within a single analytical framework because his Barotse experience had convinced him that 'law is impregnated with morality, as morality is with law' (1973 [1955]: 267). Obligations mediate the two. Gluckman employed the concept of the 'reasonable man' to theorise the legal and moral necessity to fulfil status obligations. By enquiring into the 'general issue' of 'whether particular people had behaved as reasonable incumbents of specified social positions' (1965: 17), he argued that Lozi judges were able 'to import justice into judgement' (1973 [1955]: 195). Reference to social positions indicates that the reasonable man is a variegated construct, which is never applicable in such abstract terms in practice. Disputants were assessed with respect to expectations for the behaviour of 'reasonable' husbands, fathers, wives, headmen, sisters, and so on in particular circumstances. Importantly, the notion of 'reasonableness' is inextricably linked to moral personhood because 'the upright man is implicit in the reasonable man' (ibid.: 187). Moreover, 'fulfillment of obligations in kin relationships is measured by what is done with property' (1965: 176), for it is through the transfer of property that obligations come about. This is highly relevant in the context of gender and marital relations where questions of labour and provisioning often loom large in assessments of relationships, legal or otherwise.

In the decades since Gluckman's pioneering studies, justice has received little concerted attention.[12] In recent years in particular, it has been overshadowed by a narrower focus on rights. When it has appeared as a principal concern, it has usually been in the context of debates about transitional justice in the aftermath of mass violence (see, e.g., Anders and Zenker 2014; Clarke 2009; Wilson 2001). In this literature, the emphasis is on the social and legal processes being put in place in the hope of restoring peacetime social norms. By contrast, the African context in which I worked was not reeling in the wake of atrocity. It is thus not the restoration of social order that I am interested in, but its maintenance against a background of relative peace and stability. It is the quotidian struggles for justice of ordinary people in unremarkable situations that form the focus of this study: the everyday rather than the spectacular.

In pursuing this agenda, I take inspiration from a recent volume, *Mirrors of Justice* (Clarke and Goodale 2010), whose contributors eschew the temptation to provide 'yet another abstracted *theory* of justice' (Goodale and Clarke 2010: 23, emphasis in the original). Instead, they call for sensitivity to justice's variety through ethnographic exploration of normative practice. The metaphor of the mirror, or mirrors, highlights justice's 'reflective and refractive properties' (ibid.: 23): the ways in which justice, as a discursive concept, simultaneously reproduces, shapes, and distorts 'cultural, political, and ideological imperatives' (ibid.: 6). This approach suggests that justice is qualitatively different from human rights because 'justice is contextual in a way that human rights is not' (ibid.: 10): justice is 'an ever receding and ever shrouded social ideal', rather than 'an alternative normative orientation characterized by a set of concrete expectations and practices' (ibid.: 10). I build on this recent intervention as I suggest a turn to justice, ethnographically and analytically, in order to focus more specifically on how claims are made, what is aimed for in dispute hearings, and what we might gain by paying attention to justice as an ethnographic category.

In this vein, the Chichewa lexicon provides a vital entry point for my focus on gender justice in Malawi. Several terms are key, including two deployed by Anachisale in the opening vignette of this Introduction. Anachisale invoked the spectre of gender-based violence, and the vast array of organisations and projects that have targeted violence against women in Malawi since the 1990s, with her use of the word *nkhanza*, or cruelty. *Nkhanza* is not a new coinage, but it has been infused with additional meaning since the transition to multiparty politics through

---

[12] For recent exceptions, see Clarke and Goodale (2010) and Johnson and Karekwaivanane (2018).

its association with another term Anachisale employed: *ufulu* – literally 'freedom', but here used as the common shorthand for *ufulu wachibad- widwe*, 'the freedom one is born with', which is the established term for 'human rights' (Englund 2006). When Anachisale spoke of a time in which she was unaware of *ufulu* (rights), she signalled the sharp change in public discourse that came about with the end of Kamuzu Banda's autocratic rule, change that is directly associated with the coming of rights.

Ufulu and *nkhanza* are emblematic of contemporary concerns with, and the new vocabulary of, rights and gender-based violence that are loudly promoted by government ministers, international donors, civil society activists, and NGO officers. These terms shape debates about gender relations, providing new tools for those who seek to critique the status quo, as Anachisale did when she explained to me how her new- found awareness of *nkhanza* and *ufulu* had altered her assessment of her late husband's behaviour and the ups and downs of their marriage. At the same time, they evoke a longer history of usage, and their meanings are broader and richer than the usual English glosses of 'rights' and 'gender- based violence' suggest. Invocations of *ufulu* not only refer to formal human rights provisions; they may also gesture towards customary pre- rogatives, such as a maternal uncle's *ufulu* to influence his niece's marital choices (see Chapter 3). Similarly, *nkhanza* enables wide-ranging con- cerns about spouses' behaviour to be drawn into discussions in the victim support unit, encouraging an expansive approach to questions of justice within marriage that goes far beyond matters of physical violence (see Chapter 5).

The Chichewa term for justice, *chilungamo*, is a less ambivalent trans- lation for the English word. Whereas there is room to debate the appro- priateness of equating the terms *ufulu* and *nkhanza* with rights and gender-based violence, I have not encountered similar discussions about using the term *chilungamo* for justice. Dictionary definitions suggest that the term also has connotations of truth and righteousness (Paas 2009: 51), and this is reflected in the common usage of the word *chilungamo* in the form of the rhetorical question: 'Is that *chilungamo*?' (Is that right/ true/just?) The use of the question form implies a shared understanding of what *chilungamo* entails, or at least a shared ability to recognise its presence or absence. Yet, the need to ask the question signals that shared understandings are no guarantee of just behaviour. The linguistic roots of the word lie in the verb *kulungama*, which is often used to speak of things being straight, in a physical sense, and more figuratively of things being right or correct (Scott 1892: 251). Indeed, the nexus of meanings that come together in the term *chilungamo* – truth, righteousness, and justice – might be said to underline Gluckman's insights about the proximity of justice and morality.

The argument at the heart of this book is that justice is an ideal and that the kind of gender justice that is aspired to in Chiradzulu, - characterised by complementarity - is a source of considerable contestation. The elusive nature of justice is a challenge to magistrates, chiefs, and police officers (as it is to spouses), and in their efforts to handle disputes, they elide (and sometimes collide with) distinctions between law and justice (see, especially, Chapters 5 and 6). I have framed this book around the concept of justice because I have sought to engage with theoretical and conceptual arguments about morality, rights, and law. However, as we shall see, in its narrower incarnation in the daily lives of men and women in rural Chiradzulu, the concept of gender justice that emerges from this research is difficult to distinguish from that of love (*chikondi*; see Chapter 1). Like morality, love and justice both incorporate a reciprocal form of materiality, concerned with tangible and affective contributions to mutual well-being.

Further parallels between justice and love are suggested by Rane Willerslev's (Venkatesan et al. 2011) evocation of Gilles Deleuze's (1989) concept of the 'virtual', which Willerslev interprets as a 'phantom ideal of purity' that 'may only be imagined as a kind of unthinkable abstraction or paradox, working on a purely imaginary plane' (Venkatesan et al. 2011: 228). Willerslev argues that love can be virtual in this sense, and that '[a]ctual love takes place only in the shadow of the impossibility of its virtual or ideal version' (ibid.). Although I am wary of abstracting a theory of love that would obscure the need for sensitive ethnographic attention to its contours, the similarity between Willerslev's description of love as an ever-present ideal that animates action, orients aspirations, and provides a yardstick for moral judgement (ibid.: 231) and my discussion of justice as a guiding ideal – something that is striven for and, in its absence, present – is suggestive of the fecundity of anthropological investigation at the intersections of love, morality, and justice.

Feminist anthropology?

On the one hand, this book provides a window onto a matrilineal society in which I insist that women enjoy considerable social, political, and economic authority. On the other hand, as the argument of the book unfolds, an ethnographic vision of gender justice as complementarity comes to the fore. Where does that leave us in terms of feminist analysis? Complementarity is not a concept that Western feminists have rushed to embrace. On the contrary, it has often been associated with the relegation of women to the domestic realm, something feminist scholars and activists have long sought to combat (see, e.g., Rosaldo and Lamphere 1974). The more I have grappled with the tension between Western feminist priorities and an anthropological commitment to ethnography, the more I have come to appreciate Marilyn Strathern's (1987) description of the 'awkward' relationship between anthropology and feminism. Strathern argues that anthropologists and feminists are distinguished by their different relationships with their respective 'others'. While anthropologists seek to understand the 'others' they encounter in field research, feminists engage in more overtly oppositional relationships with the patriarchal structures that work to the benefit of men as the 'other'. African scholarship highlights additional dimensions of this awkwardness, perhaps signalling a more severe disjuncture than can be encapsulated in Strathern's characterisation.

The dominance/subordination paradigm, which sees women's roles within marriage as a source of their marginality, intersects with another powerful feminist message when it comes to questions about African women's lives: the idea of African women as victims. This latter discourse has been a source of dissatisfaction for African scholars, who have sought to undermine images of universally downtrodden African women and to demonstrate how such representations do more to reassure Western women of their own relative 'progress' than they do to illuminate the lives and challenges of women in Africa (see, e.g., Nnaemeka 2005 [1994]; Okome 2003; Oyěwùmí 2003a). Oyèrónké Oyěwùmí has referred to this as 'the white woman's burden': the drive to rescue 'the exploited, hapless, brutalized, and down-trodden African woman from the savagery of the African male and from a primitive culture symbolized by barbaric customs' (2003b: 28). Similarly, Marnia Lazreg suggests that Western feminists (and, I would add, feminist-inspired media and development campaigns) are guilty of portraying 'Third World women' as '[a]n abstract anthropological subject deemed "oppressed"' (2005 [1994]: 71), thus forcing scholars from the Global South into a choice between 'defending their culture against feminist misrepresentations or revelling in the description of practices deemed disreputable, but always sensational, in an attempt to reaffirm the primacy, validity and superiority of Western feminism' (ibid.). The force with which this view is articulated suggests the depths of frustration felt by those seeking common cause for African and Western feminists. The tension between Western feminist politics on the one hand, built on a history of struggle against patriarchy and women's exclusion from the public sphere, and, on the other, the anthropological requirement to focus on the specificities of women's lives and aspirations in particular times and places is clear.

While a vocabulary of equality, independence, and autonomy has, for the most part, proved more compelling to Western feminists than a language of complementarity, the material presented in this book speaks to the progressive potential of a recognition of mutuality. Complementarity is a form of interdependence that signals the valuable ways in which having something different to offer can be a source of strength to men and women alike. What complementarity underlines is not that there is a 'natural' division of labour between men and women in heterosexual relationships, but that men and women are reliant upon one another if all the necessary tasks are to be fulfilled. In distinguishing the roles of husbands and wives, and thus emphasising their differential contributions, their mutual necessity comes to the fore.

In a recent reflection on another insightful contribution by Strathern, this one originally written in 1974 but published four decades later (2016), Judith Butler acknowledges the potential for relational understanding to alter the terms of feminist debate (Butler 2016). While feminist discourse has often decried gendered divisions of labour as a means of consolidating inequality and female subordination, Butler points to the complexity of gender roles, and suggests that 'we might wish to value' the interdependency that is often their necessary correlate (ibid.: 298). As outlined above, feminist suspicions of gendered divisions of labour have their roots in vital feminist politics, but by mapping these divisions onto a binary schema of dominance and subordination, they make it difficult to take seriously the political potential of arguments based on interdependence. In these terms, 'the ideal of unlimited freedom and mastery is yet another way to disavow an abiding and valuable interdependency among people' (ibid.: 300). The very fact that we live our lives in and through relationships with others means that, at every turn, we are affected by those relationships and confronted by difference. For better or worse, true autonomy is surely a fiction, as is equality, if that is taken to imply sameness. What is needed is a way of affirming mutuality at the same time as we critique domination. This book thus seeks, by means of ethnographic instantiation, to make the case for the inclusion of concepts such as complementarity, interdependence, and mutuality within the wider feminist lexicon.

Fieldwork setting and research methodology

This book draws on 20 months of ethnographic fieldwork in Malawi, from January 2009 to September 2010, followed by shorter trips in 2013 and 2015. I began in Zomba, with intensive language tuition at the University of Malawi's Centre for Language Studies, and went on to settle in a village in rural Chiradzulu District, where I worked in the Chichewa language.[13]

I had settled on Chiradzulu District as a suitable location for my research on the basis that it was a matrilineal area well served by local

---

[13] Chichewa is a Bantu language that is also known as Chinyanja. As well as being the lingua franca of Malawi, it is spoken in parts of neighbouring Zambia and Mozambique.

NGOs with a focus on human and women's rights. However, for a number of reasons I was to have less contact with NGO workers than I had anticipated. Between my initial enquiries during a preliminary trip to Malawi in early 2008 and my arrival for fieldwork proper a year later, these NGOs had begun to shift their emphasis. In response to changing priorities among their principal donors, including Action Aid and Oxfam, attention was beginning to turn towards 'sustainable livelihoods', including village savings and loans clubs, and the promotion of small-scale commercial agriculture. Such projects had not entirely replaced the earlier focus on rights, civic education, and women's empowerment – indeed, they were understood as a necessary complement to that work – but, given limited resources and personnel, they had a considerable effect on the kinds of activities I was able to observe. Most significantly, the geographical dispersal of these projects meant that NGO officers were rarely available in their office to provide the kind of legal counselling and advice to disputing couples that I had hoped to study.

If NGO-based dispute resolution was not to provide a venue for the observation of case hearings, a police victim support unit (VSU) proved a much more productive forum for this aspect of my research. I was first introduced to VSU officers by a local NGO worker who was well known to them, and they confirmed that they were happy for me to attend their sessions as frequently as I wished. Their instant welcome marked the beginning of what was to become a long-term arrangement; for the most part, VSU officers were supportive of my work and fascinating interlocutors. Given the closed nature of hearings at the VSU, however, I was not able to record sessions, and thus I rely on my scribbled notes taken 'live' in a combination of Chichewa and English. In contrast to the VSU, magistrates' courts, like those of traditional authorities, are open, public arenas in which my attendance and recording of cases was positively encouraged. The integration of these settings into a 'loose chain' of dispute-resolution forums (as discussed in Chapter 2) is indicative of the fluidity of discourses and practices of justice, rights, and morality that form the focus of this study.

In economic terms, the area in which I settled was unexceptional. Smallholder agriculture was the mainstay of the local economy, with most households aiming to produce surplus maize and vegetables for sale and to engage in intermittent small-scale trading. The principal cash crop was tobacco, but its cultivation is demanding in terms of resources, time, and labour, and only a small minority of villagers grew it at the time of my fieldwork. To say that formal employment was difficult to come by is something of an understatement, although the district hospital and government buildings at the district headquarters (boma), within relatively easy walking or cycling distance of my village home, offered a source of work for a few, generally male, villagers, who mostly found employment as guards and groundsmen. The nearby urban centre of Blantyre-Limbe provided opportunities for factory labour and activities in the informal sector for larger numbers of men, while others travelled further afield, seeking work in the capital city (Lilongwe), the sugar plantations of the Northern Region, or as far away as South Africa.[14] Women were more likely to engage in small-scale trade closer to home and in the townships of Blantyre-Limbe. A much more limited number of women were employed as domestic staff in the homes of better-off urban residents. Consistent with Malawi's perpetual ranking among the poorest nations, opportunities for significant economic advancement eluded the majority of villagers (see, e.g., United Nations 2010; World Bank 2007).

Chiradzulu District lies within the Shire Highlands, an area with a long history of immigration and inter-ethnic marriage (Vail and White 1991). My friends and neighbours were not unaware of ethnic labels and identities, but they did not expend a great deal of energy on their definition or maintenance. Certain villages, extended families, or individuals were recognised as Ngoni, Yao, Lomwe, and so on (NGO officers, for example, were often distinguished by their Tumbuka ethnicity and language), and certain traditional rites were similarly acknowledged as having particular 'ethnic' roots. In day-to-day conduct, however, ethnic markers were notably absent, and appeared to be of little concern. Thus, at the close of dispute hearings I attended at the police station, participants were often visibly confused by officers' requests for their 'tribe' (*mtundu*), which they were expected to record alongside each disputant's name, age, village, and Traditional Authority (chief). Unsure, respondents sometimes attempted a narrative answer along the lines of, 'Well, my mother was X, and my father was Y, I like to think I am ...,' or they deferred to an uncle or senior family member. When asked for the 'tribe' of an absent spouse, husbands and wives often struggled to provide an answer.

Despite the variety of ethnic origins, the Chichewa language is dominant and spoken universally, although sometimes as a second language, particularly for older villagers. In line with Kamuzu Banda's promotion of Chichewa as the national language of independent Malawi (Kamwendo 2006), adults over the age of approximately 35 reported having spoken Chiyao as children, although they claimed that they had since become more comfortable in Chichewa. Their children and grandchildren could often understand a considerable amount of Chiyao, but

---

[14] On the long history of migration between Malawi and other countries in the Southern African region, see Groves (2011), McCracken (2012), and Vail (1975; 1984). For a contemporary perspective, see Johnson (2017).

they would rarely have cause to speak it.[15] Although it is the official language of Malawi, English is not widely spoken; this is particularly the case in rural areas, where it is poorly taught in state primary schools and opportunities to practise are rare. According to some estimates, the proportion of the Malawian population able to understand English is as low as 1 per cent (Kanyongolo 2006: 114). Nevertheless, English remains the language of parliament, the judiciary, police records, the print media, and so on.

Christianity is the dominant religion in Chiradzulu, as it is in Malawi as a whole.[16] Catholic and Presbyterian churches were the closest to my field site and drew the largest congregations, but other churches could also count adherents among my fellow villagers, including Assemblies of God. One or two smaller Pentecostal churches were also beginning to evangelise in the neighbourhood during 2010, despite the misgivings of local traditional authorities who have since denied pastors permission to build church structures in their territories. A significant minority of villagers practised Islam, and available statistics indicate that 11 per cent of Chiradzulu residents identify as Muslim, compared with 13 per cent of the national population (NSO 2008c; 2008d). Inter-faith and inter-denomination marriages were common and did not seem to be a matter for concern; they were usually followed by the formal conversion of one or other partner.

Initial contact with my future village home was established with the help of Ngeyi Kanyongolo, an academic from the Law Department at Chancellor College, University of Malawi. Kanyongolo and I drove to the district headquarters (*boma*) and took advice from people there as to where we might begin our search for a suitable village. This was not a scientific method but luck was on our side and the first traditional authority whose name had been mentioned welcomed us onto the veranda of his home and immediately summoned his nephew. The latter promised to find me a suitable house within ten days and waved us off with a boot full of fresh pumpkins. Although it took slightly longer than ten days, he was true to his word and I was soon able to move into a house belonging to his niece in the compound of his elderly mother. This was my first glimpse of chiefly authority. As I came to understand, the elder of the two men held the rank of Sub-Traditional Authority (Sub-T/A) and was the most senior representative of traditional authority (lower case) in the vicinity. A Traditional Authority (T/A; upper case) who ranked above him lived a good three hours' walk away, and was the

---

[15] This marks a contrast with surrounding areas of the Southern Region, where Chilomwe is spoken more commonly than Chiyao.

[16] Some 83 per cent of the national population is Christian, as are 88 per cent of those living in Chiradzulu (NSO 2008c; 2008d).

highest-ranking chief with whom villagers were likely to engage. The younger of the men was a group village head (GVH). In the chiefly hierarchy, village heads answer to group village heads, who have responsibility for a cluster of villages. GVHs, in turn, answer to Sub-T/As (where one is in place) or T/As. There also exist a number of senior and paramount chiefs at the apex of the national traditional authority ladder but these are somewhat removed from local governance (see Chapter 2). Confusingly, all of these figures are referred to as 'chief' (*mfumu*) in Chichewa.

Once ensconced within the village, I became a regular attendee of meetings and case hearings at the *bwalo* (chiefs' court), as well as a familiar face in the fields and gardens, at female initiation rites, an HIV support group, a number of village committees, and the local Catholic church. As mentioned above, I combined this village ethnography with regular attendance at a police VSU and two magistrates' courts. I also established less intensive working relationships with several local NGOs that aimed to promote awareness of human and women's rights and gender equality. In addition to participant observation, I carried out a series of semi-structured interviews with key informants, including members of the HIV support group, magistrates, police officers, initiation counsellors, NGO employees, parties to legal cases, traditional authorities, and 'ordinary' villagers. I have also made use of a variety of textual sources, from media reports and NGO literature to local population statistics obtained from a village committee.

I soon learned that my attempts to describe myself as a PhD student from the University of Cambridge were meaningless to villagers, and although some interlocutors were more impressed by my affiliation to the University of Malawi's Chancellor College, the Chichewa expression for student, *mwana wa sukulu* (literally 'school child'), led many to wonder out loud which primary school standard I was in. While frustrating at times, this junior status was a boon in many respects for it implied that I was unthreatening and conveyed the idea that I was there to learn. As a result, villagers, particularly women, were encouraged to take me under their wing somewhat, to explain and instruct as best they could what they considered to be the most important aspects of life in rural Malawi. Of course, perceptions of my status were always formed in conjunction with considerations of my age and gender. As a relatively young, childless, white woman who had not completed her education but who claimed to be 'married' and who had taken the baffling decision to reside in a rural area in a grass-thatched house and to travel by foot, bicycle, and minibus taxi, as opposed to using the private vehicles favoured by the more accomplished Europeans (*azungu*) who were occasionally spotted whizzing to and from the district hospital, shopping in town, or inspecting the progress of local development projects, my status was ambiguous.

As implied by their association with chieftaincy, the compound in which I settled was home to a relatively privileged family, although that privilege was not immediately apparent in material terms. Like the majority of villagers, they lived in small, mud-brick, grass-thatched houses,[17] without electricity, and relied for clean water on communal bore holes. The women cooked on firewood and gained access to cash through the sale of agricultural produce cultivated on land they had inherited from their mothers. Where they were better off than many was not only in their proximity to chiefly authority, with the unpredictable but tangible material and social benefits that sometimes entailed, but also in the relative abundance of land to which they had access. This was the product of both their historical fortune and their more recent misfortune in having lost several adult family members to early deaths in the years before my arrival, resulting in some relief from the pressures of land fragmentation. Theirs was a predicament shared by many families in the area, reflecting both the generally low life expectancy in Malawi, and the particular, unprecedented horrors of the HIV/AIDS epidemic (Peters, Kambewa, and Walker 2008).

Perhaps the fact that none of the women of the compound brewed beer also marked them out from other villagers. By no means all women brew beer to raise cash, but it is a relatively common activity for those with access to the necessary capital. I was told that the main reason they did not brew alcohol in the compound was that a highly respected and formidable female ancestor, who had died a few years prior to my arrival, could not abide beer brewing and thus they abstained in her memory. For the same reason, they did not rent out land for cash (*kuchita renti*), but only 'lent' (*kubwereka*) land to others in the off season in exchange for a discretionary share of the yield. The women themselves, unlike some of their male kin, did not borrow or rent land from others, and nor did they have much cause, during the time of my fieldwork, to engage in paid agricultural piecework (*ganyu*) on the land of their fellow villagers, although at other times they have undertaken *ganyu* and they regularly participate in exhausting dry-season government work schemes to plant trees and repair roads. *Ganyu* labour is a casual source of additional income for many villagers, male and female alike, but it can serve to reinforce inequalities when it keeps people from their own fields at key points in the agricultural cycle (Bryceson 2006; Mandala 2005; Peters 2006). Rural social differentiation exists within relatively narrow limits, but it must be borne in mind that the categories 'villagers', 'men', and 'women', all of which I employ in this book, are not uniform

---

[17] The GVH's elderly mother was the only exception to this. Her son had sold a cow to build her a small burnt-brick house and to roof it with iron sheets several years before I arrived, after she had become permanently disabled.

(Hirschmann and Vaughan 1983). The opportunities and aspirations of particular individuals are shaped by their differential access to resources and their respective positions within webs of relationships through which such resources are acquired.

Only one of the four adult women who had established their own households within the compound was married at the time of my original fieldwork, and her husband lived and worked in Limbe most of the time. Of the other three, one was an elderly widow who had been disabled for several years and did not expect to remarry, another was middle-aged and twice divorced, and the third was a widow in her thirties. There were also 12 children, ranging in age from newborn to 19; these were the offspring of the resident women and their late female kin. For several months, we were also joined in the compound by the adult son of one of the women who brought his young wife and infant daughter with him. For the rest of the time, like two other young male members of the matrilineage, he resided elsewhere in Malawi for the purposes of employment. Although not at all untypical of village compounds, as we shall see, the paucity of marriages in my immediate surroundings restricted my ability to observe the to and fro of everyday marital relations at close hand. However, I did not have to venture far to visit with villagers who lived with their spouses or to encounter commentary on the behaviour of local husbands and wives. The marriages of several men from the matrilineal family, who lived with their wives in the surrounding villages, also provided plenty of opportunity to observe and discuss marital relations, including divorce, remarriage, and domestic conflict, as well as to witness the involvement of matrilineal kin as marriage guardians (*ankhoswe*) in these various circumstances.

Structure of the book

Married life forms the focus of Chapter 1, which introduces the institution of marriage in this matrilineal setting as a fulcrum of contestation, arguing that shifts in the broader political-economic context feed into this contestation and alter the stakes of marriage for men and women over time. The chapter offers ethnographic insight into married life in the twenty-first century, illuminating the nexus of love, marriage, and political economy hinted at above, and demonstrating the continuing importance of marriage in rural Malawi, in contrast to other parts of Southern Africa where it appears to be in decline. This chapter highlights the mundanity of contestation and negotiation; illuminates the kinds of models and resources upon which spouses, and those charged with assisting them, draw as they strive for resolution to their marital disputes; and makes tangible the social and cultural context in which aspirations for justice are formed.

Chapter 2 introduces the various legal forums that together constitute a loose chain of institutions available to men and women as they seek to resolve their gendered and marital disputes. The institutions are placed in historical context, and also considered from the perspective of contemporary disputants who often deal with them sequentially, moving between so-called 'traditional' settings and more 'modern' venues and encountering various constellations of custom, human rights, and state law as they go.

Through detailed engagement with a case heard in a VSU, Chapter 3 brings an ethnographic lens to bear upon the complex and ambiguous interaction of the so-called 'formal' and 'traditional' spheres outlined in Chapter 2. The aim is to tease out some of the implications of the ways in which rights are grappled with in the language of *ufulu*. This chapter also introduces questions of justice, which animate the rest of the book, arguing for the analytical potential of justice as a concept that opens up – as opposed to foreclosing – attention to life as it is lived, in all of its existential, moral complexity.

The focus on justice is developed further in Chapter 4 through consideration of contrasting judgments in magistrates' courts and an analysis of the form of gender complementarity to which men and women aspire in their marital relationships. Key to the analysis is the idea that complementary gender roles are not defined in advance (cf. Goheen 1996). In other words, complementarity is not a static model but rather a working moral principle that is applied differently in different circumstances. By providing an ethnographic illustration of divergent approaches to gender justice, this chapter underlines the degree to which gender norms, custom, rights, and justice are contested in contemporary Malawi.

Chapter 5 concerns the administration of justice by police officers and magistrates in relation to gender violence (*nkhanza*). Finding only limited references to violence in dispute hearings, I ask what, if not violence, is foregrounded in such proceedings. The answer lies in a range of strategic efforts to demonstrate moral personhood. This chapter extends the ongoing discussion of justice by bringing the ethnographic argument into conversation with Derrida's (1990) theoretical distinction between justice and law, a distinction that hinges on their relative calculability. While law is amenable to calculation, justice is not, in large part because justice is an ideal to be striven for. In the words of Susan Hirsch, justice is 'always shimmering beyond the reality of particular courts, claims, or persons' (2010: 168). This chapter thus demonstrates the complexity of the challenge facing those tasked with the administration of law in their efforts to approximate justice.

In Chapter 6, the ethnographic core of the book culminates in an attempt to gain further purchase on justice's unfinished, out-of-reach quality. The chapter centres on a criminal case heard in a magistrates' court when a brother stood accused of publicly insulting his sister and making reference to her HIV-positive status. Analysis of the case focuses on how existing legal resources were brought to bear upon novel situations and new moral categories within the context of a dispute between members of a matrilineal family with differing views on the disposal of lineage land. In handling the case, the magistrate drew on dominant ideas about stigma, which served to obscure the gendered and relational context of the dispute. By contrast, HIV-positive women's narrative accounts of their experiences are suffused with references to complex and unfinished relationships. Significantly, their narratives also contain tentative expressions of hope for the future, which echo the prospective temporality of efforts to bring about justice through legal forums, thus illustrating the experiential proximity of justice and hope. However, as the case study demonstrates, the administration of law can serve to foreclose the forward momentum of justice.

The 'awkward' relationship between feminism and anthropology (Strathern 1987) returns to the spotlight in the Conclusion, where I address the disjuncture between the analytically derived ideal of gender complementarity and the activist goal of gender equality as sameness. This is an ethnographic disjuncture as much as it is a theoretical problem: men and women in matrilineal Malawi articulate their visions of justice in conversation with discourses of human rights and NGO programmes emphasising the constructed nature of gender difference and the desirability of equality as sameness. In taking seriously local aspirations to complementarity, I thus take up the challenge laid down by Saba Mahmood to 'rethink, with far more humility than we are accustomed to, what feminist politics really means' (2005: 38).

'Justice' weaves throughout the book, appearing in a number of guises, both ethnographic and theoretical: as an elusive ideal, a shared goal, a realm of contestation, a right, a form of equality, an issue of morality, and an object of administration. As I demonstrate, not only does justice's motivational force require such ambiguity, but the impossibility of reducing justice to a universal checklist of expectations and practices holds the key to both its enduring significance in social life and its conceptual potential for anthropological analysis.

1   Love, marriage, and matriliny

'What do I need a husband for?' Anachisale asked, gesturing to the fields around us. 'I can farm this land for myself; it belongs to me. I can feed my children through my own labour. A husband will just come along after the harvest, eat my maize and then slink off when it's time to farm again. A husband is just another person to feed!' Anachisale enjoyed talking like this; humorous and defiant, she would gather momentum as she complained of the ills of marriage and the shortcomings of men. She spoke from experience, she reminded me, as she had been twice married and twice widowed. Her second marriage in particular had had its fair share of ups and downs (see Introduction). Charismatic and great fun, her second husband was also liable to go missing, spending his time with other women – 'And boy did he have a temper!' Anachisale had nursed him during his illness until shortly before the end, when his sister had taken him home, and she maintained good relations with her in-laws and her husband's son from a previous marriage. Nevertheless, Anachisale insisted, she would not be entertaining any future marriage proposals.

As Anachisale implied, marriage proposals were considered very much a male prerogative. Indeed, women were highly sceptical of a male NGO worker's suggestion that they might initiate romantic or marital relationships themselves, on the basis that rigid distinctions between male and female activities ought to be challenged. When asked what kinds of work women are inherently unable to do, his audience of women villagers debated several suggestions, including the digging of long-drop toilets, the preparation of adult graves, and the building of houses. On the latter point in particular, the majority view was that women could indeed build houses if they were so inclined. But one thing was clear: women could not propose (*kufunsira*). Even those who said they were aware of cases of women proposing to their spouses argued that it was unusual and somewhat scandalous, implying loose morals on the part of the women concerned. Their firm resistance to the idea that they might propose to potential suitors was palpable, although they were willing to concede that they could make use of less direct means of indicating romantic interest, such as fetching water for men or offering to accompany them to church.

For the most part, the process of getting married is marked by very little ceremony. Following a proposal, marriages are distinguished from other relationships by the allocation of matrilineal representatives to act as marriage guardians (*ankhoswe*; singular: *nkhoswe*). As Lucy Mair observed among the Chewa and Ngoni of Dedza District in the mid-twentieth century, the 'formal meeting of the *ankhoswe* . . . is the essential act that makes the marriage legal' (1951: 108). The coming together of the *ankhoswe* usually occurs in a low-key private *chinkhoswe* ceremony, and may or may not be publicly celebrated with more extravagant festivities at a later date. Similarly, elaborate wedding rituals may be carried out years after a marriage is contracted, or not at all. Polygamous unions are contracted in much the same way and are not particularly unusual.[1] The appointment of *ankhoswe* signals the acceptance of the marriage on the part of the couple's respective matrilineal kin, and their commitment to offering support to the couple in times of conflict. *Ankhoswe* are highly valued as a first port of call whenever tensions arise, and their duties involve bringing the spouses together to discuss disagreements in the hope of brokering peace, as well as counselling their charges with respect to future conduct. Their very existence is indicative of local expectations that marriages will inevitably entail conflict and that wider networks of kin have a crucial role to play in their success.

Central to the argument of this book is the idea that marriage constitutes contested terrain in rural Malawi. In addition to dispute hearings held by *ankhoswe*, traditional authorities, police officers, and magistrates, this contestation manifests itself in a variety of ways: in everyday interactions between husbands and wives as they negotiate their respective roles; in public debates about the age of consent for marriage or the validity of homosexual relationships;[2] in the aspirations of adults on behalf of young people as expressed in initiation ceremonies (see below), and so on. The broader political-economic context shapes these and

---

[1] Available figures indicate that 7.6 per cent of Malawian men have two or more wives, while 14.4 per cent of women have one or more co-wives. The figures for Chiradzulu are 3.4 per cent and 8 per cent respectively, reflecting lower rates of polygamy in southern Malawi more generally (NSO and ICF Macro 2011). Co-wives ought to know of each other's existence, but they will each maintain their own homesteads and gardens, rather than forming a single compound with their husband and children. The husband's kin are expected to assign different individuals as *ankhoswe* for each of his marriages and, ideally, polygamous husbands will divide their time equally between their multiple wives.

[2] This book does not enter into debates about homo- or trans-sexuality in Africa, the relevance of which to rural Malawian life worlds was explicitly denied by my informants in the wake of the high-profile prosecution of two men alleged to have held a public engagement ceremony (*chinkhoswe*) in December 2009 (Biruk 2014). Non-heteronormative relationships and practices no doubt exist in rural Malawi. For the most part, however, they go unremarked and are not accorded public recognition. For an entry point into the literature on sexualities in Africa, see, e.g., Engelke (1999), Epprecht (1998; 2004; 2013), and Tamale (2011).

other forms of contestation, as it buffets Malawian citizens, offering up and restricting opportunities for employment, mobility, and economic security. Over time, historical shifts in the availability of paid work, land, and other resources have altered the relative importance of predominantly male and female contributions to household reproduction, intersecting with personal biographies to affect the extent to which marriage appears attractive, possible, or necessary to men and women at particular junctures. This chapter focuses on the institution of marriage in the early twenty-first century, pointing to the nexus of love, marriage, and political economy, and incorporating historical change at regional, national, and life-historical levels. I also draw on ethnographic and statistical evidence to demonstrate the ongoing centrality of marriage to the lives of men and women in this part of Africa, showing that marriage is both an important and dynamic institution and a fulcrum of contestation.

Man trouble

Economic indicators tend to paint a rather bleak picture of Malawi as a nation with few resources and an impoverished population. Some 20 years on from the advent of multiparty democracy and economic liberalisation, the country languished in 174th position in the United Nations Human Development Index, with 62 per cent of the population living below the international poverty line of $1.25 per day (UNDP 2014).[3] Small-scale farming is considered 'employment' for the purposes of national statistics, which helps to explain why 80 per cent of the population was counted as employed, of which 64 per cent were working in the agricultural sector, and 89 per cent were in informal employment (NSO 2014). Secure employment in the formal sector remains the preserve of very few Malawian citizens. However, while formal employment has always been scarce for the majority within Malawi's borders, migration – principally to the mines, farms, and towns of present-day Zambia, Zimbabwe, and South Africa – has provided an alternative source of employment, particularly for men, from at least the late nineteenth century. Indeed, Malawi and the Shire Highlands have long been integral to the broader Southern African regional political economy (Marks 1999).

The attitude of colonial authorities towards labour migration 'vacillated between cautious acceptance and reluctant opposition' (Power 2010: 25). Nevertheless, by the mid-twentieth century, migrant labour was a major factor shaping economic and gender relations within the country and beyond. Robert Boeder was thus not exaggerating when he

---

[3] The World Bank puts this figure at an even more dismal 72 per cent (World Bank 2014).

stated that: '[v]irtually every Malawian who has ever lived in the twentieth century has been affected by labour migration either as a participant
or as a member of a migrant's family' (1974: 242, cited in Groves 2011: 5).
But gone are the days of organised mass migration, as a result of which
Malawi constituted the most significant supplier of migrant labour to
South Africa by the early 1970s (Andersson 2006: 379). Migrant
numbers have declined significantly since the mid- to late 1970s and
today's smaller-scale migration follows another historical precedent,
often overlooked in historical accounts: that of informal, independent
migration (Johnson 2017). Such migration pre-existed and continued
alongside organised recruitment, bypassing the efforts of governments
and industries to control the movements and destinations of workers
(Groves 2011; Makambe 1980). As in the past, the journeys of independent migrants from rural Chiradzulu to the urban centres of South Africa
today tend to rely on contacts with friends or kin already there who can
provide accommodation and support (Andersson 2006: 387). Thus, of
the five men from the village in which I resided who were in *Joni*, as
South Africa is commonly called (Msiska 2017), during 2014, two were
staying together in Cape Town, along with a friend from a neighbouring
village, and others had joined relatives in Johannesburg.

A number of local men had also migrated within Malawi to find work
in the principal cities, Lilongwe and Blantyre-Limbe, or on the sugar
plantations of the Northern Region, while others commuted, often by
bike, to the factories of Limbe or for the purposes of trade. In this final
role in particular, they were joined by smaller numbers of women.
Women traders were especially active at the rotating markets held at
local trading centres, but significant numbers also travelled to the townships on the outskirts of Blantyre on a more or less regular basis.[4]
Nevertheless, the relative mobility of men could give the villages a
particularly feminine feel. Walking between fields and homesteads,
men seemed few and far between, and it was women who were most
visible tending their crops, fetching water from the boreholes, selling
foodstuffs from their homes and along the roadsides, and chatting in
the compounds.

My early impressions were very much of villages of women, and this
sense was reinforced when I attended village meetings called by local
traditional authorities or NGO staff. Without fail, these were attended by
many more women than men, even at weekends when those commuting

---

[4] Scholars working elsewhere in Malawi have commented on increasing numbers of women
migrating to South Africa, both as the wives of labour migrants and as labour migrants in
their own right (see, e.g., Andersson 2012; Banda 2008). I was not aware of any women
migrating for work from the area in which I resided, although a small number of local men
were said to have 'taken' (*kutenga*) their wives with them to South Africa.

for work could be expected to be at home. The absence of men at such meetings, and on the various village-level committees concerned with 'development' (*chitukuko*), did not go unremarked by villagers. While some complained that it showed a lack of awareness of, or interest in, development on the part of men, others explained that men who had married into the villages did not feel entirely welcome on village committees, or were not selected for them, because this was not their home (*kwawo*). Men who had moved upon marriage, as is the norm, were technically outsiders, and, where geographically possible, might play a more active role in meetings and committees in their mothers' villages, where they would always belong by matrilineal descent. Those men who did take part in village meetings and serve on committees tended to be those who could most legitimately claim belonging. These men had either remained in the village after marriage, returned there following separation, or resided with their wives in nearby villages within the area of the same group village head (GVH). Other men were not necessarily seen as suitable recipients when resources were at stake, and might be criticised for taking too active a role in decision making.

I was certainly not alone in feeling the absence of men. Villagers commonly expressed a similar sense that men were vastly outnumbered when they spoke of a generalised shortage of men that both held women back from marriage and made polygamous unions inevitable. Although a widely held belief, contemporary statistics do not account for the lived experience of male absence. The 2008 population and housing census results indicated that women constituted 51 per cent of the national population (NSO 2008a: 2), and they made up 53 per cent of the population of Chiradzulu District (NSO 2008e). Locally collected statistics (discussed in more detail below) indicate a population comprising 55 per cent women across the 17 villages overseen by the local GVH. These figures undermine claims of a substantial gender imbalance. As Nicole Bennesch has pointed out, however, the persistent 'demographic myth' (2011: 117) of male absence had a firmer grounding in empirical reality throughout much of the early to mid-twentieth century, during the period of extensive male labour migration.[5] At that time, in the words of a district commissioner writing in 1937, it was 'unusual to find any young men in the villages, there being only young wives and their children, and middle aged and old people' (Vail 1984: 18).

Indeed, from the 1930s onwards, concerns were increasingly raised about the impact of labour migration on the women and children left behind in Malawi: for their welfare, but also for their moral fibre and the

---

[5] Rijk van Dijk (2014) encountered a similar myth in Botswana and he echoes Bennesch's historical interpretation (cf. Izzard 1985: 267).

fate of the institution of marriage.[6] Thus, a 1936 report by the Emigrant Labour Committee lamented a 'gloomy picture of deserted wives, undisciplined children, [and] uncultivated fields' (Read 1942: 611). Margaret Read, the anthropologist tasked with investigating the situation, compared the effects of extensive migration on predominantly patrilineal Ngoni and matrilineal Chewa areas of what are today referred to as the Northern and Central Regions of the country, between Mzimba and Ntcheu. Her conclusions were profoundly shaped by her preference for patrilineal norms (Brantley 1997). She argued that the Ngoni weathered 'the strain' (Read 1942: 624) of male absence considerably better than the Chewa, reasoning that they enjoyed greater stability of 'family and village life', higher levels of 'care for the welfare of [the] wives left behind; and more concern for the upbringing of the children' (ibid.: 625). Her argument hinged on the assumption that marital instability in matrilineal areas was evidence of societal malaise. Echoing colonial officials, Read argued that matrilineal and matrilocal practices undermined agricultural productivity (Kishindo 2010). In the context of labour migration, she argued that wives in matrilineal areas were liable to grow 'lazy' (1942: 629) and cease cultivating their land, instead becoming dependent on their mothers. By contrast, patrilineal Ngoni wives remained under the watchful eyes of their in-laws, and this arrangement was said to encourage more industrious activity in their husbands' fields as well as ensuring moral probity (as we saw in the Introduction, however, such concerns had little basis beyond the observers' androcentric world view).

If absent men have been one long-standing source of concern about marriage in Malawi, the position and status of the in-marrying husband (*mkamwini*) in matrilineal areas has been another persistent cause of anxiety for officials and ethnographers alike. Henry Rowley, one of the earliest missionaries to Malawi, observed with keen interest that, among the matrilineal Mang'anja in the vicinity of the Magomero mission in present-day Zomba District, '[f]requently ... the position of the woman seemed superior to that of the man' (1867: 208, cited in Mandala 1990: 25).[7] While Rowley found it 'amusing to see the deference which the men sometimes paid the women' (ibid.: 26), the 'unenviable position of husbands in matrilineal-matrilocal societies' (Mitchell 1959 [1951]: 328) has been viewed by others with greater seriousness. In Mandala's Marxist analysis, for example, the 'exploitation' of male youth in Mang'anja society reaches its peak in the practices of *chikamwini,* or bride-service

[6] See Archambault (2010) for a discussion of the pitfalls of the term 'left behind' in reference to the wives of labour migrants.
[7] Rowley was deacon to Bishop Charles Mackenzie at the 'ill-fated' (White 1987: 8) Universities' Mission to Central Africa at Magomero, just 10 kilometres to the north of Chiradzulu, from 1861.

(1990: 30). Mandala describes a relatively formalised, and dystopian, institution of *chikamwini* among the mid-nineteenth-century Mang'anja of the lower Shire Valley, southern Malawi:

Under the control of his prospective mother-in-law (*apongozi*), the boy had to open and maintain a new field for at least one growing season before he was allowed to start his own household in the girl's village. He was the first to go to the fields in the morning and the last to return home in the evening. When others took a break at midday, he would go on working in the dead heat of the sun . . . Should he displease his mother-in-law or show any sign of laziness he would be returned to his natal village with nothing but a blanket, regardless of the amount of work he had done. A prospective son-in-law (*mkamwini*; plural *akamwini*) was, in the words of one Mang'anja informant, 'a D-7 [tractor]. He was there to fell the largest trees' for the mother-in-law. (Mandala 1990: 30–1)

Similarly struck by married men's apparent low status in their marital villages, J. Clyde Mitchell suggested that the Yao husband in mid-twentieth-century southern Malawi could not 'escape the fact that he is only a "billy goat" . . . a typical man without prestige: a stranger, whose duty is largely procreative' (1956: 184; see also Vaughan 1987: 137–8).[8] From the perspective of the twenty-first century, such attitudes are easily dismissed, along with predictions of matriliny's demise. The assumptions behind them have been convincingly debunked (Brantley 1997; Peters 1997a; 1997b; 2010). Not only have matrilineal practices been shown to be remarkably resilient, but the clear-cut distinction between the two 'systems' has also been reassessed, giving way to a more fluid understanding of social relations and social organisation.

Peters refers to visions of 'henpecked husbands or exploited sons-in-law' as 'crude misunderstandings' (1997b: 135), and she is no doubt correct in her assessment that many of the pronouncements on the relative status of men and women in matrilineal Malawi tell us more about the commentators' own attitudes towards gender relations than they do about the practices they purport to describe (1997a: 192; Peters 2010: 184–5). As Peters has pointed out, the 'matrilineal puzzle' (Richards 1950) in which men struggle to reconcile their roles as fathers and as mothers' brothers, 'was not in fact that at all but a gender puzzle' (Peters 1997b: 141), precipitated by the seeming incomprehensibility of kinship norms and practices that gave 'greater social and political space to women' (ibid.: 133; see also Arnfred 2011). Nevertheless, it is perhaps ungenerous to leave the analysis there without also acknowledging that the duties of in-married husbands towards their wives' families can indeed be onerous, especially in the context of high unemployment and

---

[8] See Richards (1934: 273–4) for comparable remarks about the matrilineal Bemba of Northern Zambia.

material want. It is thus worth considering the position of men within matrilineal compounds, and the expectations placed upon them.

The relationship between a husband and his parents-in-law (*apongozi*) is marked by social distance conceptualised in terms of 'respect' (*ulemu*). While men and women both enjoy relaxed relations with their *alamu* (their brothers- and sisters-in-law, including their spouses' categorical siblings and grandparents), interactions with their *apongozi* are generally more restrained, respect being expressed through mutual avoidance and the husband's labour. Women, too, can be said to work *chikamwini* for their in-laws, but as they tend to live at further remove, this is a less frequent duty, involving, for example, fetching water for their mothers-in-law when they visit, and assisting with the preparation of food on ritual occasions. For men, who more commonly live in the same village as their in-laws, and often in the same compound, the requirement to behave respectfully in the presence of parents-in-law demands constant vigilance. The work of *chikamwini* is sporadic but unending: men are expected to display particular diligence in assisting their in-laws in the early years, but throughout their marriage they will be looked to whenever a roof needs fixing or a fence building, particularly if their mother-in-law is divorced or widowed, and their assistance may also be expected by their resident unmarried female *alamu*.

The institution of *chikamwini* in contemporary Chiradzulu is less formalised than that described by Mandala for nineteenth-century Mang'anja. *Chikamwini* never came up in marital disputes as 'customary' evidence of a marriage in the way that the allocation of *ankhoswe* did, and while magistrates showed concern with whether or not a man had built his wife a house, I never heard the question of his having performed bride-service for his in-laws raised in this context. People would joke approvingly that a man was working *chikamwini* if he laboured in the garden or homestead of his mother-in-law, but there was no formal recognition of, or requirement for, this work. It was simply understood as an expression of respect and an aspect of ongoing relationships of reciprocal assistance and provision, made visible at other times through the transfer of food and agricultural inputs between households and through shared childcare. Where men were in waged employment, which often meant that they spent much of their time in the nearby urban centre of Blantyre-Limbe, they might substitute monetary support and small gifts, such as tobacco or relish, for some of this labour, although they were still likely to find their services required on occasions when they were present. It was largely through such labour and provision that men established themselves in the compounds and villages of their wives as 'good' husbands and fathers, men who 'love' (*kukonda*) their in-laws and children and whose presence was highly valued.

As we saw in the Introduction, the furnishing of relish foods (vegetables, legumes, fish, and meat) was the quintessential act of provisioning expected of husbands and fathers. Tensions between spouses were thus often associated with men's failure to provide sufficient purchased foods to supplement those grown and bought by their wives, or their seeming prioritisation of other items, such as alcohol, ahead of food for their families. In addition to stoking marital disputes, the topic of men's provisioning – or lack thereof – commonly featured in local jokes and morality tales in which men were also lambasted for their supposed stinginess with the food they did provide. Everybody knew about the husband who counted the lumps of meat in his wife's cooking pot, for example, or the man who insisted on cutting the meat himself so that he could be sure that it was neither consumed in the kitchen nor shared with his wife's kin (cf. Mandala 2005: 224). Similarly, everyone had heard of the 'good' son-in-law who arrived home from town at the weekend with a bag full of his mother-in-law's favourite relish.

'Mbewa Zanga' ('My Mice'), the most popular Chichewa song on the airwaves in 2010, tells the story of a husband who caught mice and handed them over to his wife to prepare. The male singer complains bitterly in the catchy chorus that he has been served only the tails. He goes on to recall another occasion on which, suffering from malaria, he had gone without soap so as to buy dried fish, only for his wife to discreetly divide the relish with her mother, leaving him with an insufficient share. The song contains a frustrated commentary on contemporary marriage from the perspective of a young husband who is all too aware of the challenges entailed in fulfilling the role of provider (cf. Groes-Green 2013). The youthful male singer contrasts the present with the past, a time in which, he says, men were shown greater respect by their wives and juniors. He neglects to mention, of course, that mothers-in-law might also hark back to a time when they could expect greater deference and generosity from their daughters' husbands, or that wives might envisage a past of marital stability and cooperation. No doubt the song's appeal resided in its comical take on a recognisable and morally ambivalent scenario.[9] For men, it also chimed with a common concern that some women approached marriage like a 'business' (bizinesi). The epitome of this mindset was encapsulated in tales of wives who chased their husbands away once they had built them a house. Taken together, 'Mbewa Zanga' and related reflections on marital discord point to both

[9] Wilison Mwase's song is available online at <www.youtube.com/watch?v=n0Z7DclvJsY>. It has interesting historical resonances with women's pounding songs in which they critiqued their husbands' shortcomings (see, e.g., Vaughan 1987: 32–4). See James for more on the potential of songs to serve as a 'platform for the appraisal, and denouncing of the inadequacies, of present-day kinship roles and relationships' (1999a: 108).

the ambivalence surrounding marriage in popular discourse and the need to recognise the difficulties faced by aspiring 'good' husbands and fathers in this matrilineal setting without positing that they are exploited 'billy goats' denied their 'natural' authority and control over their wives and children.

Love

Despite the strong expectation that the love (*chikondi*) of a husband and father will be reflected in his material contributions to the reproduction of the household and compound, the image of the male household head as the sole breadwinner is not an accurate depiction of many families in this area, where women are active farmers and traders, beer brewers, and *ganyu* labourers (casual pieceworkers), and, as landowners, can rent out their gardens during the low season for brick or cash-crop production. Nevertheless, there is a strong expectation that men will provide regular cash inputs for the purchase of clothes and relish, daily necessities such as soap, salt, and paraffin, and less frequent but more significant expenses including fertiliser, secondary school fees, and home improvements. As I have stressed, this is not an easy task in a country where opportunities for regular employment are few and far between and, more often than not, provide extremely low rates of remuneration.[10]

It might be objected that the material and the affective – money and love – ought not to be conflated, lest the former somehow demean the latter. Such a view, however, takes for granted the prevalent Euro-American ideology of 'love'. It fails to acknowledge that, across much of Africa, 'romantic love as a strategy for establishing more egalitarian gender relations ... has met with uneven success' (Thomas and Cole 2009: 13). Indeed, several accounts describing the recent emergence of ideals of 'pure' love, untarnished by materiality, show how these can undermine earlier conceptions, reducing women's scope for resisting male infidelity 'without throwing the entire relationship into question' (Thomas and Cole 2009: 27), and promoting the idea that love entails female 'self-sacrifice' (Cole 2009: 129; 2010: 144). Most importantly, concerns about the proximity of love and money obscure the ways in which 'expressions of love enacted through cooperation and mutual assistance – practices that are simultaneously material and meaningful ... – are crucial to the intertwined histories of love and exchange' both on the African continent and beyond (Hunter 2010: 16; see also Moore and Vaughan 1994: 164; Zelizer 2005).

---

[10] Similar predicaments across postcolonial Africa have invited local and scholarly reflection on a so-called 'crisis of masculinity' (Masquelier 2005; McNeill and Niehaus 2009; Moffett 2006; Ngwani 2001).

A current surge of interest in 'love in Africa', to cite the title of a recent volume (Cole and Thomas 2009; see also Cole 2010; Groes-Green 2013; Hunter 2010; Klaits 2010; Poulin 2007; Kringelbach 2016),[11] is a welcome addition to the literature on sex and marriage on the continent, which has often been distinctly blind to the affective dimensions of gender relations, and decidedly blinkered in its failure to acknowledge the Eurocentric lens that makes any relationship touched by materiality appear sullied. This is, of course, a peculiar blind spot for a discipline founded on the study of reciprocity (Malinowski 1999 [1922]; Mauss 2002 [1954]), steeped as it has been, in the words of Elizabeth Povinelli, in a 'language of love, passion and seduction' (Venkatesan et al. 2011: 222).

Affinities between the concept of *chikondi* (love), as expressed by my Malawian informants, and Jennifer Cole's description of *fitiavina* ('love', 'a moral-material and emotional exchange' (2009: 119)) in rural Madagascar are striking:

> To give someone rice that you have produced from your own land; to buy clothes for a lover, a parent or a child; to pay for a child's school supplies or medical care – these are well-known forms of *fitiavina*. In a context where people can acquire resources only through the collaborative, labour-intensive activities of farming or fishing, to take resources and put them toward the well-being of another is to nurture, protect and give of oneself. It is the primary way to create attachment. In *fitiavina*, love and material support are ideally fused. (Cole 2009: 113)

As with the English-language concept of 'love', *chikondi* and *fitiavina* are understood to characterise marital relationships, but they are also expressed more widely within families and among friends. If, as I will argue, justice, in the context of marital relations and in its moral-material and affective dimensions, is intimately entwined with mutual care and recognition, it might be said that this book is as much about *chikondi*, 'love', as it is about *chilungamo*, 'justice'. Conceived at the broadest level, justice intersects with love and there may be little to gain from insisting on a firm delineation.

As we shall see, expectations of 'provider love' (Hunter 2010) are at the heart of idealised visions of marriage, centred around gendered divisions of labour. Invocations of this ideal often allude to harmonious cooperation in agricultural endeavours, with women more closely associated with domestic chores and childcare and men striving to supplement household finances with cash earnings. Actual arrangements exhibit a great deal of variation from household to household, as well as within households over time. What remains constant, however, is

---

[11] See Hirsch (1998: 96–105) for a discussion of the role of the language of love in Islamic marital disputes in Kenya that precedes this more recent literature.

female custodianship of land and a strong symbolic association of men with the cash economy. As the broader political economy waxes and wanes, these facts have certain effects on the relative significance of marriage for men and women. When employment is relatively abundant, the advantages of marriage are clear to women as it is largely through marriage that they stand to gain access to predominantly male-controlled resources (Moore and Vaughan 1994: 171–2). On the other hand, when cash income is scarce, and unemployment or irregular employment the norm, it is men for whom the advantages of marriage are most apparent, since marriage entails access to land and thus both the means of subsistence and the possibility of commercial agriculture. This latter scenario more accurately describes the situation during 2009 and 2010, a time when agriculture remained absolutely essential to household reproduction, aided by favourable rains and a farm input subsidy programme, while regular wages eluded the majority.

To marry or not to marry?

At the time of my fieldwork, a sense that their resources were valuable and ripe to be abused by unscrupulous, scrounging men infused several conversations I had with unmarried women who shared Anachisale's fear of being taken advantage of. Specifically, these women were wary of being hoodwinked by men who would propose marriage after the harvest had been collected, move into their homes, and consume – or worse, make off with – their maize supplies with no intention of contributing to the production of the subsequent harvest. Such men, it was said, would make themselves scarce at times of intensified labour and food shortage, discarding their wives once their resources were diminished. Nightmarish accounts of marriage of this kind tended to exaggerate observed behaviour. Thus, the question of whether or not an errant husband had farmed with his wife, and his consequent entitlement to a share of the maize crop on separation, was often a key point of debate at the police victim support unit (VSU), and these were also hot topics of conversation among villagers as they discussed the marital woes of their neighbours and kin. The flip side of these debates centred on whether women were 'chasing' men away after benefiting from their labour and thereby denying them a share of a harvest to which they were entitled. Of course, to say that women's access to land was highly valued is not to suggest that life as a landholding woman was easy, that it negated the need for additional economic resources, or that access to land marked the limit of villagers' ambitions.

Awareness of potential marital pitfalls fed into efforts to advise young people and help improve the terms on which they might enter marriage. In particular, villagers and traditional authorities were concerned that young women should not rush to marry too young, seeing this as a sure route to poverty. In this vein, a 2010 Women's Forum[12] campaign provided an opportunity for the coming together of villagers, traditional authorities, and representatives of formal authority, including head teachers and police officers, united by their opposition to early and forced marriage. The campaign culminated in a district-wide public meeting at which the Women's Forum district chair addressed the assembled traditional authorities (from GVHs to Traditional Authorities (T/As)), informing them that the women had 'come with a message: we do not want girls to marry too young and we want you to help us'. The campaign was sparked by the women's dissatisfaction with the government's proposal to raise the age at which girls could get married from 15 to 16. Sixteen was felt to be still too young, regardless of the fact that it was an improvement on the existing law (Mangulenje 2009; Nduna 2009). Indeed, the strength of feeling across the country proved such that President Bingu wa Mutharika eventually chose not to sign the Bill, prompting an extended period of debate and consultation (see, e.g., Laing 2012; Mwasinga and Nkowani 2012).[13]

The Women's Forum event featured speeches, song, dance, poetry, personal testimony, and three short plays. In the opening act of the first play, a mother was seen complaining about the extent of her poverty. Expressing her desire for shop-bought bread and sugar, she concluded that it was high time her school-going daughter was married. Although her daughter made clear that she did not want to marry, the mother went ahead and found an eligible bachelor who bought presents for them both, including a much sought-after blanket-like cloth wrap that the mother took great pride in wearing. Eventually, her daughter agreed to leave school and get married, and she moved to town to live with her new husband. In a later scene, we watched as the heavily pregnant daughter attended an antenatal clinic where she tested positive for HIV. As the play drew to a close, her husband refused responsibility for her predicament, blaming the girl's mother for focusing on the gifts he had provided rather than telling them to get tested before they married. The drama offered a perceptive analysis of the confluence of poverty, avarice, intergenerational tension, HIV risk, and women's

[12] Women's Forum is an organisation funded by ActionAid and comprising committees of women at T/A and Sub-T/A level who raise awareness about issues concerning women and girls, run savings and loans groups, and send representatives to monthly meetings at the district headquarters.
[13] The Marriage, Divorce and Family Relations Bill, which passed through parliament in February 2015 under Bingu's brother, President Peter Mutharika, raises the age of marital consent to 18. Ambiguity surrounded the issue until 2017 because the constitution allowed marriage from the age of 15 with parental consent. It has since been amended in light of the new legislation (Kanyongolo and Malunga 2018: 174).

economic opportunities (or lack thereof), familiar to many in Malawi. The intended lesson was clearly spelled out: the future is school, not marriage. Also conveyed, however, was a strong sense of the very real social and economic obstacles to achieving the desired goal. While nobody in the audience supported the mother's strategy, they could not fail to recognise the conditions that made a wealthy son-in-law an appealing prospect.

Although the theme of the event was forced marriage, women taking part were ambivalent about whether parents really did cajole their daughters into marrying before they were ready. Some suggested to me that it was the girls themselves who pursued boyfriends (*zibwenzi*), not necessarily husbands (*amuna*): but once they found themselves pregnant, what were they supposed to do? 'They realise later what they have done,' one woman remarked, 'and they know that they were advised otherwise, but at the age of 15 or so they are interested in boys and they follow their friends into that behaviour.'

Female initiation rites (*chinamwali*) were a key feature of these debates. I lost count of the number of times men and women told me that girls married soon after their initiation ceremonies because they had been shown the secrets of marriage and were impatient to put into practice all that they had learned.[14] It was acknowledged that this was nothing new, but there was a sense that it was more worrying in the current epoch than it had been for previous generations. For one thing, HIV complicated relationships between men and women, and, in addition, as one woman put it: 'It's like the world has turned upside down [*dziko latembenuka*] and these days girls should stay at school.' A sense that more girls were marrying young than in the past is not borne out by the available statistics, which indicate a decline in the number of Malawian women married by the age of 15 (from 21 per cent of women aged 40–44 at the time of questioning for the 2010 Demographic and Health Survey, to 4 per cent of those aged 15–19, down 2 per cent since the previous round in 2004 (NSO and ICF Macro 2011: 76)). The statistics do, however, confirm the villagers' association of education with delayed marriage: the median age at first marriage rises with levels of education, ranging from an average of 17 for women with no education to 24 for those educated beyond secondary level (ibid.: 77).

On the one hand, initiation ceremonies were closely associated with the transition to marriage, something villagers agreed ought to be delayed. On the other, they were essential rites equipping young women for adult life. In the words of a former initiation instructor: 'What makes

[14] In this area of the country, female initiation rites are carried out for between one and three girls at a time, at the age of approximately 15. For more on initiation ceremonies, see Johnson (2018b).

a person a person is initiation [*Kuti munthu akhale munthu, ndi unam-wali*].' Knowledge acquired through initiation not only prepares women for marriage and childbirth, but also ensures the well-being of the wider community, for example through schooling in the importance of customary periods of abstinence (during the illness of a child, for example), which, if neglected, put the health of those around them at risk. Rules laid out by the GVH specifying fines for the families of girls initiated before the age of 15 were respected, but the GVH would also fine the parents of girls who became pregnant before they had undergone initiation, underlining the perceived significance of the rites.

In practice, the initiation ceremonies I attended were important venues for the transmission of aspirations for young girls' futures; these did not centre on marriage per se but rather on educational achievement and relative financial independence. During sections of the rites dedicated to tailored advice, girls were encouraged to continue with their education and direct links were made between formal schooling and eventual marital success: 'There are no medical doctors at Chiradzulu hospital who come from this district,' one initiator explained, 'but you, if you work hard, could secure such good jobs. Marriage and pregnancy are not what you should be thinking about at this time.' Initiators also suggested that girls should consider training as nurses: 'You'll have no need of a husband until you've accomplished that, and then you can marry a man who is also well educated.' In this way, education and employment were frequently lauded as strategies for delaying marriage and ensuring a satisfactory future partnership with a like-minded man.

For his part, the GVH linked initiation, schooling, and early marriage with the broader challenges of governance. Expressing his concerns to villagers at a public meeting, he asked: 'If girls get married in Standard Seven [of primary school] will we prosper?' Some months later, he made his position clear again at a meeting of women from across his 17 villages who had been called together by a local NGO, when he seized the opportunity to berate the assembled women for singing songs relating to sexual intercourse at girls' initiations (something they denied, saying that they do not sing about sex; they simply sing because they are enjoying themselves). At the close of the meeting, the GVH took centre stage to tell the women he had some messages for them to take back to their respective village heads: the most important of these concerned the fact that, as he saw it, too many children were avoiding school. He thus declared that the parents of those who failed to attend would be fined three goats. 'Going to school is important,' he insisted, and his reasoning could not have been more serious: 'The gardens are insufficient.' While children who succeed at school will one day buy their own plot, 'girls who concentrate on the activities of the bedroom just get pregnant and then you have to give them a garden'.[15] What he wanted to avoid, he explained, were conflicts over land that would lead to serious accusations of witchcraft (see, e.g., Peters 2002). Hunger and conflict could only undermine his efforts to coordinate development work, such as the new World Vision programme that was due to begin in his area a few months after the meeting. He wanted his villagers to be strong, able, and willing to labour on projects to bring bridges, schools, and health centres to the area. He also wanted young villagers to pursue educational advancement, so that they might generate prosperity for themselves and their kin.

In a private exchange I observed at his home, the GVH counselled his young female heirs in much the same way. 'These are the days of school,' he told them:

You need the [secondary school leavers' certificate]. If you finish school, there are colleges; do you think I can't find the money for your fees? In just two years you can train to be an agricultural adviser ... or you could do teaching, the [District Education Manager] can sign and you'll train to be a teacher. You will be self-reliant. Then you can marry and have good marriages, marriages characterised by development. Otherwise, your marriages will be marked by poverty, we will give you gardens and you will grow maize.

Like their traditional leaders, villagers also wanted their daughters to enter marriage from a position of strength, with the means of providing themselves with a cash income to supplement their agricultural endeavours, and the ability to choose a spouse who would prove industrious, resourceful, and supportive. Their fear was that girls would be bounced into marriage by early pregnancy and economic dependence and that this would mean a future of poverty, marital discord, and perhaps even HIV.

Young girls themselves differed in their reactions to these messages, as illustrated by the experiences of two sisters aged 19 and 21, who had both been initiated at around the age of 17. The younger sister delighted her matrilineal kin with her, frankly scandalous, response to her first marriage proposal: roughly speaking, 'Not even if the earth farted!' (*olo pansi pataphwisa*). In retelling the story, she waited for her audience to regain their composure, and then explained her decision by way of the rhetorical question: 'Am I supposed to go to school *and* think about marriage?!' Thus, she made clear where her priorities lay. Her sister, on the other hand, despite continuing her education at a local state secondary school, frustrated her relatives with her vocal and defiant loyalty to her long-term boyfriend, whom she maintained was her intended future spouse. Try as they might, nobody could persuade her that her time would be better spent on her studies than with her boyfriend. The fact that her boyfriend

---

[15] His comments allude to the lack of unallocated land and the consequent pressure to subdivide plots.

had been largely unemployed since dropping out of school did little to allay their concerns. The diversity of voices, and the differing life choices of young women in these Chiradzulu villages, suggest the difficulties of reconciling conflicting aspirations and the challenges involved in achieving adult womanhood in the contemporary era.

A matter of time

The advice given to young girls at initiation focuses on the formation of households through marriage, but it is also important to maintain a sense of life-historical transformation within households and relationships over time. This point was brought home to me when I returned to Malawi in September 2013 and revisited the village I had left in 2010. In just three years the makeup of many households had been transformed by marriages, divorces, births, deaths, and migration, as well as by the healthy growth of infants into young children capable of carrying out household tasks, and the transition of productive adolescent family members into absent secondary-school students or household heads in their own right. Changes in the gender balance, income, and available labour within particular households and compounds had far-reaching effects, ranging from the freeing up of formerly nursing women to engage in trade beyond the village to the inability of others to maintain the extent of their gardens. In addition to affecting gendered divisions of labour, these shifts had observable implications for relations of inter-household support and exchange, both within and beyond compounds. They also affected the movement of children sent to live with kin, near or far, who were in need of additional household and agricultural labour and who would largely assume responsibility for feeding, clothing, disciplining, and schooling the children for the duration of their residence.

Anachisale's experience makes clear the importance of diachronic analysis. She had married young, but her early experience of married life, during which she lived among her husband's kin in a village within walking distance of her own, had ended abruptly with her husband's sudden death in a road accident. Some years later she had married again, and during the course of her second marriage her husband had built a home in her matrilineal compound where they lived for some time; they also spent several years living in a township close to Limbe so that he was more favourably placed for his work on the local minibus taxis. The configuration of her household shifted significantly over time as she cared for a number of the children of two categorical sisters who had passed away, as well as for her second husband's son. Two of these children had reached adulthood by the time of my fieldwork, while others had moved to live in related households. This latter group included her stepson, who was living with his paternal grandparents following the death of his birth mother. During 2009–10, Anachisale formed a household unit with two teenage daughters of her late sisters, whom she would often refer to as her own children, and for whom she had cared since their early childhood. By 2014, one had married and moved to live with her husband's kin in the expectation that, in time, she and her young family would return to her matrilineal home compound, in the vicinity of Anachisale's house. With her other daughter attending a secondary school too far away for her to reside at home, Anachisale was maintaining her homestead alone.

Despite her strong misgivings about marriage, Anachisale had in fact accepted a proposal in the intervening years. The relationship was short-lived, however, as it emerged that her new husband was already married to a woman living in a neighbouring district. Nevertheless, she and her matrilineal kin did not condemn him entirely for he had given her the biological child they never thought she would bear. They thus chose not to pursue him for abandoning his wife and failing to support their child. As a result, Anachisale was largely reliant on the material support of her matrilineal kin in the early months of her son's life, and her son went by the name provided by his maternal uncle rather than his father's kin, as custom would dictate.[16] The birth of her son in 2012 entailed a significant shift in the configuration of Anachisale's household, which remained female-headed but in other ways was barely recognisable from the one I had entered in 2009. Single once more, my enquiries about any future marriage plans were met with derisive laughter.

Anachisale's position as a single mother and female household head is unremarkable in the context of rural southern Malawi; this is a setting in which marriage has long been a volatile institution and divorce does not invite shame. Historical accounts indicate that high rates of divorce and remarriage have invariably characterised matrilineal areas of the country (Kaler 2001): while marriage is desirable, it is often experienced serially. Population statistics collected by the community-based organisation (CBO) committee for the 17 villages of the local GVH in March 2010 give some indication of the relative prevalence of household forms.[17] However, questions about female- and male-headed households seem to have been variously interpreted, and in only five cases do the numbers provided add up to the total number of households indicated.

---

[16] Villagers follow a tradition of inviting the father's kin to name a couple's first-born child.

[17] I was told that the CBO was instigated by Oxfam. It is made up of men and women from each of the 17 villages and the committee is charged with coordinating development activities at GVH level, and reporting to the GVH and to visiting NGO representatives. The statistics were compiled by members of the CBO committee, the member for each village taking responsibility for collecting the data for his or her own home village. Any errors, therefore, are unlikely to be the result of unfamiliarity with the setting.

Table 1.1 *Household headship in Malawi*

Household head	Urban	Rural	Northern Region	Central Region	Southern Region	Chiradzulu District	Total
Male	82.0	71.1	73.0	75.6	70.1	62.9	72.7
Female	18.0	28.9	27.0	24.4	29.9	37.1	27.3

Note: Figures are summarised from the 2008 Census Gender Report (NSO 2008b: 68–9).

The translation of male- and female-headed households as 'families ruled over by men or women' (*mabanja akulamulidwa ndi amuna/akazi*) may have invited some to list only single-headed households by the sex of the household head, leaving households headed by married couples unaccounted for, but this is not something I can verify in relation to each village. Despite certain inconsistencies in the figures, the numbers are suggestive of a situation in which the majority of households are headed by men (56–76 per cent), with a significant minority (24–44 per cent) headed by women. The figures for household headship in the area are broadly consistent with the available national statistics, as recorded in the 2008 census (see Table 1.1).[18]

The national survey found female-headed households to be more common in rural areas, where they make up almost 29 per cent of households. The Southern Region as a whole has a greater proportion of female household heads, and, within the region, Chiradzulu District has the highest percentage of female-headed households, at 37.1 per cent. Nationally, only Ntcheu District in the Central Region recorded a larger proportion of female-headed households, at 39.6 per cent.[19]

The CBO statistics do not indicate the proportions of adult men and women who are married, divorced, widowed, or single. However, national data suggest that 68 per cent of women aged 15–49 were in 'a union' at the time of the Demographic and Health Survey in 2010:

[18] See also the 2010 Demographic and Health Survey report (NSO and ICF Macro 2011: 11), which gives slightly higher figures for female household headship overall (28.1 per cent), in urban centres (20.7 per cent), and in rural areas (29.5 per cent). The 2010 report does not provide regional or district-level data on household headship.
[19] For the census, the recorded household head was the person reported as head by other members of the household, and it should not therefore be taken to imply that the designated head is unmarried. The report acknowledges that, in matrilineal settings, the characteristics and responsibilities of household headship may be better regarded as 'shared rather than being vested in one individual' (NSO 2008b: 68). The authors offer matriliny as an explanation for the prevalence of female-headed households in Chiradzulu and Ntcheu, adding: 'By giving the women land ownership and control over key issues such as what to plant and selling land, the matrilineal system gives women an edge over men, which enhances their position in society, unlike their counterparts in patrilineal systems' (ibid.: 70).

Table 1.2 *Percentages of women aged 20–24 and 45–49 currently divorced in 2001*

District	Average age at first marriage	Divorced (women aged 20–24)	Divorced (women aged 45–49)
Balaka (South)	17.5	10.6%	22.2%
Mchinji (Central)	17.5	5.0%	9.4%
Rumphi (North)	18.3	3.4%	11.3%

Note: The women were divorced at the time of the 2001 questionnaires conducted as part of the second round of the longitudinal Malawi Diffusion and Ideational Change Project, as analysed by Reniers (2003).

59 per cent in a marriage that had been formalised by civil, religious, or traditional rites; and 9 per cent cohabiting without having formalised the relationship. The figures for men indicate that 57 per cent were currently in a union, with 48 per cent formally married (NSO and ICF Macro 2011: 77). Comparison of these figures with those cited by Hunter for South Africa suggests that marriage is not such a 'rarity' (2010: 2) in Malawi as it has become further south. South African census data show a decline in marriage rates from 57 per cent of Africans recorded as married in 1960 to just 30 per cent in 2001 (ibid.: 93).[20] But marriage rates tell only part of the story. Georges Reniers' study of divorce and remarriage in Malawi, which uses data collected in Balaka District in the south, Mchinji in central Malawi, and Rumphi in the patrilineal north (see Table 1.2), shows 'exceptionally high figures' (2003: 190) for divorce. Indeed, he goes as far as to suggest that in matrilineal Balaka, 'the divorce probabilities must be among the highest recorded on the continent' (ibid.: 198).[21]

Reniers' statistics reveal a degree of geographical and life-historical variation. Women are more likely to be currently divorced in the matrilineal south than in the mixed central or patrilineal northern districts, and in all three districts studied, the divorce figures are higher for older

[20] The figures Hunter cites also contained the categories of 'living together' and 'separated', so those of 'married' and 'divorced' can be assumed to imply that the appropriate rites had been conducted, which would involve the payment and possible return of bridewealth. The connection Klaits posits between men and women's reluctance to marry in Botswana and vast gender inequalities in access to resources (2005: 51) chimes with Hunter's analysis of the situation in South Africa (see also Gulbrandsen 1986).

[21] Reniers' categorical distinction between cohabitation and marriage goes some way towards navigating what can be rather fluid arrangements. While, formally, it is the *chinkhoswe* rites that establish a couple as married, in the absence of explicit tensions, relationships of cohabitation will often be referred to as marriages (*mabanja*). Similarly, with divorce and separation, *chisudzulo* rites mark the formal dissolution of a marriage but the end of cohabitation will often be referred to in the same terms (*kutha kwabanja*).

women. Reniers warns, however, that such statistics are 'confounded by the speed and frequency of remarriage' (2003: 179). Perhaps more informative, then, are the figures indicating that, in Balaka, one in three first marriages ended in divorce within five years, with almost 65 per cent dissolved within 25 years. The figures for Rumphi are 14 per cent and 40 per cent respectively (ibid.: 189). For comparative purposes, Reniers compares the combined divorce rate (across the three districts) – 45 per cent of all first marriages within 20 years – with the available figures for Ethiopia, considered to have a high divorce rate, where the equivalent figure is 40 per cent (ibid.: 190). Across the three districts, more than 40 per cent of women remarried within two years, 75 per cent within five years, and almost 90 per cent within ten years of divorce (ibid.: 194). These latter statistics introduce a sense of dynamism that snapshot figures focusing on household headship do little to illuminate (Peters 1983).

The ethnographic data provide necessary context for these statistics and reinforce the message that women in rural Chiradzulu were not rejecting marriage wholesale. Their attitudes towards marriage were more nuanced and characterised less by a general hostility than by a broadly generalisable strategy of embracing a first marriage, bearing children, and perhaps later, following divorce, seeking greater independence at the level of the household, all the while remaining embedded within those matrilineal relationships through which material and immaterial resources flow. For some women, it was only after two or three marriages that life as an unmarried woman (*mbeta*) emerged as an attractive possibility; for others, first marriages lasted a lifetime. For a significant number, however, household 'independence' was achieved and treasured, often with the material support of adult sons, brothers and/or mothers' brothers. As we shall see in the chapters to come, the decision to remain unmarried was generally taken in relation to women's evaluation of men's capacities to fulfil the moral-material role of the 'good' husband, and of their own access to economic and social resources. The figures for remarriage suggest that such decisions are subject to ongoing assessment.

If marriage is contested terrain in Malawi, it goes without saying that contestation of the sort that will be described as we move into the police VSU and the magistrates' courts does not represent an aberration. There is no typical marital harmony against which cases heard in those spaces might be measured or with which they might be compared. Nevertheless, an important theme of this book is the power of ideals to orient aspirations, expectations, and moral assessments of particular relationships and disputes. These ideals include visions of masculine 'provider love' and gendered divisions of labour within marriage; they also extend to the role of wider networks of kin in guiding and supporting spouses, and the particular expectations that women hold of male kin, principally brothers and mothers' brothers, to whom they may look for moral and material support (see Chapter 6). Ideals are rarely met, but they cast a long shadow and inform the contested visions of gender justice, itself an ideal, that lie at the heart of the chapters that follow.

2   Marital disputes and the legal search for justice

> What I believe is that marriage is a contract, it can end at any time. But the end of a marriage does not mean the end of life. It is just a step into another life. You shouldn't hate one another; when there are reasons to cooperate, you should do so ... Whatever is coming tomorrow, we can't know, so we should not prioritise hostility.

With these words, a village head brought a marital dispute hearing to a close one Saturday afternoon in July 2010. Gathered under the trees in front of the village head's house were the couple whose marriage was coming to an end and their respective *ankhoswe*. For reasons of convenience, the discussions had taken place in the relative privacy of the village head's compound rather than in the more public space typically referred to as his *bwalo* (court), but the hearing was taken no less seriously for that. The session had begun with accounts of the events that had brought the couple to the village head, and, after listening to each side, his first intervention had been to comment on the emotional tenor of what he had heard:

> What I really listened for is the love [*chikondi*] that was there ... I listened to hear where that love has gone. From what I've heard, the issue seems to be that your love is finished. So we can't tell you to carry on [with marriage] because that will only lead to you chopping each other's hands and fingers off and burning each other ... My job now is to get you to discuss matters together so that we can see what to do next.

Through the course of the discussions, a consensus was reached that the couple's marriage was over and thus, rather than seeking reconciliation, the hearing focused on questions of property, child maintenance, and the husband's provision of a house for his soon to be ex-wife. Emotions ran high, but both parties and their respective *ankhoswe* had their say, and by the end of the session they were in agreement about how to proceed. The dispute itself did not involve claims of violence, but the village head gestured to the possibility of violence when he steered them towards an acceptance of the breakdown of their relationship. His allusion to the kinds of severe injuries Malawian men had reportedly inflicted upon their wives in recent years (see Chapter 5) invoked the contemporary discourse of human rights and gender-based violence. His words met with assent and the case thus marked the coming together of two sets of matrilineal kin to oversee the dissolution of a marriage: an unremarkable outcome was given new resonance as a means of avoiding future violence.

This chapter describes how ideas about human rights and gender-based violence became mundane in Malawi, and examines the nexus of dispute-resolution forums through which they, and disputing couples, travel. The aim is to understand the different institutional contexts in which gendered disputes take place and to gain analytical purchase on the ambiguities of legal authority that underpin them. However, the ubiquity of ideas about human and women's rights does not negate alternative framings or ambitions for justice with respect to gender relations, and the chapters that follow focus more specifically on tensions between globally circulating ideals and locally salient aspirations.

Human and women's rights

The concepts and language of human and women's rights were by no means new to Malawi by the time I arrived in 2009. In fact, so familiar were they by then that the village head cited above could invoke them implicitly. Without directly employing the vocabulary of rights, his reference to gender-based violence was sufficient to signal a field of meaning that villagers associated with the contemporary era. Indeed, the coming of *demokalase*, heralded by the 1994 election of President Bakili Muluzi in the country's first multiparty elections since independence, was immediately associated with the dawn of human rights (*ufulu wachibadwidwe*). These were enshrined in the country's new constitution, which came into effect the following year (Gloppen and Kanyongolo 2007). While the discourse of rights (*maufulu*; singular: *ufulu*) swiftly became ubiquitous, it has been argued that the potential for building on this discourse to facilitate tangible improvements in people's lives was restricted by the particular way in which rights were framed, including their translation into Chichewa (Englund 2006). The use of the existing word for 'freedom', *ufulu*, qualified by the term *wachibadwidwe*, roughly 'of birth', produced the individualising expression 'freedom that one is born with' or 'birth freedom' as the standard rendering of human rights. This phrasing, and the associated focus on civil and political liberties at the expense of economic and social rights, while understandable following 30 years of autocratic rule, has had peculiarly disempowering effects (ibid.). As Englund demonstrates, this situation was compounded by an anti-democratic attitude of distanced superiority on the part of those whose education and positions might otherwise have endowed them with opportunities for advocacy on behalf of the less fortunate majority. It is perhaps instructive, then, that the village head chose to signal the relevance of recent rights campaigns without employing the language of *ufulu wachibadwidwe*.

It was during the first decade of democratic rule, as the discourse of human rights was becoming pervasive, that Chiradzulu became notorious as the site of a series of gruesome and shocking murders of women (Bombeya 2000; Chapalapata 2000; Chikoko 2000; Paliani 2000; Semu 2000). Local memories of these crimes lent additional resonance to the village head's concerns about possible gender violence. Reactions at the time revealed a considerable degree of ambiguity surrounding the new language of rights (*Daily Times* 2000; *Malawi News* 2000). Had freedom/ rights (*ufulu*) gone so far that people thought they could behave entirely as they pleased with no regard for others? Or did the murders signal the need for the further protection of women's rights/freedom? In other words, did Chiradzulu suffer an absence or an excess of rights? For a number of Malawian women, incidents of this kind were a spur to action, and several went on to found NGOs aiming specifically to educate Malawian citizens about human rights and violence against women and children. Many of their early activities were focused on Chiradzulu District, where violence was thought to be particularly prevalent, and where, as a result, contemporary awareness of campaigns against gender-based violence may be particularly high.

In subsequent years, *jenda* (gender) has become almost as familiar a term as *ufulu*, and, like rights, talk of *jenda* could also elicit both scepticism and approval. At the broadest level, 'gender mainstreaming' has been embraced and high-profile campaigns have sought to raise awareness of domestic violence and to increase the participation of women in electoral politics. Locally, *jenda* has also dominated development activities and interventions (see Chapter 4). As we shall see, however, messages of gender equality have been variously interpreted, engaged with, and resisted. This book turns the spotlight on tensions between government- and NGO-endorsed messages of gender equality as sameness on the one hand, and locally observed aspirations to complementarity in gender and marital relations on the other. It does so by paying attention to the views of Malawian citizens, as well as to encounters with traditional authorities, police officers, magistrates, and NGO facilitators. It is to this complex landscape of legal authorities and institutions, which men and women must navigate as they seek resolution to their marital disputes, that I now turn.

A loose chain of dispute-resolution forums

Perhaps the most remarkable characteristic of marriage in matrilineal areas of Malawi is its seeming fragility, as suggested by the village head's ready acceptance that not only was the couple's marriage over, but that the end of their marriage was a relatively routine matter. Although marriage rates remain high, signalling the enduring importance of marriage as an institution, discord, divorce, and remarriage are also remarkably common (see Chapter 1). As we saw in the previous chapter, the defining feature of a marital relationship is the allocation of *ankhoswe* or marriage guardians. These are matrilineal kin designated as the first port of call in the event of marital disputes. Their very existence indexes the expectation that marriage will entail friction, and that it will be necessary for disagreements to be mediated by external parties. The range of further possible mediators and adjudicators is striking, and they each have their own historical and contemporary resonances: thus, in combination with *ankhoswe*, traditional authorities, police officers, and magistrates can be said to provide a 'loose chain' of marital dispute-resolution forums.

One certainty about this loose chain is that *ankhoswe* stand at the near end of it. In practice, not everybody begins with their *ankhoswe*, but it is widely acknowledged that they should. *Ankhoswe* bear responsibility for arranging discussions between spouses when trouble arises, and for accompanying their disputing kin as they navigate additional dispute forums when these kin-based hearings have reached an impasse. In the first instance, it is understood that this ought to involve a session at the *bwalo* or village head's court, such as the one encountered above. Not all cases enter the *bwalo*, however, and not all of those that do so end there. In the event of an unsatisfactory experience with the village head, several options are available. Taking the 'traditional' route, complainants would request a referral to the next rung of the traditional authority ladder; alternatively, they might opt to visit a police victim support unit (VSU). Magistrates' courts offer a third possibility.

Traditional authority

In the current structure of traditional authority (lower case), village heads answer to group village heads (GVHs) who have responsibility for a cluster of villages; a number of GVHs, in turn, answer to a Traditional Authority (T/A; upper case). In some areas, a Sub-T/A occupies an intermediary position between the two. The T/A is the highest-ranking chief with whom villagers are likely to engage, although there also exist a number of senior and paramount chiefs.[1] Following this structure,

[1] In some locations, senior chiefs have been appointed above T/As. Nationally, there are seven paramount chiefs who rank above senior chiefs, four of whom were inaugurated by President Bingu wa Mutharika from 2007 onwards (Eggen 2011: 326). Paramount chiefs – unlike village heads, GVHs, T/As, and senior chiefs – represent ethnically (rather than territorially) defined constituencies.

disputes that are not concluded to the satisfaction of both parties by a village head can be referred up the traditional authority hierarchy to the GVH and then to the T/A (via the Sub-T/A where applicable). Altogether, there are over 20,000 *bwalos* in which traditional authorities handle disputes in contemporary Malawi (Schärf et al. 2002: 39).

Today's ranked structure of traditional authorities is, in part, a colonial legacy. British officials directly challenged chiefs in the early stages of colonisation, but then gradually became more and more reliant on local leaders, some of whom they had appointed themselves (Eggen 2011: 316–17). John McCracken thus describes a 'slow drift towards indirect rule from the 1920s' (2012: 220). In the face of extensive male out-migration, it was often in order to secure a ready labour force for the agricultural estates that colonial officials sought the cooperation of local headmen (and headwomen) and chiefs in the Shire Highlands. In this regard, the area lagged behind much of the rest of the country due to the resistance of estate owners to measures that would loosen their control over their workers. It was not until 1930 that principal headmen were appointed in Chiradzulu and the surrounding districts; even then, their responsibilities were limited as a result of pressure from the estates (ibid.).

In the years that followed their recognition as principal headmen, and their later designation as native authorities, these chiefs, and the village headmen beneath them, were delegated responsibilities for hearing minor cases, administering marriages and divorces, issuing beer licences, and so on. Of course, many of these activities would have been occurring anyway, without the official consent of the colonial authorities. Nevertheless, the recognition of principal headmen was not always straightforward, and many appointments were contested (McCracken 2012: 224; Power 2010: 30–1; White 1987: 179–80). The outcomes of these wrangles had a lasting impact: successors to the original Chiradzulu principal headmen – Mpama, Likoswe, Kadewere, Nkalo, and Nyimbili (Ntchema) – are joined by Chitera as contemporary T/As, at the apex of the local chiefly hierarchy. Under indirect rule, these native authorities operated within severe financial constraints. They enjoyed neither the kinds of supporting infrastructure, such as tribal police and tax collectors, nor the salary levels that enabled chiefs in neighbouring Tanganyika (Tanzania) to distinguish themselves through the conspicuous consumption of such luxury goods as motor cars (McCracken 2012: 225). They were, however, prominent figures in rural areas, working alongside district commissioners, who were the most senior representatives of the colonial government.

Following independence, the 1967 Chiefs' Act maintained a key role for traditional authorities in assisting district commissioners, as well as promoting 'culture' and 'customary law' in their areas of jurisdiction

(Englund 2012a: 76–80). By contrast with Malawi, postcolonial governments in the neighbouring countries of Mozambique and Tanzania
legislated to abolish traditional leadership, while the Zambian government curtailed leaders' activities. Having never restricted traditional
authority to such an extent in the first place, it follows that Malawi has
not shared in the more recent regional trend of reviving chieftaincy.
Nevertheless, traditional authorities in post-1994 Malawi have been
boosted by their association with development initiatives, despite legislation introduced in 1998 to re-institutionalise local government.[2] While
democratisation and decentralisation might have posed a challenge to
traditional authority, local councillors have not made much of an impression. First elected in 2000, their tenure expired in 2005 and no further
local elections were held until 2014. Not only did this mean that my
fieldwork was carried out during a hiatus in local government, but the
literal absence and abiding ineffectualness of elected councillors have
meant that traditional authorities have maintained their de facto significance for the planning and administration of district and sub-district
development projects. They remain the only effective links between
citizens and government, donor, and NGO officials (Chiweza 2007).

Thus, while dispute resolution was a vital and long-standing element
of traditional authorities' duties, it by no means exhausted their job
description. As a GVH summarised for me, their work could be divided
into four principal areas, of which dispute settlement was one; the others
were maintaining order, attracting development initiatives (*chitukuko*)
through liaison with governmental and non-government agencies, and
facilitating contact between such agencies and their rural subjects. Traditional authorities thus remain vital intermediaries, if somewhat ambiguously placed, between formal and informal authority.

In these circumstances, and contrasting further with their counterparts
elsewhere in Southern Africa who have been subject to different kinds of
political interventions, traditional authorities in Malawi have maintained
considerable legitimacy into the postcolonial and post-Kamuzu Banda
periods (Englund 2012a: 76–80; Kanyongolo 2006: 146–7). While villagers recognised the varying competencies and idiosyncrasies of individual incumbents, they held the institution of chieftaincy in high regard,
attributing local peace and security to its presence as well as crediting it
for local NGO-led development activities. The respect accorded to traditional authorities was also evident in times of personal or family crisis,
when villagers called upon village heads for assistance, keeping them
informed of their changing fortunes and circumstances. Popular attendance at the *bwalo* when dispute hearings were in session similarly served

---

[2] Local councils were initially abolished by President Muluzi's government, before the first
local elections were held in 2000.

to underline the legitimacy of traditional authorities. The waxing and waning of their involvement in formal court structures (on which more below) notwithstanding, traditional authorities' ongoing role in dispute resolution in rural areas was widely recognised, not least by police officers and magistrates who expected to receive referral letters from village heads when dealing with civil and low-level criminal matters.

Hearings at the village *bwalo* were conducted by the village head with the assistance of councillors; these were generally elder male villagers who were usually not members of the village head's own matrilineage and who were said to have been selected on the basis of their particular skills and strength of character. Each village had a recognised space designated as *bwalo*; these were usually relatively open areas benefiting from the shade of large trees. While personnel in more formal legal forums often liked to distinguish their own procedures by referring to *bwalo* hearings as unruly free-for-alls, where anyone in attendance could join in at will and people frequently spoke over one another, this characterisation was not entirely accurate. *Bwalo* procedures did allow for wide discussion, enabling complainants and defendants to speak at length, question each other, and call witnesses; they also often attracted large audiences, but spectators rarely made substantial contributions and their involvement was regulated by the village head. Questioning was usually directed by the councillors, and the village head would listen and take notes, waiting until the proceedings were drawing to a close before pronouncing on the case. Ultimately, village heads strove to reach a judgment, rather than simply facilitate discussions, and their decisions were often accompanied by orders for compensation to be paid, generally in the form of chickens or goats. In marital disputes, orders tended to relate to the husband's provision of a house for his wife, as in the case discussed above.

In the event of dissatisfaction with the result of a hearing by a village head, many disputants opted not to pursue appeals to higher-ranking traditional authorities, who were often more geographically distant than other available forums. Instead, they carried referral letters from their village heads to other adjudicators. Some approached NGOs: in Chiradzulu District at the time of my fieldwork, this would almost certainly have involved a visit to a small branch office shared by two Malawian NGOs that had been established around the time of the democratic transition (1993–4) and focused on human and women's rights. However, during 2009–10 this option was rarely taken due to the NGOs' changing priorities and projects (see Introduction). More commonly, disputants opted to discuss their cases at a police VSU, or to initiate a civil hearing at a magistrates' court.[3] Indeed, many ended up visiting both a VSU and a

---

[3] For a small number of people whose marriages had been celebrated in a religious establishment (a church or a mosque), religious leaders could also be consulted.

magistrates' court, as the former very often referred cases onwards to local courts, and the latter could also direct complainants to pursue police mediation before returning to court. It is possible to speculate that, had the case outlined above not progressed so smoothly, the village head's next step would have been to refer the couple to the VSU.

Community policing and victim support units

In Chapter 3, we will engage in detail with a case heard at the VSU after the complainant, Anabanda, arrived at the police station front desk to report the destruction of her property. Identifying the case as a marital dispute, the police encouraged her to summon the relevant parties and discuss the matter at the VSU the next day. Anabanda thus eschewed the village head due to the seeming urgency of the situation she faced. Hers was not the only case to reach the VSU via the police station proper, but such cases were fairly unusual. Alefa, another woman whose case I observed, also bypassed the headman, but in very different circumstances. She decided to avoid a hearing at the *bwalo* because she was living in her husband's home village and he was related to the chiefly lineage. Employing a common idiom, she explained that 'kinship is like a scar' (*chibale ndi chipsera*; i.e. one cannot brush off a kin relationship), so she could not expect a fair hearing.[4] She also expressed discomfort about the open nature of *bwalo* sessions, at which details of disputes are revealed in the presence of many villagers. For Alefa, going to the VSU and then to court was a matter of self-respect (*ndinadzipatsa ine ulemu*).[5] Lusiya, another woman whom I met at the VSU, was also living among her husband's kin when problems arose in her marriage; she had first approached the village head for assistance, but the dispute had escalated and she had moved back to live with her matrilineal relatives before he

---

Instances of this were relatively rare, although I did come across a few cases at the VSU that had previously been heard by church elders.

[4] Other villagers held contrary views, arguing that chiefs treat everyone alike and would not necessarily favour their own relatives in cases brought before them. In fact, they might deal more severely with the misdemeanours of their own kin in an effort to ensure that their authority was not undermined, and to set an example. One traditional authority in particular often warned his relatives that their behaviour must be exemplary, for if their fellow villagers were to see that he could not maintain order within his own extended family (*mbumba*) they would not respect his leadership. He was known to have meted out unusually harsh punishments to young male relatives who had behaved disrespectfully towards their neighbours.

[5] Alefa chose to take her case to the VSU after it was recommended to her by people in her village who said that the police consider all sides of a case (*amaona mbale zonse*). In the event, her case was not heard at the VSU because her husband did not honour the summons (according to Alefa, he did not think it appropriate for matrimonial cases to be heard at the police station). After a month had passed, the police issued a referral letter to the magistrates' court.

had been able to call the parties together. She subsequently chose to pursue her case at the VSU because it was closer to her home village and she had heard positive stories about its work.[6]

Despite the range of pathways traversed in practice, police officers working in the VSU saw themselves as a fixed node within a linear, hierarchical route, located between village heads and magistrates' courts. Thus, they spoke of referring cases backwards or downwards to village heads or *ankhoswe*, and onwards or upwards to the magistrates' court. Where cases had been brought to them first, officers would castigate villagers for usurping the authority of the 'lower' institutions, principally the *ankhoswe*, but also village heads. Officers issued countless referral letters 'up' the chain to the magistrates' courts, although they occasionally acknowledged that this was not strictly necessary as complainants could open a case at court without a written referral, or with a letter from a traditional authority – and many did so. While officers felt it appropriate for them to refer cases 'up' and 'down', they were highly critical of staff at the magistrates' court when they considered them to be shirking the responsibility that came with being, in the words of a sub-inspector, at 'the end of a chain'. 'They shouldn't just send people back to the beginning,' he fumed upon hearing that a woman had been directed by court staff to go 'back' and deal with her *ankhoswe*.

The VSU register at the Chiradzulu station documented an average of 24 cases per month during 2009, a figure that vastly under-represented the officers' workload by including only those cases deemed to have been in some sense resolved, and by omitting any reference to the number of hearings held with respect to each dispute. It was not unusual for cases to require multiple sessions, but they would appear only once in the register. The VSU office was busy year-round and, by the time it opened at 8 a.m., there was often a queue of people waiting outside to register cases and attend discussions. While the police generally elicited ambivalent views among villagers (who feared them while also considering them both ineffective at combating crime and susceptible to corruption), VSUs were held in high regard and frequently turned to when hearings with *ankhoswe* or traditional authorities had failed, especially where that failure was due to one party's refusal to engage with proceedings. A summons letter from the police, it was said, was more likely to be heeded. Indeed, this seemed to be the case, despite the absence of enforcement mechanisms.

---

[6] Lusiya's aunt had been to the VSU to complain about her husband's excessive drinking and, according to Lusiya, the outcome had been a significant transformation in his behaviour. Lusiya's own case was eventually referred to the magistrates' court after she and her husband failed to reach a settlement at the VSU.

Police summons letters were addressed to village heads, asking them to inform the person against whom the complaint had been made, as well as his or her *ankhoswe*, that a hearing was to be held on a particular date. On the day in question, couples and their supporting kin would arrive at the VSU, where community policing officers and lay volunteers would handle their dispute.[7] Hearings were conducted in a closed room, with no audience beyond those there to support the disputants. The complainant would first be asked to outline their grievance, and the other party would then be given the floor. The two would be invited to ask questions of one another, and their *ankhoswe* would be enjoined to speak to the veracity of what had been said. Although following this rough order, the discussions often felt like open conversations; interjections were usually not discouraged and police officers and lay volunteers sometimes also contributed a great deal. The informal tone was facilitated by the use of Chichewa, despite the fact that the police kept their records in English. The aim was not to issue any kind of binding judgment or legal order, but to reach an agreed resolution, or to refer the case to another forum for further handling.

In a relatively short period of time, VSUs had become key institutions within the local legal landscape, providing a venue to which village heads could refer difficult cases, and a means for villagers to attempt to bypass traditional authorities if they so wished. Indeed, in my first conversation with the Sub-T/A of the area in which I resided, he told me that he heard significantly fewer marital disputes these days because the local VSUs were so popular. In addition, a proportion of the marital cases he did hear reached him at the community victim support unit (CVSU) rather than at the *bwalo*. CVSUs are another community policing forum, convened at T/A or Sub-T/A level and involving traditional authorities in the handling of disputes alongside police officers (see Chapter 3). VSUs and CVSUs blur the lines between formal and informal institutions; while they do not pass judgment in the way that traditional authorities and magistrates do, and they do not have the authority to dissolve marriages, they are staffed by uniformed state police officers who are not shy about threatening uncooperative disputants with the full force of the law. These community policing structures are also eminently 'modern' and strongly associated with the dissemination of human and women's rights.

Indeed, the Malawi Police Service's Community Policing Services Branch (CPSB), of which VSUs are a central institution, emerged during the restructuring of the Malawi Police Force with the transition to

---

[7] The only regular volunteer at the VSU I observed was a Muslim sheikh (see Chapter 3). The original idea had been that local traditional authorities and a range of religious leaders would also attend.

multiparty politics.[8] The UK Department for International Development (DFID) provided funding for the police reform programme, which came into operation in 1997 with the aim of helping the police 'to adapt to current norms of policing, including those that seek to protect human rights, uphold the rule of law and promote accountability and efficiency' (Kanyongolo 2006: 103). The first VSUs were established in 2001. According to police guidelines:

> Every police formation should have a VSU which is situated at a good, quiet place away from the main building and not close to the counter or cells.[9] There should be a visible signpost that directs people to the VSU. The VSU must have a minimum of three rooms: an interview room, first aid room and waiting room. (Malawi Police Service and MHRRC n.d.: 15)

The VSU at the Chiradzulu police station met most of these requirements: a local NGO had assisted with funds to build a separate building for the VSU, which was painted with the words '*Malo othandiza nkhani za chinsisi*', describing the VSU as a place for assistance with confidential matters.

The VSU building consisted of three rooms, although they fulfilled slightly different functions from those envisaged in the guidelines. Two of the rooms were fairly large and one of these served as the main room for hearing cases. This room contained two long wooden benches positioned along adjoining walls, two large desks placed side by side and facing the benches, and a number of chairs. The second room, access to which was gained through the first, contained a single bed with a foam mattress and blanket, two small desks piled high with paperwork and reports, and some additional chairs. Officers working in the VSU explained to me that this room was intended to provide a temporary refuge for a victim fleeing domestic violence during the night, but the bed remained unused throughout my fieldwork. In practice, the second room was most commonly used as an overflow facility so that, when necessary, two cases could be heard at once. A smaller, third room, with a separate entrance, was used as a storeroom. People waiting to make a complaint, or to have their cases heard, sat on the ground outside, taking shelter along the side wall of the VSU or against the main police station building

---

[8] Jean and John Comaroff describe a comparable move by the South African Police Force to transform itself from 'jackboot of the state' into 'the South African Police *Services*, a gentler, human-rights-oriented, community-friendly agency' (2006: 281, emphasis in the original).

[9] This remained an ambition. A presentation by George Kainja, then Deputy Commissioner of Police and Officer in Charge of the Community Policing Services Branch, delivered in July 2010, states that the objective of the CPSB is to support 'the expansion of Victim Support Unit[s] to all Police Stations and consolidate the existing ones' (Kainja 2010: slide 27). I was aware of four VSUs in Chiradzulu District but I have not been able to find data on the current number of VSUs in the country.

VICTIM SUPPORT UNIT.

ROLES AND RESPONSIBILITIES:

(A) COUNSELLI NG

Traumatized Victim of Domestic and
Gender based violence, and all other
victims of crime.

(B) CHILD ABUSE

Stopping Child abuse practices.
Dealing with Children in conflict with the
law.
Dealing with traumatized Children by
providing Therapy.

(C) GENDER AND DOMESTIC VIOLENCES

- Checking the trend of both Gender and
  Domestic Violence and how best these
  mal-practices could be stamped out.

Figure 2.1 Poster in the VSU (reproduced by the author)

opposite. Throughout the building, hand-drawn wall charts displaying
VSU statistics hung next to NGO- and police-produced posters warning,
for instance, against child trafficking, or explaining the virtues of community policing. A typed A4 poster on the door between the two
main rooms described the 'roles and responsibilities' of the VSU (see
Figure 2.1).

The poster highlights counselling, child abuse, and gender and domestic violence. It was the latter that a senior officer at the Chiradzulu police
station stressed when he explained to me that community policing is like
an 'umbrella body' within which the VSU 'looks after GBV [gender-
based violence]' (*imaona za GBV*). Another officer focused more closely
on counselling and the community aspect of community policing when
he told me that: 'The main aim of this office is to build relationships with
the community. That is why with most of the issues we don't open a file,
discussion comes first.' By their own admission, officers had few opportunities to engage with children beyond outreach visits to local schools.

George Kainja, then Deputy Commissioner of Police and Officer in Charge of the CPSB, made it clear that the focus on community policing constituted a break with previous approaches to policing in Malawi: 'Community policing demands the relaxation of the traditional paramilitary structure and culture of police services to more open, creative, innovative and participatory working environment [sic]' (Kainja 2009: slide 29). The senior CPSB officer at Chiradzulu police station echoed these sentiments (and those of his colleague cited above), when he told me that the number one objective of community policing was 'to establish kinship [*ubale*] between the police and the people in the villages'. He went on to describe a perceived transformation in attitudes towards the police, which he attributed to the work of the CPSB: 'Before, when the police entered a village, people used to run away; we were notorious for cruelty/violence [*nkhanza*] ... but now we are the true friends of the people.' These days, he added (in English), the police are 'part of the public', and he suggested that this was largely a result of the fact that nowadays 'people know their responsibility' (*udindo wawo*). To a certain extent, outside observers have also credited VSUs in Malawi with achieving a positive shift in public perceptions of the police. A report from the Malawi Human Rights Commission, for example, commends VSUs, which, it says, 'saw many victims, especially of domestic violence, seek the assistance of the police whose role was previously only seen as that of arresting and prosecuting' (2007: 21–2).[10]

The 'latest Western policing fashion' is how Mike Brogden (2004: 635) describes community policing, explicitly situating such police reform in the wider context of donor-driven restructuring in the Global South, and branding the trend little more than 'a panacea from the West' that is 'largely irrelevant to most African countries' (ibid.: 647). Similarly, Julia Hornberger has described how 'human rights – as part of a technocratic consensus promoting "good governance" and "the rule of law" – have become a global commodity' (2007: 17). Critics of community policing thus associate it with the neo-colonial spread of neoliberal modes of governance. Elements of the CPSB's self-description are certainly consistent with such an interpretation. For example, Kainja explains that one of the roles assigned to the community policing forums, which bring together 'stakeholders' at T/A level, is to '[e]stablish community self-help

---

[10] The same report, however, highlights several well-substantiated allegations of police brutality and torture, and reminds the reader that 'gross violations of detained persons are pervasive in the Police Service' (Malawi Human Rights Commission 2007: 24). Similarly, in an interview in which the police Inspector General expressed gratitude for the British government's financial support for police reform and praised advances in community policing and victim support services, he also admitted that '[p]olice officers have been found with criminals, committing rape, conniving with robbers. But,' he went on, 'we are trying to clean Malawi Police Service' (*Nyasa Times* 2009).

spirit where residents contribute towards the protection of each other's life and property' (Kainja 2009: slide 58) – a reference to the 'responsibility' (*udindo*) of rural villagers identified by the Chiradzulu officer.[11] Brogden's sole concession to optimism is that 'in South Africa, Malawi and Botswana, they have apparently demonstrated successfully that local communities and police can co-operate in developing and implementing crime reduction services for victims of crime, particularly of rape and domestic violence' (2004: 648). He does not reference this claim but, in relation to Malawi, it is possible to infer an allusion to the VSU programme, and we might sense some hope that there is more to this particular story than the neo-colonial imposition of a neoliberal agenda.

Nevertheless, the turn to community policing, and human rights-driven police reform in general, has to be understood in its wider context, as part of a global trend with its roots in 'Western' police reform.[12] As Hornberger reminds us, 'ultimately to speak of human rights and policing remains a historically specific possibility' (2010: 260). And it is an ironic possibility at that, with police officers having shifted from the position of archetypal human rights abusers to essential human rights defenders as understandings of human rights have expanded to incorporate the behaviour of individual citizens towards one another in the domestic sphere. We might also locate this move within a postcolonial trend to 'lawfare' (Comaroff and Comaroff 2006) – 'the preoccupation with legalities and with the legal subject, [which has] come to be so salient a dimension of postcolonial dis/order' (ibid.: 21). In articulating this trend, Jean and John Comaroff pay attention to constitutions, pointing out that while those developed in the decades following the Second World War 'gave little autonomy to the law, stressing instead parliamentary sovereignty, executive discretion, and bureaucratic authority', human rights have been prominent in constitutions drafted since the late 1980s, which have placed much greater emphasis on the rule of law (ibid.: 23). They argue that it is the 'spirit' and language of the law,

hegemonically retooled for the neoliberal epoch, that gives postcolonial nation-states their delicate sense of unity and coherence ... Law, in short, is the hydra-headed instrument by which postcolonial states seek nowadays to extend control over space and time, the cultures and identities, of their subjects. (Comaroff and Comaroff 2004: 539)

There is certainly something to the idea that law and legality have been elevated to new heights within postcolonial states in Africa, and VSUs are

---

[11] Police reform in Malawi has involved the establishment of a hierarchy of community policing structures including: community policing forums (CPFs) at T/A level, crime prevention panels (CPPs) at GVH level, and crime prevention committees (CPCs) at village level. Baker outlines a similar structure in Uganda (2008: 120).

[12] See, e.g., Chesluk (2004), on community policing in New York in the 1990s.

a clear instantiation of this trend. However, as we, like a significant number of Malawian disputants, move from the VSU to the magistrates' courts, we are reminded, in part by the switch to the use of English, the language of colonial rule, that a plurality of legal institutions and pre-occupations predates postcolonial developments.

Magistrates' courts

If VSUs are emblematic of the coming of human rights with the transition to multiparty democracy, magistrates' courts are heir to a significantly longer, but no more parochial, history. In 1902, three years after Malawi (Nyasaland) became a British protectorate, the first full court system was established. Beneath a High Court (with unlimited jurisdiction) sat subordinate courts made up of district and sub-district courts (with jurisdiction over disputes concerning Europeans and/or Asians), and district and sub-district native courts (with jurisdiction over disputes between Africans). The courts were staffed by European administrators and remained in place until the early 1930s (Benda-Beckmann 2007 [1970]: 35–8). Although there was no formal recognition of the pre-existing judicial institutions of the local population, colonial administrators appreciated the virtues of so-called 'unofficial' courts and some 'even avoided deciding "purely native cases" unless a trial had already taken place before the village headman or the chief' (ibid.: 39). Indeed, cases reaching these formal courts tended to be brought on appeal following hearings conducted by village heads (Hynd 2011: 435).

As indirect rule was extended to Nyasaland, the Native Courts Ordinance of 1933 opened the way for recognised court structures over which 'native' chiefs would preside as judges. The ordinance stated that the jurisdiction of the native courts would be limited to cases involving Africans only, and that the courts must apply 'customary law' in the first instance. In the context of high male labour migration, a significant proportion of the cases brought to these courts were marital disputes initiated by women on the grounds that their husbands had deserted them (McCracken 2012: 227). At around the same time, the subordinate courts were rearranged into a four-tier system of magistrates' courts, whose jurisdiction and appeals procedures differed according to the identities of the disputants (Africans, Europeans/Asians). From 1933, then, colonial 'legal pluralism' was formalised, with only the High Court connecting the parallel legal systems.[13]

---

[13] I began this discussion from the early colonial period; others, however, have highlighted a much longer history of pluralism (see, e.g., Kanyongolo 2007). It goes without saying that the introduction of native courts, and the (selective) elevation of chiefs and village

It was not until the period of political upheaval towards the end of colonial rule that further reforms were introduced. From 1961, the first elected African politicians pushed for the disarticulation of administrative and judicial powers, particularly within native authority structures (Benda-Beckmann 2007 [1970]: 45). New local courts and appeal courts were established in 1962 (renamed traditional courts in 1969) in which judgment was passed by chairmen 'selected with due political consideration' (ibid.: 45), rather than native authorities. Traditional leaders were thus removed from these formal state structures but continued to hear cases informally in their capacity as chiefs and village heads. Oversight of the official local/traditional courts was assigned to a new team in the Ministry of Justice.

During Kamuzu Banda's reign (1964–94), however, the focus shifted from the unification of the judicial system towards greater separation of the 'traditional' courts from their 'English' counterparts (Kanyongolo 2006: 45). Whereas the local courts were under the direct supervision of the Ministry of Justice, the 'English' system maintained some independence from the executive branch of government (ibid.). Over time, the criminal jurisdiction of the traditional courts was expanded and the regional traditional courts came into their own as venues for dealing with criminal charges against political opponents of then Life President Banda (ibid.: 44; see also Chikaya-Banda 2012). Rights of appeal to the High Court and to legal representation were withdrawn.

If the era of one-party rule saw the development of a form of enhanced legal pluralism, albeit within the context of an authoritarian state characterised by the extreme centralisation of power, the transition to multiparty politics returned formal legal centralisation to the political agenda. In October 1993, the regional traditional courts and National Traditional Appeal Court were suspended, which, 'for all practical purposes', amounted to the wholesale abolition of the traditional courts (Kanyongolo 2006: 45). The new constitution integrated the judiciary by empowering magistrates' courts to rule in cases involving customary law, with appeals heard by the High Court and the Supreme Court of Appeal. Traditional court chairmen became magistrates and the physical court structures were absorbed into the formal legal system.[14]

At the time of my fieldwork, magistrates were divided into professional and lay magistrates. Professional magistrates were known as resident magistrates (and subdivided again into chief resident, principal

---

headmen to native authorities and judges, was far from a straightforward formalisation of 'traditional' judicial structures. Nor were the dual systems of 'customary' and 'English' law ever completely distinct. For example, in colonial Malawi, customary marriages were always recognised as valid and as entailing 'legal consequences', which was not the case in all British colonies in Africa (Benda-Beckmann 2007 [1970]: 97).

[14] See Schärf et al. (2002) for an overview of critical responses to the integration process.

resident, and senior resident), and required a law degree. To the best of my knowledge, there were no resident magistrates in Chiradzulu District. According to Fidelis Edge Kanyongolo, in the mid-2000s there were only 30 in the entire country (2006: 41), and they were concentrated in urban areas (Schärf et al. 2002: 25). Lay magistrates held legal qualifications below degree level and were divided into first, second, third, and fourth grade, with decreasing civil and criminal jurisdiction.[15] The ranking of lay magistrates was a contentious topic, and academic commentators have claimed that official distinctions are 'neither based on qualifications nor competence' (ibid.: 11). This assessment was echoed by the second-grade magistrate at Chiradzulu, who told me that 'there isn't really a difference because we [all] underwent the same training'.[16] Magistrates hear cases alone, without counsellors or assessors. They are assisted in court by clerks who serve to translate the magistrates' English into Chichewa for the benefit of all present.[17] Magistrates keep their own records and must take constant notes during court proceedings. These handwritten notes, taken in English, form the bulk of the case file. In 2009–10, physical court structures remained

---

[15] Chief resident magistrates could hear civil disputes concerning amounts up to 50,000 kwacha (K), first-grade magistrates were limited to K40,000, and second-, third-, and fourth-grade magistrates to K30,000, K20,000, and K10,000 respectively. Both resident and first-grade magistrates could hear any criminal cases except murder, manslaughter, and treason, and impose any sentence except the death penalty or imprisonment beyond 14 years. Second-, third-, and fourth-grade magistrates were limited to five-year, one-year, and six-month prison sentences, or fines of up to K1,000, K500, or K250, respectively (Kanyongolo 2006: 42). For a discussion of Malawi's subordinate courts in relation to women's access to justice, see WLSA (2000: 55–69).

[16] I have described the structure of the courts at the time of my fieldwork. However, the 1995 constitution provided for the creation of 'traditional or local courts presided over by lay persons or chiefs', which would be limited in their jurisdiction 'exclusively to civil cases at customary law and . . . minor common law and statutory offences' (see Section 110(3) in Government of Malawi 2004 [1994]). By late 2010, politicians had still not enacted legislation to bring such courts into being. In early 2011, parliament, responding to a 2007 report by the Special Law Commission, tabled a Local Courts Bill (Government of Malawi 2011). The Act, which passed quickly through parliament (*Nyasa Times* 2011b) but has yet to be acted upon, (re)introduces local courts and district appeals local courts. It tasks the Chief Justice with appointing chairpersons to preside over the courts with the assistance of panels of assessors, who are to be selected by the registrar of the High Court (Kanyongolo 2011; *Nyasa Times* 2011a). If and when the Act is implemented, the new local courts will constitute a 'parallel structure' to magistrates' courts, and disputants will have the right to appeal decisions of the district appeals local courts to the High Court and Supreme Court of Appeal (Kanyongolo 2011: ii). For an overview of the debates in the print media that surrounded the passing of the Bill, see Banda (2011), Kakande (2011), Mbavi (2011), and Sonani (2011).

[17] The accuracy of translation could be a source of tension between clerks and magistrates. On the use of English in Malawian magistrates' courts, see, e.g., Gloppen and Kanyongolo (2007: 258), Kanyongolo (2006: 114–15), Kishindo (2001), and Schärf et al. (2002: 15).

basic, often operating without electricity or running water and with official court papers produced by typewriter.[18]

The order in which I presented the above discussion illustrates the 'ideal' route through this legal landscape: beginning at home with *ankhoswe* as family representatives, then reaching out to local traditional authorities before taking a referral letter to the police VSU, and finally receiving a formal judgment in the magistrates' court. However, it is important to stress that this is not the only, and perhaps not even the most common, route that disputants take. In practice, efforts to resolve disputes through engagement with outside authorities and legal forums were often characterised by false starts, delays, and reversals. People might go straight to the magistrates' court, for example, where their case might well begin, only for the magistrate to declare that they had 'rushed' and needed to return to their *ankhoswe* or village head. Others, struggling to get satisfaction from hearings with their *ankhoswe*, might pursue multiple sittings at the village level over many years before ever seeking alternatives. Indeed, some of the disputants I met at each of the venues discussed here arrived as seasoned participants, familiar to the authorities who had dealt with their cases before and would either make further efforts to handle their ongoing difficulties or throw up their hands in defeat and issue a referral 'up' or 'down' the chain.

The various venues for dispute resolution were thus distinguished more by their position in this loose chain of legal forums than they were by their modus operandi. They tended not to be approached as alternatives offering access to different kinds of legal or discursive resources (custom, rights, or statutory legal provisions). Formal distinctions, such as the status of customary law in each venue, were not mentioned as factors influencing decisions about where to take a case. Nor were these choices made in reference to abstract notions of law versus custom, state versus traditional authority, or direct versus indirect rule. The importance of customary institutions, not least *ankhoswe*, was affirmed in each forum; indeed, *ankhoswe* were expected to participate at every stage. Similarly, the language of human rights and an awareness of the need to combat gender-based violence were encountered at every turn. However, as we shall see in the coming chapters, this did not mean that there were no differences or disagreements over how custom, rights, and law ought to be interpreted in these settings.

Looking at the network of available legal institutions from the perspective of those who accessed them, it is evident that the choice of dispute-resolution forum was guided by multiple motivations and

---

[18] By 2015, the typewriter was no longer in use and had been replaced by an aged computer, which remained underutilised because staff had limited computing skills and the electricity supply was woefully unreliable.

aspirations in situations of imperfect information. I came across a number of women at the magistrates' court, for example, who were unaware of the VSU and had come to court either directly or via their village heads.[19] The overriding concern was to obtain *chilungamo* – justice, truth, righteousness. As in cases of medical pluralism, the range of possible legal forums straddled what might appear to be mutually exclusive, or contradictory, realms. However, state and 'traditional' services were not perceived as antagonistic alternatives, and complainants made pragmatic decisions about where to seek redress, adjusting their strategies according to circumstance, and at times circumventing 'traditional' forums without rejecting traditional institutions or traditional authority per se. Extrapolating from the model of medical pluralism, we might expect individuals seeking solutions to their domestic problems to embrace this ambiguity (Last 1981). Perhaps unlike the example of medical pluralism, though, in this case state service providers (police officers and magistrates) also perceived their work as somehow integrated, and compatible, with village-based 'customary' dispute-resolution processes.

Comparable situations have sometimes invited interpretations of 'forum shopping' in which 'disputants have a choice between different institutions and they base their choice on what they hope the outcome of the dispute will be' (Benda-Beckmann 1981: 117; see also Griffiths 1997: 121). But such a vision relies on the idea of atomised individual actors making strategic calculations; it fails to accommodate the limitations to 'choice' experienced by rural Malawians as relational beings (not to mention the challenges faced by poor villagers with respect to the potentially prohibitive costs of transportation and/or fees).[20] Rather than 'shopping', we might better understand these relationally situated disputants as traversing, navigating, or negotiating a complex legal landscape. Their routes are shaped in significant ways by their various starting positions and by the degree to which they are supported by others along the way.

The ambiguity of legal authority

The result of the historical developments and travelling ideas described above is a complex legal landscape that is suggestive of the relevance of

---

[19] This would have been extremely unlikely in and around the village in which I resided but it reflects the wider geographic reach of the court and the still patchy provision of VSU services.

[20] During 2009–10, it cost K20 to register a complaint at the magistrates' court. Hearings at the village head's *bwalo* cost K300 (or the equivalent in chickens). While there was no charge at the VSU, accessing the VSU (or the magistrates' court) might require minibus fares and/or arduous journeys on foot.

the long-debated concept of legal pluralism.[21] The concept originated as a means of understanding the colonial legal context in which codified European and unwritten 'customary' law were understood to operate side by side. It marked an important departure from earlier studies, which tended to focus exclusively on the 'customary' aspects of law in colonial settings, even where they acknowledged the disruptions of colonial rule (Comaroff and Roberts 1981; Moore 1986). Nevertheless, this approach, which Sally Merry (1988) terms 'classic legal pluralism', was rightly criticised by historians who argued that colonial and customary law – and, by extension, postcolonial national and 'local' legal regimes – had always been interconnected. Martin Chanock (1985), for example, exposed the ways in which customary law in colonial Malawi and Zambia was both thoroughly implicated in the colonial project and significantly transformed through the interaction of African subjects and colonial authorities. The effect, according to Chanock, was the solidification of 'custom' to the benefit of political elites, both European and 'native', and the consequent consolidation of chiefly power.[22] For some, such critiques reduced legal pluralism to little more than a convenient 'colonial fiction' (Wilson 2007: 346).

Further attacks on legal pluralism came from legal-centralist scholars, notably Brian Tamanaha (1993), who argued that anthropologists, in their efforts to accord legal status to customs and social norms (in its more developed guise, Merry (1988) terms this 'the new legal pluralism'),[23] were stretching the category of law beyond utility: when law is everywhere, these critics pointed out, it is simultaneously nowhere. Anthropologists thus stood accused, with some justification, of failing to appreciate the particular character of codified state-backed legal orders.[24]

Yet despite these powerful critiques, anthropologists have continued to find the concept of legal pluralism seductive. Valiant efforts have been made to rehabilitate versions of legal pluralism that might speak to the profusion of legal discourses and practices that anthropologists confront in contemporary ethnographic encounters (see, e.g., Griffiths 1997). With the emergence of human rights instruments, discourse, and practices in particular, legal pluralism has continued to afford a certain analytical purchase (see, e.g., Merry 2006a). Thus, Richard Wilson

---

[21] See Wilson (2000; 2007) and S. F. Moore (2005) for overviews of these debates.

[22] For comparable arguments, see Hay and Wright (1982b), Hodgson (1996), and Young (2010).

[23] This is a tradition that traces its roots to Malinowski (1926). See Gluckman (1965: 18–19) and Greenhouse (2012: 433–5) for more sympathetic accounts of Malinowski's approach.

[24] More recently, Tamanaha has apologised for the 'regrettably strident tone' of his earlier critique (2008: 391). His position remains unchanged, however.

maintains that legal pluralism 'provides an important descriptive model of society as made up of a diversity of modes of conflict resolution, shattering the myth of state law's unchallenged empire' (2000: 77).

It is in this sense that I find the concept illuminating, as a means of making sense of the complex and overlapping sources of legal authority and legal claim-making that characterise the postcolonial legal landscape. In this form, legal pluralism must shed the metaphorical baggage contained in the idea of 'plurality'. If 'pluralism' signals 'a condition or system in which two or more states, groups, principles, etc., co-exist',[25] it is difficult to escape an understanding of legal pluralism that posits distinct legal normativities operating side by side – interacting, perhaps, but above all *coexisting* as disparate modes of conflict resolution. However, the intertwining of formal and customary legalities witnessed in Malawi refuses to conform to such a conception and instead suggests a form of legal plurality that is characterised by cross-fertilisation and integration. No longer do separate institutions cater for different constituencies or administer different forms of law. Contemporary VSUs and magistrates' courts serve all citizens of Malawi, and they do so by reference to uncodified 'customary' law, state-backed legal statutes, and human rights provisions as enshrined in the 1995 constitution. Similarly, traditional authorities draw upon and develop contemporary understandings of rights and gender-based violence as they handle disputes in the shade of the mango trees at the village *bwalo*. Formal magistrates' courts can thus be viewed as lying at the end of a chain: a single, woven chain that begins with *ankhoswe* and incorporates traditional authorities and VSUs along the way.

By focusing on the routes traversed by disputing couples in Malawi as they seek justice, then, this study sheds light on the complex ambiguity of postcolonial legal and political authority. Øyvind Eggen (2011) has recently argued that the dual character of the colonial state in Malawi has continued into the era of multiparty democracy, with one significant alteration: 'the boundaries have become porous' (ibid.: 315). The two state hierarchies – that of the elected government and that of 'traditional authority' – now apply to the vast majority of Malawians, who are at once citizens *and* subjects. Eggen thus challenges Mahmood Mamdani's (1996) influential arguments about the legacy of late colonialism by positing that 'the result is not a bifurcated state, but an ambiguous one' (2011: 329). His insight is pertinent to the institutions discussed in this book. Take the community victim support unit (CVSU), a community policing institution established by the state police and staffed by both police officers and traditional authorities, in which, as we shall see in

---

[25] Definition taken from the *Concise Oxford English Dictionary*.

Chapter 3, a chief can cite the constitutional Bill of Rights in a case related to the occult. As Eggen suggests, the line between 'indirect, chiefly rule and direct, modern, liberal democratic governance' (ibid.: 324) is often blurred in practice.

The ambiguity of authority in Malawi is perhaps best illustrated by the intersecting hierarchies of formal and 'traditional' authority in the community policing programme, the instability of which is evident when we consider the different perceptions of the VSU and CVSU held by the police and villagers. For the police, CVSUs are local versions of the VSU. Closer to the rural poor, they are imagined as more accessible, less intimidating forums for resolving the same kinds of disputes. However, CVSUs are overseen by T/As, the most senior representatives of chiefly power accessible to rural citizens. For this reason, it is rare for villagers to bring their marital disputes to the CVSU, for to do so is not to access a subordinate forum, but rather to leapfrog to the highest level of traditional authority.[26] By contrast, the VSU, located at the police station and staffed predominantly by police officers, is considered a more suitable venue for domestic disputes, a plausible alternative to the village head's *bwalo*. The CVSU, in the words of a GVH, is a 'serious forum' (*bwalo lalikulu*), suitable for 'bigger issues' (*nkhani zikuluzikulu*), principally long-standing land disputes and, occasionally, cases concerning witchcraft.[27] The involvement of the T/A in the CVSU programme, then, rather undermines the police's intention to provide a form of 'grassroots' VSU. It also highlights the degree to which the Malawian legal landscape is suffused with the porous ambiguities of postcolonial governance.

One certainty about the handling of marital disputes was that they should begin in the hands of *ankhoswe*. Only where the efforts of matrilineal kin had proved unequal to the task of reconciling a couple or amicably dissolving their marriage should hearings begin in other forums. Deviation from this norm would affect the way in which a case was perceived by other authorities. Very often the next step, after consulting the *ankhoswe*, was to visit the village head, who, if similarly unable to solve the dispute, would likely refer the couple to the VSU, and from there they might find themselves in the magistrates' court. As I have stressed, other routes through this legal landscape were possible, and the forums had their own styles and procedures for dealing with disputes. Yet none could be singled out as purely 'customary' or entirely 'formal'. Nowhere could the importance of matrilineal kin be denied, and

---

[26] That villagers felt it inappropriate to take their marital disputes to the T/A at the CVSU is indicative of the high esteem in which T/As are held.

[27] Land disputes could be dealt with by district commissioners, but they would always consult the T/A. Police officers and magistrates were reluctant to discuss land issues.

nowhere could the language of human and women's rights, or an aware-ness of campaigns against gender-based violence, be held at bay.

As men and women navigate the ambiguities of legal authority in Malawi in the search for justice, they are confronted simultaneously by customary expectations and constitutional human rights provisions. In the process, both can be subject to re-evaluation. On the one hand, ideas about human and women's rights have become mundane in Malawi; they are familiar to rural citizens and references to them emerge spontan-eously in a range of contexts. However, familiarity does not necessarily entail wholehearted endorsement or consistent application, and nor does it imply a lack of alternatives, be they explicitly or implicitly conveyed. It is to the ethnographic exploration of the mutual imbrication, and con-testation, of custom and constitution in a VSU that I turn in Chapter 3.

3   Navigating *ufulu*

Ufulu, freedom, has become the familiar Chichewa shorthand for human rights. Yet, as a term that pre-existed the arrival of democracy and human rights in the mid-1990s, it also has wider resonances. It is commonly employed in community policing structures as police officers, religious leaders, chiefs, and rural disputants navigate intricate entanglements of human rights, 'custom', and a progressive constitution. Their complex references to *ufulu* are often steeped in a recognition of the fundamentally relational context in which freedom and rights are negotiated in practice. As we shall see, flexible use of the languages of custom, rights, and relationships is oriented towards the elusive ideal of justice (*chilungamo*), which shimmers in the background of case hearings.

Disputing marriage

Anabanda's complaint, in a nutshell, was that her husband had taken another wife. Not only that, but she and Anambewe, the second wife, had fought, following which Anambewe had gone to Anabanda's house and destroyed her belongings. As she narrated these events, Anabanda explained to two police officers and a local sheikh (and the anthropologist), in the presence of her husband and Anambewe, that she and Mr Phiri had married in 2001 and she had borne him three children. Mr Phiri, she said, began spending nights away from their home (*kugona moyenda*) when she was pregnant with their third child, a boy of approximately two years of age who was sitting on her knee. One day, her husband told her that he had found another wife and that he wanted to bring his new wife to meet Anabanda at their home. She told him not to bring her, and she stressed that his relatives did not support his endeavours to marry a second wife either. After their son was born, they sat down with their *ankhoswe* and Mr Phiri explained that he wanted to start growing tomatoes for sale and thus that the gardens provided by Anabanda's family were no longer sufficient for his needs. As a result, Anabanda's relatives agreed to give them some additional land and the couple had since farmed the new garden for two full planting seasons:

> But he hasn't stopped. And his other wife, whenever we meet we fight … Two days ago, we met on the path by the Catholic church and she provoked me, asking, 'What are you staring at me for?' … I wouldn't have hit her if she hadn't provoked me. People around us stopped us fighting and she went and told my husband that I'd hit her. He reported to *ambuye anga*,[1] and I explained that I wouldn't have hit her if she hadn't provoked me … [Later that day] she smashed my things – plates, two pots, a plastic bucket, metal pails, [and] a basin. I brought the smashed things here in the evening and was given a letter to come back today.

When she had finished describing her case, the sub-inspector asked her what exactly she was complaining about: 'You have said many things; are you complaining about your husband or about the smashed property?' '*Zonse*,' she replied: 'Everything.' 'I've been married to my husband for ten years and he said he just wanted more land to farm, but when we gave him the extra garden he didn't leave her. The *ankhoswe* have refused polygamy [*mitala*].' The sub-inspector summarised: 'The complaint is that your husband has another wife and she smashed your property.' 'What do you have to say about that?' he asked Mr Phiri.

Mr Phiri's account began much like his wife's. He explained that they had been married for many years, that their first child, a daughter, had started school, their second born, a son, had passed away, and that their third child was the little boy on his wife's knee. In reference to Anabanda, however, he said, 'We frequently disagree.' Pointing to the two women in turn, he claimed that each was his wife, and he insisted that he did not show favour. Mr Phiri continued:

> I found a second wife, I proposed to her, and she accepted. At first all was well; I would spend a week at a time with each. But recently things have changed and they fight … That day, a friend came and found me cutting down trees. He told me that my wives were coming and it looked like there'd been some trouble. I asked my first wife and she didn't answer me, so I went to her *ambuye* to tell him that she'd been fighting and that if there hadn't been people around to stop her who knows what might have happened.

The sub-inspector sought further clarification: 'You say you have two wives, but your wife says you have only one wife and a girlfriend [*chibwenzi*]. Do you have two wives or one?' Mr Phiri repeated that he had two wives, and, moreover, that the *ankhoswe* were aware of this fact and capable of verifying it. When the sub-inspector asked if there had been *ndondomeko*, a proper programme, for contracting the second marriage,

---

[1] *Ambuye* – grandmother or senior maternal uncle; *ambuye anga* – my grandmother/senior maternal uncle. In this case, Anabanda's *ambuye* is both her uncle and her *nkhoswe*.

Mr Phiri declared that the person who was ruining the *ndondomeko* was his first wife because she did not want to be a co-wife. He maintained that she had previously agreed to the arrangement and that his younger brother had been witness to the decision. The sub-inspector expressed surprise that someone who had agreed to polygamy would fight with her co-wife, and he stated that: 'She has the freedom/right [*ufulu*] to refuse polygamy.' Asked to respond, Anabanda countered:

Maybe he agreed with his brother when I wasn't there. When the *ankhoswe* were called they refused and he said, 'But I want a garden.' If things had been conducted properly, there would have been no cause for fighting.

In contrast to the sub-inspector's view that they had reached an impasse and needed to summon the *ankhoswe*, the sheikh suggested that they first hear from the second wife, who up to this point had remained silent. Addressing Anambewe, he asked, 'When he married you, what did he tell you? That he was married?' Anambewe explained that he had told her that he had a wife, but that he wanted to end his first marriage because he didn't want polygamy. On hearing this, the sheikh turned back to Mr Phiri:

So, what? You only told your first wife it was polygamy? You told your second wife that you would leave the first . . . Do you know what polygamy is? Polygamy is to agree with your first wife; if she agrees, you go to the *ankhoswe* with your first wife to agree together. Then you look for a second wife. When you have found her, the two wives should be introduced to each other so that they won't fight. And there is *ndondomeko*: maybe you spend one week with each, maybe two days with one and two days with the other. But your wives are refusing. Did you really arrange polygamy? Or did you just arrange it on one side?

Mr Phiri was adamant that he had followed the proper procedure (*ndondomeko*) with respect to both women. In answer to the sheikh's follow-up questions, however, he admitted that he had told Anambewe that he would end his first marriage, and he accepted that Anabanda's relatives had given him an extra garden so as to prevent him from marrying a second wife.

Frustrated by the sheikh's insistence that neither of his wives wanted polygamy, Mr Phiri declared that he would leave both women, prompting Anabanda to interrupt: 'I can't accept that. My mother is dead, how am I supposed to care for the children?' Anambewe, too, asserted that she would not accept divorce because Anabanda had caused her great hardship. At this point, the sheikh conceded that they could go no further without hearing from the *ankhoswe*. He told Anabanda and Mr Phiri to come again in a few days' time with their *ankhoswe*, and he asked Anambewe to attend, but not to bring her *nkhoswe* because the dispute was between Mr Phiri and Anabanda. When the marital case was resolved, they would turn to the issue of the broken property. As they left, he warned the women that they would be arrested if they fought again before the next meeting.

When the case resumed,[2] the two parties summarised the dispute in much the same way, with Mr Phiri adding that he had begun looking for a second wife because his first wife was being rude to him and he thought that he would teach her a lesson. He maintained that Anabanda had initially agreed to polygamy and that it was only later, when Anambewe had begun coming to their home to ask for soap, that the women had started to fight. Although Anabanda's relatives had given them an extra garden, he said, the additional land was still insufficient. He acknowledged, however, that he had not raised the issue again with their *ankhoswe*.

This time, when the sheikh asked if she would agree to polygamy, Anabanda acquiesced: 'I'll agree, provided that they give me my things [those that were smashed].' The sheikh reminded her that she had not agreed the last time they met. 'Were you lying then?' he asked. But Anabanda stated that that was before her husband had explained to her that he wanted polygamy and they had been given an opportunity to call their *ankhoswe*: 'Before, my *ankhoswe*[3] was not here. I couldn't accept in his absence. It is better for me to agree when my uncle is here.' The sheikh explained to the *ankhoswe* that things had been different in the first session. That day, both women had refused polygamy, but when Mr Phiri had said that he would leave them both, they had insisted that they could not allow that. 'That is why we called you as *ankhoswe*. Please tell us if the marriage is acceptable [*banja ndi lololedwa*].'

Mr Phiri's *nkhoswe* was the first to respond. He confirmed that he was aware that Mr Phiri had been spending nights away from home because of the garden issue and he had said that he would leave Anabanda, but instead it had been agreed that he would marry Anambewe and he had begun spending alternate weeks with each wife. However, this had annoyed Anabanda and she had complained:

When we discussed the matter, he said that he would leave Anambewe when they argued; he said it was problematic for him to leave her if they hadn't argued. Anabanda then agreed to polygamy, but quickly began fighting with her co-wife and soon declared that she didn't want polygamy anymore, after she had already agreed.

Anabanda's *nkhoswe*'s account was somewhat different. He said that from the time they had discussed the issue of the garden, when he had given them an additional field, they had not discussed any further

---

[2] The sheikh and the sub-inspector were present for this second hearing, in addition to Anabanda and Mr Phiri's *ankhoswe*. A sergeant who had observed but not intervened in the first hearing was absent when they regrouped.

[3] The plural is used here as a marker of respect.

concerns whatsoever. He knew nothing about the polygamous relationship with Anambewe; the first he had heard of it was when the two
women had fought. Having listened to the *ankhoswe*'s statements, the
sheikh admonished Mr Phiri, asserting that the government (*boma*) does
not want people to be fighting like this: 'Men are causing trouble for
people in this country; people are being killed and all sorts of things
because of individual men.' 'Which one is your wife?' he demanded of
Mr Phiri, who was steadfast in his claim that he was married to both
women. In response, Anabanda reaffirmed her assent: 'Seeing that he's
agreed that we are both his wives, that's fine, we'll be two.' However, the
sheikh informed them:

Here we don't bring together polygamous unions; we discuss issues with one
wife. If you are going to have polygamy, you should go home and agree with your
ankhoswe there. Polygamy, how it works is that the wives help each other, send
relish to each other, share maize, send money when a child is in hospital, go to
visit ill children, and so on.

The sub-inspector, in agreement, clarified that: 'Polygamy is not
unacceptable, but it is also not to be forced; men have the freedom/right
to marry twice, but the first wife also has the freedom/right to say that
she does not want polygamy.' Continuing, he summarised the case as
he saw it:

It was not done properly; he came and said he wanted an extra garden but he had
already found his second wife. Other men begin properly, announcing: 'I want to
find a second wife for these reasons.' If you fail to resolve the issues, people agree.
For example, if the first wife hasn't borne any children. But in this case, things
didn't proceed as they should have done and this is the result: conflicts [*ziwawa*].
The *ndondomeko* isn't supposed to go like that. Mr Phiri, if you had behaved as
other men do, you could have said openly that the garden was still inadequate,
but you didn't say that and that is why they are fighting now. It is your fault. You
didn't handle things as you ought to have. Now, Anabanda might agree, because
of the children, she doesn't want you to leave her. But if she were in a position to
choose freely [*pa ufulu, pa mtendere*], perhaps she would say that she does not
want polygamy.

Before Mr Phiri could respond, Anabanda's *nkhoswe* spoke up to explain
that he had the right to tell his niece to accept. 'Mr Phiri should fail by
himself [*alephere okha*],' he said, implying that if the marriage were to fail,
it ought to be the result of Mr Phiri's shortcomings rather than his niece's
intransigence.

At this point, Anabanda and Anambewe both confirmed that they
accepted polygamy, but when Anambewe brought up the fact that she
and Anabanda tended to fight, the sheikh and the sub-inspector accused
her of wanting Mr Phiri for herself and of 'disturbing the marriage'
between Mr Phiri and Anabanda (*kusokoneza banja*), for which, the

sheikh informed her, she could be arrested. Anambewe denied the allegation, countering that she had told him to end his marriage to Anabanda before taking up with her. In contrast, she accused Mr Phiri of disturbing her. The sub-inspector responded rather directly to this suggestion: 'How did you agree to sleep with him in your house? ... Anabanda has accepted and now you say he should be yours?' To which Anambewe replied, 'We will be two [wives]. I am accepting with all my heart.' Unsatisfied, the sheikh accused her of 'ambushing' her co-wife and disturbing her marriage (*kupanga chiwembu*). Turning to Mr Phiri, he observed that Anabanda had agreed to polygamy but Anambewe wanted him for herself. Mr Phiri demurred, arguing that it was Anabanda who was causing the problem by accepting. By his own admission, he had no solution. Expressing frustration that they were not getting anywhere and that this issue was likely to occupy them for too long, the sheikh advised the parties that if they wanted polygamy, they should sit down together at home and form *ndondomeko*: 'If there are rites [*miyambo*], go and carry them out.'

Repeating the warning that they could make an arrest, the sub-inspector counselled Anambewe that if she could only be patient (*kufatsa*), she would find her own husband, but the path she had taken – that of disturbing other people's marriages – was inappropriate. She was causing *ziwembu* (maliciousness).[4] 'There are women who drink poison because of such behaviour. There are many men out there,' he said, 'yet women think they must snatch [*kulanda*] one, and that is not right.' Elaborating further on this theme, the sheikh suggested that 'this is how accidents happen, and fights, burnt houses and killings can result'. He stressed that Anambewe was wasting her time with such relationships. The sub-inspector agreed, warning her that her reputation could be damaged. In her defence, Anambewe stated that if Anabanda had not hit her, she would not have smashed her things, to which the sub-inspector replied:

If you hadn't snatched her husband, would she have hit you? Sometimes we bring these things upon ourselves. Would you like it if your husband had a girlfriend? If you hadn't been disturbing her marriage she would not have hit you.

The sheikh brought the matter back to the possibility of formal charges. 'There are several offences [*milandu*] here: snatching a husband, violating the rights of his wife and children, smashing property.' The sub-inspector advised that, while they were simply discussing these things at this stage, they wanted Anambewe to learn from this experience, adding: 'You don't fix a problem with another problem; you should follow proper

---

[4] *Ziwembu* is the plural form of the noun *chiwembu*, which I translated above as 'ambush'. It can also be rendered as plot, attack, or conspiracy.

Serial No.	Date and OB No.	Name and Particulars of Accused/Suspect	Offence	Name and Particulars of Victim	Particulars of Offence	Particulars of the Investigating Officer	Police Action	Result of Case and Date
7	08/07/10	Christopher Phiri, 30, Lomwe, X village, T/A Kadewere, Chiradzulu	Polygamy	Grace Phiri, 25, Yao, Y village, T/A Mpama, Chiradzulu	The suspect wants to have another wife as a second one, however because there was no consent from the 1st wife the two ladies fought after they had met.	Sub-Inspector Z, Sheikh -.	Matter has been referred back home to discuss whether to go ahead with polygamy or not.	

Figure 3.1 VSU register entry

procedures.' In support of this argument, the sheikh added: 'You should learn from this; we do things according to rights, according to goodness/virtue [*timapanga za ufulu, za ubwino*].'

Recognising that the sheikh and the sub-inspector considered the case closed and had begun taking the parties' details for their register, Anabanda raised the issue of the broken property one last time. The sub-inspector informed her that since all of this had begun because of her husband, he should be the one to deal with it. Mr Phiri's *nkhoswe* declared that he would support whatever Mr Phiri and Anabanda agreed, and Anabanda's *nkhoswe* concurred: 'Our role is that of support poles,' he said, citing a common idiom.[5] As they prepared to leave, the sub-inspector issued a final warning against fighting, reminding them that they could all be arrested. He also cautioned Mr Phiri that he must share his resources across two families now. Making a quick calculation, based on the fact that each of his wives had two children to care for, he said: 'There are three adults and four children, a total of seven people who must rely on you to share your resources; you should think about that with maturity [*muganize mokhwima maganizo*].'[6]

The register entry can be seen in Figure 3.1.[7]

Negotiating rights and custom in the search for justice

Anabanda's complaint was heard in the victim support unit (VSU) at a police station in Chiradzulu District, where I carried out participant observation approximately twice a week from July 2009 to August 2010.

[5] *Ife kwathu ndi nchalamila.*
[6] After the parties left, the sheikh and the sub-inspector agreed that Anabanda had been influenced by her *nkhoswe* to accept polygamy. They also agreed that Anabanda was 'higher quality' than Anambewe (they judged this by their appearances) and thus that, in all likelihood, Anambewe had fed Mr Phiri *mankhwala* (medicine/love potion).
[7] The police kept brief records of each case, in English, in a VSU register. I have erased the names of the villages and those of the sheikh and the sub-inspector. Mr Phiri's and Anabanda's names are pseudonyms.

The office is staffed by police officers from the Community Policing Services Branch (CPSB) with selected lay volunteers.[8] As we saw in Chapter 2, VSUs constitute an intermediate link in a loose chain of dispute-resolution forums available to couples in rural southern Malawi. There is general agreement that the first port of call for all ought to be the *ankhoswe*, followed by the village head (VH). From that point on, disputants have a number of options. They might follow the 'traditional' route, moving up the chiefly hierarchy, first to the group village head (GVH) and then to the Traditional Authority (T/A) or Sub-T/A. Alternatively, they might choose to discuss their case at a VSU, or to open a civil case file at a magistrates' court. The VSU, then, can be bypassed, either by a chain that follows the 'traditional' institutions before reaching the formal legal system (*ankhoswe* – VH – GVH – [Sub-T/A] – T/A – magistrate – [High Court – Supreme Court of Appeal]),[9] or by a route that moves more quickly to the formal realm (*ankhoswe* – VH – magistrate). Other pathways are possible, too, and the VSU can feature in a variety of positions, or not at all. For example: *ankhoswe* – VSU – VH – magistrate; VSU – *ankhoswe* – VSU – magistrate; *ankhoswe* – VH – NGO – magistrate, and so on.

From the colonial period to the present day, 'informal' dispute-resolution processes have operated alongside government courts, and court personnel have long expected rural disputants to consult family and/or village-level traditional authorities before entering the formal system (see Chapter 2).[10] VSUs are a contemporary instantiation of this fact: ambiguously placed, they can be viewed as a meeting point of state law, customary law, and a progressive constitution. While staffed by

---

[8] I was told that two group village heads and a Catholic priest used to attend fairly regularly, but the sheikh was the only lay volunteer to attend the VSU during the period of my fieldwork. The presence of a Muslim sheikh should not be taken to suggest a majority Muslim population. According to recent statistics, 13 per cent of the Malawian population is Muslim; the figure is 11 per cent for the population of Chiradzulu District (NSO 2008c; 2008d). The sheikh tended to adopt an inclusive approach to religion, stressing to disputants that they all worship the same God and that the teachings of the different holy books reinforce each other in their calls for harmony and respect.

[9] I place square brackets around these courts because, in practice, rural couples rarely make use of them. By law, however, all Malawian citizens have recourse to appeal to these courts. Because they are of little practical relevance, I omit them in the proceeding examples.

[10] At present, the only *official* link between the numerous courts presided over by traditional authorities (of which there are more than 20,000 at VH level (Schärf et al. 2002: 39)) and the formal legal system is a constitutional provision that the High Court may 'review any decision by any person or institution, including traditional authorities, to determine whether it respects and upholds the human rights guaranteed by the Constitution' (Kanyongolo 2006: 147). Nevertheless, in practice there is much greater integration; on the dependence of magistrates on traditional authorities for the 'service of process on villagers', see Schärf et al. (2002: 27).

uniformed state employees, they are also forums for extended discussion where *ankhoswe* play a central role. Indeed, they embody the ambiguous nature of postcolonial legal authority described in Chapter 2. It is thus worth stressing that an official separation of traditional authority-run justice forums from the formal legal system was not a distinction felt by villagers, who experienced the requirement to follow 'traditional' procedures; recognised the cross-over of personnel in community policing structures; and were frequently referred from one to another of these forums in multiple directions.

The complex legality of community policing forums is highly dependent on the competence and personalities of those hearing the cases. Procedure is flexible and training ad hoc (Kanyongolo 2006: 104). During my time observing community policing practices, I witnessed elements that were distinctly 'uncustomary': for example, the practice of hearing marital disputes concerning couples who had not formalised their *chinkhoswe*,[11] or the insistence of police officers that fathers (and not maternal uncles or other matrilineal kin) remain financially responsible for their children after divorce, which runs counter to local norms. Other aspects were clearly at odds with human rights provisions, such as when the sheikh informed a woman that the injuries she had suffered at the hands of her husband were insufficient grounds for leaving him. 'Other women,' he told her, 'have huge plasters on their broken limbs and still they do not ask for divorce' – although, as we shall see in Chapter 5, both rights and custom could (and did) provide firm grounds for the condemnation of violence within marriage. It is to the various ways in which matrilineal custom and human rights can be negotiated in the pursuit of justice that I now turn. The result will be an appreciation of the flexibility of *ufulu* – freedom or right(s) – precisely because its meaning is not confined to human rights. We will see how the ways in which *ufulu* is employed in the VSU contribute to delicate negotiations of justice, at the same time as they provide a window onto local conceptions of personhood, which ground freedom in matrilineal relationality.

In Anabanda's case, the first we heard of *ufulu* (freedom/right) was the sub-inspector's explanation that Anabanda had the freedom or right to refuse polygamy. At a later stage, he stressed the same point: 'Polygamy is not unacceptable, but it is also not to be forced; men have the freedom/right to marry twice, but the first wife also has the freedom/right to say that she does not want polygamy.' Such uses of *ufulu* call for a closer analysis of human rights as a polysemic concept, spanning the terrain of the 'customary' and the constitutional.

---

[11] It is commonly understood that, according to custom, marriages are recognised once *ankhoswe* have been formally assigned by means of a *chinkhoswe* ceremony.

When the sub-inspector spoke of rights or freedom (*ufulu*) in relation to polygamy, he was not making a straightforward reference to a human right enshrined in the constitution. Indeed, the 1995 constitution is silent on the issue of polygamy. However, Section 22(5) recognises the validity of 'all marriages at law, custom and marriages by repute or by permanent cohabitation', and given that polygamous marriages are widely recognised in Malawi, this can be interpreted as signalling that partners in polygamous unions ought to enjoy the same constitutional protections as their monogamous counterparts.[12] Anabanda's right to reject polygamy is perhaps enshrined in Section 22(4), which states that 'no person shall be forced to enter into marriage'. However, since this refers to entry into marriage, it might more accurately apply to Anambewe, whom the sub-inspector excluded from his statement by specifying that this freedom/right pertained to the first wife. Malawian academic and expert in constitutional law Fidelis Edge Kanyongolo argues that it is only 'traditionalists and adherents of religious faiths that consider polygamy to be a right' (2006: 48), implying that the constitution does not provide the right to polygamous marriage. Lea Mwambene (2007) has gone as far as to suggest that Section 24(2) requires the banning of polygamy, since it states: 'Any law that discriminates against women on the basis of gender or marital status shall be invalid and legislation shall be passed to eliminate customs and practices that discriminate against women.' Section 26, however, guarantees: 'Every person shall have the right to use the language and to participate in the cultural life of his or her choice.' As things stand, therefore, support for and against the right to polygamy can be found within the same constitution, and thus the issue of polygamy as a human rights concern is somewhat ambiguous.

Although the sub-inspector referred to *ufulu* in the language of human rights, he made no direct mention of the constitution or of particular legal provisions. In fact, both the sheikh and the sub-inspector drew on knowledge of customary law – specifically of the *ndondomeko* that ought to be followed if things are to be done properly, according to custom – as much as, if not more than, they relied on the provisions of state law. While *ufulu* is the recognised term for rights and is specifically associated with human rights as a central tenet of democratic rule, the word also retains other resonances. As 'freedom', it can be used more broadly than 'human rights': it is not bound by reference to specific laws or

---

[12] The Marriage, Divorce and Family Relations Bill proposed in 2010 would have outlawed polygamy in line with the 2005 recommendations of the Malawi Law Commission (see Kanyongolo 2006; Mwambene 2007). The Bill met with stiff opposition, however, with debates pitching women's right to equality against the 'right to culture' (for an overview of the debate, see Chikoko 2010; *Nyasa Times* 2010a; 2010c; Sonani 2010). A revised version of the Bill, which passed through parliament in February 2015, leaves the status of polygamy unchanged: it is banned only in civil marriages.

conventions and thus enjoys greater elasticity and a fertile ambiguity. This was evident in the sub-inspector's gestures towards rights, in which his authority emanated from two sources: state law, of which he was a uniformed representative; and custom, his familiarity with which was demonstrated by his concern with 'proper' customary procedure. Within his very person, the sub-inspector embodied the complex legality of the VSU and, in this sense, he followed in a long tradition of intercalary subjects in South-Central Africa.[13]

Crucially, his loose 'human rights talk' (Wilson 2007) incorporated a moral conception of rights and wrongs, of what was acceptable, just, or expected. When he referred to Anabanda's 'right' to refuse polygamy, his use of the language of rights encompassed a sense of her prerogative as a wife to influence her husband's ability to marry polygamously. This prerogative was not necessarily set out in legal statutes or specific consti- tutional provisions; rather, it derived from a sense of how things ought to be done, of what men and women ought to be able to expect of one another in marriage, and thus invoked a more 'traditional' kind of *ufulu* that non-codified customary law, and customary institutions such as the allocation of *ankhoswe*, were expected to protect.

While the sheikh and the sub-inspector affirmed their knowledge of custom (through their ability to define polygamy, their descriptions of the appropriate mode of contracting polygamous marriages, and their aware- ness of how other men and women behaved), they also strove to distance themselves and their work from the customary realm. Towards the end of the proceedings, the sheikh made plain that he understood the role of the VSU, at least in part, as that of setting a good example with respect to human rights and the good life. 'You should learn from this,' he told Anambewe. 'We do things according to rights, according to goodness/ virtue.' Prior to this, he had also explained that they did not discuss polygamous unions in the VSU and he advised the trio that if they were going to agree to polygamy, they should 'go home and agree with [their] *ankhoswe* there'.[14] Thus, the sheikh distinguished between 'here', the 'modern' office at the police station, and 'home', the space of the village, *ankhoswe*, and polygamy. But this binary distinction – pairing *ufulu* with the VSU and polygamy with the village – was not maintained consist- ently. Soon after this statement, the sub-inspector suggested that, had polygamy been contracted according to the proper customary procedure (*ndondomeko*), Anabanda would have been in a position to choose freely

---

[13] The archetypal intercalary subject is the village head (Durham 2002; Englund 2002; Gluckman, Mitchell, and Barnes 1949; cf. Kuper 1970).

[14] In my experience, staff in the VSU often dealt with issues arising in polygamous marriages, but it was rare for more than one wife to be present at any one time. The same was true of village-level discussions.

or enjoy her rights (*pa ufulu, pa mtendere*), and, in that case, she might have rejected polygamy. According to this framing, Mr Phiri had violated his first wife's rights by failing to adhere to customary procedure – and thus the opposition between rights and custom was collapsed.

Anabanda's *nkhoswe* also referred to *ufulu*. In his case, he invoked his right as *nkhoswe* to tell his niece to accept polygamy. This *ufulu* was firmly rooted in the 'customary' realm and could claim only a rather dubious case for constitutional backing through Section 26, the right 'to partici- pate in the cultural life of his or her choice'. Yet this rights claim went unchallenged, despite obvious contradictions with Anabanda's consti- tutional right not to be forced to marry, and regardless of the fact that it followed directly from the sub-inspector's suggestion that she might have rejected polygamy if she had been enjoying her freedom/rights. While the sheikh and the sub-inspector recognised Anabanda's right to make her own decisions regarding marriage, their quiet acceptance of her *nkhoswe*'s statement, and their private assessment at the end of the case that Anabanda had indeed been influenced by her *nkhoswe* to accept polygamy, suggested that they understood marriage to be more than a straightforward contract between two individuals. The esteem in which *ankhoswe* are held is one of the most tangible indications of the fact that marital relationships are valued for the ways in which they bring together wider networks of kin who have a legitimate stake in the marriage's success and the well-being of the spouses and their children. No doubt many of my rural informants would consider Anabanda's *nkhoswe* to have overstepped his role here. Nevertheless, they would not dispute the fact that he had a vital responsibility to guide and support his niece. Anabanda may have engaged the human rights regime by taking her complaint to the VSU, but her claims were not those of the autonomous liberal subject imagined by the distant architects of human rights.

Thus, at certain instances in community policing forums, custom and rights reinforced each other, such as in the insistence that a woman had the right to decide whether or not she would accept a polygamous marriage. At other times, rights and custom merged in ways that contra- dicted human rights principles: for example, the idea that an *nkhoswe* might have the right to determine his niece's choice. This was particu- larly evident where 'custom' interacted with popular gendered stereo- types. In Anabanda's case, for instance, the sheikh suggested that 'women think they must snatch' men from one another, explicitly asso- ciating Anambewe with the generalised women of popular imagination who 'ambush' men, 'disturb marriages', and cause 'fights, burnt houses and killings'. Anambewe was thus condemned for behaving like other women, just as Mr Phiri had been admonished for behaving like other men when the sub-inspector told him that 'men are causing trouble for people in this country; people are being killed and all sorts of things because of individual men'. At another point, however, Mr Phiri was denigrated for failing to live up to the supposedly higher standards of other men. Had he 'behaved as other men do', the sub-inspector asserted, he would have said openly that the garden was still inadequate and the ensuing conflict might have been avoided.

Gender stereotypes interacted in a variety of ways with the human rights agenda. Another version of femininity that emerged frequently in the VSU mobilised the image of the woman-as-victim, physically abused and economically dependent on a stereotypically aberrant husband.[15] Much like the village head cited in Chapter 2, the sheikh and the sub-inspector invoked the spectre of gender-based violence (*nkhanza*) at certain points in the hearing, summoning the weight of anti-domestic violence campaigns. In cases where these kinds of images informed officers' interpretations, men were frequently threatened with arrest, fiercely criticised for neglecting their customary or legal duty to provide for their families, and told that they were violating the rights (*maufulu*) of their wives and children to adequate care. Such statements were not morally neutral and they underlined the close relationships between custom, law, morality, and justice.

In the community victim support unit (CVSU), too, 'tradition' and rights, customary procedure and constitutional provisions interacted in sometimes quite unexpected ways.[16] In one case, for example, heard by the GVH and the community policing forum secretary, who was a senior male villager, the discussion was brought to a head when the GVH read from the Chichewa translation of the constitution. Rather abruptly, he informed the defendant: 'You need to apologise. Law 24: "women have the right to adequate protection."[17] You didn't protect her. How will you apologise?' The case concerned a disagreement between a woman and her ex-husband's brother, who had threatened that over the course of the next year two corpses would be taken out from her house. Section 24 of the English version of the constitution begins: 'Women have the right to full and equal protection by the law, and have the right not to be discriminated against on the basis of their gender or marital status.' The GVH did not read out the sentence in full. Indeed, his reference to human rights as enshrined in the constitution appears to have been little more than a rhetorical tool to augment his authority in condemning the behaviour of the young man.

---

[15] See Scully (2011) and Chapter 5 for more on the centrality of the figure of the suffering African woman to human rights discourse and interventions.

[16] See Chapter 2; CVSUs are convened at T/A level with the involvement of traditional authorities, members of the local community policing forum, and a community policing officer. It is not necessary for a police officer to be present for cases to be heard.

[17] *Amayi ali ndi ufulu kulandira zitetezo zokwanira.*

The case was complicated, but it could not easily be reduced to an issue of gender-based violence or the abuse of women's rights, and nor did the GVH seek to frame it as such. During the course of the hearing, he asserted both his belief in witchcraft (*ufiti*) and his familiarity with the constitution. Like the sheikh and the sub-inspector in the VSU, he also sought to establish that the defendant had overstepped the bounds of appropriate (customary) behaviour for someone in his position: in this case, someone who was not *nkhoswe*.[18] Indeed, the GVH and the sub-inspector displayed similarly broad concerns, not only with the propriety of disputing parties, but also with their welfare: 'You should think about that with maturity,' the sub-inspector counselled Mr Phiri with respect to his responsibilities towards his wives and children. 'You should be aware that such conduct provides opportunities for others to practise witchcraft,' the GVH advised the young man, pointing to the dangers he might invite upon himself and those around him if he did not reform his behaviour.

Rights and custom were not necessarily approached in these settings as mutually exclusive or opposed. Rights could inhere in customary practices and institutions such as polygamy and the system of *ankhoswe*. Indeed, they were polyvalent, with roots in both the customary and the transnational fields. Discussions of rights, facilitated by their Chichewa translation, incorporated constitutional provisions but did not always adhere to them in their entirety or push them to their logical extremes. Similarly, 'custom' was open to negotiation, and what constituted 'true' customary procedure (the proper *ndondomeko*) required articulation. Underlying these negotiations seemed to be a tacit recognition of the relational nature of personhood in this context: parties to disputes were conceptualised as wives, (potential) co-wives, nieces, husbands, and *ankhoswe*. To a certain extent, it was their positions in webs of relationships that determined how their actions, and their rights, were interpreted.

A language of relationships

In their attention to relationships – or 'status' (in the sense of 'social position'), to use a now unfashionable term – VSU officers and disputants could be said to employ a version of 'the reasonable man' as identified by Gluckman in his work among the Barotse in what is now Zambia (1965; 1973 [1955]; and see Introduction). In Barotseland, Gluckman argues, judges investigated 'the behaviour of the parties to

---

[18] The role of *nkhoswe* would have justified his interest in the current state of the relationship between his brother and the complainant, since this was related to the threat.

one another ... over a long period', assessing it 'against the standards ... demand[ed], for a series of situations, of the reasonable brother, sister, brother-in-law, nephew and headman [etc.]' (1973 [1955]: 187). Thus, scrutiny of the reasonableness of behaviour soon became 'an inquiry into the fulfilment of status obligations' (1965: 14). In this way, morality entered into legal adjudication, for '[i]mplicit in the reasonable man is the upright man' (1973 [1955]: 22; see also Werbner 2014). Through the use of something akin to Gluckman's reasonable man, police officers and religious and traditional authorities in the Chiradzulu community policing forums attempted to navigate the so-called 'tragedy' of judicial ethics entailed in the tension between the requirement to follow rules and the inevitability of moral engagement (Clarke 2012). Rights or freedoms (*ufulu*) were approached as pertaining to the obligations and expectations that accompany particular relationships, be they marital, affinal, or matrilineal.

It is important to note here that the women discussed above did not claim their rights directly in the language of *ufulu* – although they perhaps approached community policing forums in the expectation that knowledge of human rights would inform proceedings. Rather than rights, they articulated their claims in the language of relationships. They spoke of the aberrant behaviour of their husbands, (potential) co-wives, and relatives-in-law. The freedom/right they sought was well captured by the sub-inspector's description of the position from which Anabanda might have rejected polygamy, when he paired *ufulu* with *mtendere*, a possible synonym for 'freedom' carrying strong connotations of peace and harmony. The women sought explicit acknowledgment of the breakdown of particular relationships and they hoped for the restoration of *mtendere* – freedom as peaceful coexistence. While the analyst might perceive a contradiction between liberal human rights, widely understood to pertain to autonomous individuals, and a conception of personhood that recognises the constitutive role of relationships, the Malawian officials and villagers cited here discerned no such conflict.

The phrase 'Mr Phiri should fail by himself', with which Anabanda's *nkhoswe* followed up his claim to have the right to direct his niece to accept polygamy, gestured towards a desire to secure her respectability by eschewing responsibility for marital breakdown. Given the prevalence of divorce in matrilineal Malawi, his words conveyed a sense that the marriage might well fail in the future, but that any such failure ought to be seen to result from Mr Phiri's own inadequacies as a husband, as opposed to fickleness or truculence on Anabanda's part. Significantly, such strategising occurred in the absence of bridewealth payments, precluding the kinds of directly material explanations proffered elsewhere in Africa to account for disputing parties' efforts to avoid blame for marital breakdown (see, e.g., McClendon 1995). Nor can his concern be explained by any stigma surrounding divorce. Divorce in and of itself would not taint a woman's moral standing, although assessments of how it had come about would doubtless inform local appraisals of her character. Thus, her *nkhoswe*'s words reflected his desire to safeguard Anabanda's reputation as a woman who strove, against the odds, to make her marriage work, and thereby to maintain the support of her kin and neighbours. That support, in turn, was essential to the moral-material reproduction of her household.

The sub-inspector also alluded to the relationality of personhood when he cast doubt on the position from which Anabanda had agreed to polygamy, pointing out that she had children to look after and thus did not want to be without a husband. Anabanda had made a similar point herself when she offered the fact that her mother had passed away as a reason for her reluctance to accept divorce. In this matrilineal setting, mothers often provide significant contributions, both material and affective, to the care and provisioning of their daughters' children. It is in this context that we ought to understand the sub-inspector's concern that, had Anabanda been in a position to choose freely or enjoy her rights (*pa ufulu, pa mtendere*), she might have rejected polygamy. With these words, he acknowledged the limits of Anabanda's *ufulu*, signalling an understanding that her ability to consent to, or refuse, polygamy was affected by the social and economic situation in which she found herself, not least the difficulties she would face as a mother bringing up her children with limited familial support.

The sub-inspector recognised that Anabanda did not act from a position of autonomous individuality, if that is taken to imply detachment from the relationships of matrilineal and affinal kinship in which she was inevitably enmeshed or exemption from serious economic constraints. His statement also echoed a recent strand of Africanist anthropology that grapples with similar conundrums: what is the relationship between rights and social relations? How can we understand freedom or equality in conjunction with – rather than in opposition to – dependence and obligations (Englund 2006; 2011; 2012a; Ferguson 2013; 2015)? This work suggests that freedom and equality may be achieved through claims of hierarchical interdependence, rather than autonomy.[19] These arguments are counterintuitive to those steeped in a liberal discourse of freedom, equality, and rights, or what James Ferguson has called 'the emancipatory liberal mind' (2013: 223), yet anthropologists working in Africa have long held that personhood is inherently relational: persons do not pre-exist relations of dependence;

---

[19] African feminist scholars have engaged in similar debates; see especially Nzegwu (2006). For a critique of this approach, see Rossi (2016).

they are constituted through them and in their efforts to discharge the obligations they entail (Piot 1999: 17–19).

Such arguments owe a significant debt to the work of Marilyn Strathern, whose insights concerning the essential relationality of human life, derived from rich Melanesian ethnography, establish what she terms 'a thoroughly trans-local social fact' (2004: 232): namely, that '[p]eople are nowhere "free" to create relationships' (ibid.). Nevertheless, sociality, and the inevitability of the potentially constraining obligations entailed in social relations, do not imply a lack of agency, for '[a]gency is evinced in the ability of people to (actively) orient themselves to or align themselves in particular relationships. This is not the same as free choice' (2005: 189, original emphasis removed). In other words, a view of social relationships as somehow impinging on a 'natural' state of 'freedom' or 'autonomy' is a red herring.

The sub-inspector conveyed an understanding of the fact that Anabanda spoke from within a particular configuration of relationships shaped by the matrilineal setting. When she accepted polygamy, she was not bowing to coercion or the weight of custom, but consenting as a woman who, as well as being a wife, was also a mother, niece, and matrilineal kinswoman. In a setting in which marital instability and impermanence are the norm, she consented to polygamy in the knowledge that this was unlikely to be the last time that she and Mr Phiri sat down with their *ankhoswe* to discuss the future of their marriage. Rather, this dispute hearing was but a single episode in the ongoing negotiation of their relationship and of the wider network of kinship relations in which it was embedded. Unfinished and unfolding, her agreement was secured for now, but by no means forever.

Conclusion: towards an anthropology of justice

It has recently been suggested that justice is qualitatively different from human rights because 'justice is contextual in a way that human rights is not' (Goodale and Clarke 2010: 10). According to this view, justice is 'an ever receding and ever shrouded social ideal', as opposed to 'an alternative normative orientation characterized by a set of concrete expectations and practices' (ibid.). I am inclined to agree, but the analysis presented here suggests that the distinction between *ufulu* and *chilungamo* (justice) is not quite as easy to define. This is because *ufulu* is a flexible and ambiguous term, drawing at once on an older and broader semantic field, best summed up in English as 'freedom', yet also saturated with contemporary meaning as the quintessential concept of the multiparty era. Embraced and yet derided, *ufulu* implies modernity and a desirable break with the past, but it can also go too far, undermining the moral foundations of society. The ways in which *ufulu* is invoked in dispute hearings indicate that it can be a welcome resource, allowing for complex negotiations of customary and rights-based perspectives that do not alienate participants who approach the case from different positions.

But if *ufulu* is a tool, *chilungamo* (justice) is the goal. The commonly heard demand 'I want justice' captures what it is that complainants seek when they arrive at the VSU, rather than 'I want my rights'. *Chilungamo* does not carry the same connotations of modernity that infuse *ufulu*: it is neither new nor foreign. And yet it is just as ambiguous, if not more so, because it is formally contentless. Unlike rights (or custom), which can be specified, at least in theory, justice must always be defined anew in relation to each case. While the details of (idealised) gender roles and appropriate customary procedure could usually be outlined in discussions, justice itself remained abstract, operating as an ever-present but undefined goal. In the case discussed above, appeals to customary procedure provided, at least momentarily, a degree of normative thickness to the notion of *chilungamo* that shimmered in the background, making it function as more than a mere 'empty signifier' (Goodale and Clarke 2010: 11). However, it could not be tied down for long, and the concept slipped rapidly back to the status of elusive ideal, the content of which was open to contestation.

The Chichewa rendering of justice as *chilungamo* is uncontroversial, and the same word can also be translated back into English as truth or righteousness. Derived from the verb *kulungama*, meaning 'to be straight or upright', it has clear moral connotations. Perhaps the closest we can come to a definition of *chilungamo* in Anabanda's case is the reference to *mtendere* (peace, harmony, freedom), another elusive concept. In addition to being the stated goal of many disputants, *chilungamo* often appeared in the VSU in the form of the rhetorical question 'Is that justice?', implying a shared understanding of what justice does and does not entail. In many cases, *chilungamo* was also appealed to in relation to issues of customary procedure or gendered norms of care, approximating the meaning of 'right', as in 'proper' or 'appropriate'. Indeed, functional synonyms included *zolondola* (correct), *zabwinobwino* (good, proper, virtuous), *za ndondomeko* (systematic, orderly, according to the proper process), *zolongosoka* (in order, proper), and *zoyenera* (appropriate, proper). Like *ufulu*, these terms carry moral freight, and, following Gluckman, we might say that it is, in part, through the manipulation of their imprecision and elasticity that it is possible 'to import justice into judgement' (1973 [1955]: 195).

Research conducted by Women and Law in Southern Africa (WLSA) has also highlighted ways in which understandings of *chilungamo* are intertwined with moral ideas about the good life and 'traditional' gender roles. They carried out research in five districts of Malawi and found that women's perceptions of justice 'included being looked after or being provided with necessities for survival by a husband' (WLSA 2000: 18). This would support the evidence from the VSU that suggests that women claiming their rights to fair treatment and opposing their husbands' behaviour do so without challenging long-established, *complementary* gender roles, which tend to place men as providers and women as nurturers of children, livestock, and agricultural produce.[20] As Chapter 4 further underlines, shifting the focus from human rights to justice enables us to fold ideas about morality, the good life, relational personhood, and gender roles into understandings of gendered disputes, opening the way for a consideration of the ways in which different ideas about gender are challenged, contested, and reproduced in this matrilineal setting.

---

[20] Hodgson makes a similar point in relation to Tanzanian Maasai women, who, she says 'are seeking equality in terms of rights but not necessarily roles' (2011: 156; see also Young 2010).

4   Gender justice?

Parties to marital disputes were often asked by those seeking to assist them what it was that they wanted to achieve. Often, they simply answered: '*Ndikufuna chilungamo*' – 'I want justice.' Simultaneously evasive and truthful, their answer begs the further question of what exactly constitutes justice in the context of gender and marital relations in matrilineal Malawi. Justice as a shared goal is easy to agree upon, but marital disputes illustrate the degree to which the content of justice is open to contestation. This chapter takes an ethnographic approach to the question of what gender justice might look like, considering the competing visions of gender relations available to rural Malawians from those espoused by NGO officers to those that inform magistrates' interventions. Moving beyond these discursive arenas, it also provides a broader view of women's expectations and experiences of marriage. The range of voices illustrates the extent to which gender relations are subject to debate in contemporary Malawi while simultaneously enabling analytical purchase on a vision of justice that differs substantially from the notion of gender equality that saturates the teachings of local NGOs. What emerges is an appreciation of the importance of men's and women's differentiated and complementary – yet contested – contributions to household reproduction for the constitution and expression of moral personhood. Rather than the formal equality of men and women as husbands and wives, I argue that 'complementarity' and the concomitant recognition of the constitutive moral obligations of husbands and wives to one another are central to the understandings of justice that guide women and men in this part of rural Malawi as they strive to achieve successful relationships and satisfactory resolutions to their marital disputes.

The *jenda* agenda

In recent years, training delivered to women in Chiradzulu District by local NGOs has often focused on *jenda* (gender) and *ufulu wachibadwidwe* (human rights). Women are taught that much of what they understand to be appropriate gender roles and take for granted as the necessary

gendered division of labour is the result of culture (*chikhalidwe*), or
customs and traditions (*miyambo*), which vary according to location.
Instructors impress upon them that there are only three tasks assigned
to women by God or creation – pregnancy, lactation, and menstruation –
while impregnation is men's sole gender-specific burden.[1] These tasks
have remained unchanged 'since the Garden of Eden'.[2] Beyond these, all
supposedly gendered work can be learned by anyone, and therefore there
is nothing immutable about women's relatively heavy domestic and
agricultural workloads.

Such lessons are in keeping with the Malawi government's broad
policy of 'gender mainstreaming', which began in the early 1990s
(Kanyongolo 2007: 235; see also Miers 2011), and, more generally, with
the internationally dominant 'women's rights as human rights' approach
to female equality and empowerment that has transformed women's
advocacy since the late 1980s (Hodgson 2002; 2017). The training is
intended to 'empower' women to reject customs and practices that hold
them back; to understand and demand their human rights as women;
and to transform their lives and relationships in accordance with globally
salient ideals. At times, women do indeed embrace the idea that, as the
name of one NGO-created village committee puts it, 'women are able'
(*Amayi angathe*). On one occasion, for example, women responded in
large numbers to a village head's order that a bridge be repaired, assisting
male villagers to carry freshly felled tree trunks to the location of the
damaged bridge and taking over from the smaller group of men who were
visibly, and audibly, struggling with their log. The women seized the
opportunity to exclaim '*Amayi angathe!*' and carried the log briskly while
singing a competitive wedding song, the lyrics of which translate loosely
as 'they are not strong enough' (*akuchepera kaba amenewo*) (see

---

[1] For women: '*kutenga pathupi; kuyamwitsa mwana; kupita kumwezi*'. For men: '*imodzi
yokha, kupereka pathupi*'. The source here is notes taken by a female villager during a
training session in late 2009. My own notes, my own notes from a similar session
I attended in June 2010 are almost identical.

[2] Citation from my notes taken at the training session in June 2010, which was held in a
village nursery school building over three days. There was a striking similarity in structure
and content between my notes and those of villagers who had attended other sessions by
the same or different NGOs. The training sessions in June were simultaneously delivered
to local men at a location in a neighbouring village. The instructors, who operated on
rotation, included NGO staff, a male pastor, a female police officer from a local VSU, and
a female court administrator from a nearby magistrates' court. Topics covered included:
Gender (*Jenda*); Gender and Religion (*Jenda ndi Chipembedzo*); HIV/AIDS and Gender
(*HIV/AIDS ndi Jenda*); Human Rights, Women's Rights, and Children's Rights (*Ufulu
Wachibadwidwe, Ufulu wa Amayi, Ufulu wa Ana*); Domestic Violence (*Nkhanza za
M'banja*); The Domestic Violence Act and the Penal Code (*Lamulo Loteteza Nkhanza
za M'banja ndi Penal Code*); and Good Leadership (*Utsogoleri Wabwino*). Participants were
provided with exercise books and pens and encouraged to take notes, copying down those
written on flip charts by the facilitators. All training was conducted in Chichewa and the
translations are my own.

Figure 4.1 *Amayi angathe*!

Figure 4.1). The women continued to sing long after the log had reached its destination, facing the mildly amused and somewhat humbled men, singing, dancing, and ululating in delight.

On another occasion, a group of male and female villagers who had been selected to benefit from an NGO-sponsored pig-rearing 'income-generating project' found themselves behind schedule with the task of producing the bricks necessary for the construction of their pigsty. They needed to build a brick oven, and fast. Although this task was widely held to be 'men's work', the women in the group had heard about women elsewhere building brick ovens and burning bricks without male assistance. Fed up of waiting for their male counterparts to get their act together, they began the work themselves in the name of *jenda* – *amayi angathe* indeed!

These examples are somewhat superficial, however. This is evident when we consider the fact that, despite the larger group of women achieving what the men could not in transporting the hefty tree trunk, there was never any question of them assisting with the work of bridge construction. Similarly, it was not long before the male members of the pig-rearing group relieved their female colleagues. Rather, these brief vignettes illustrate the extent to which men and women are familiar with the teachings of *jenda* and their ironic incorporation of human rights discourse in their daily lives (cf. Allen 2013). Their familiarity with the language of human rights and gender equality, as well as their recognition of its limitations, are revealed through teasing and casual humour.

For some villagers, particularly men, *jenda* has negative connotations. It can be understood to imply the need to reverse gender roles, so that, as one NGO instructor put it, 'men should cook for women and women should rebel against their husbands'.[3] The instructor was keen to dispel

---

[3] *Abambo aziphikira amayi, amayi aziukira azimuna awo.* This is not a straightforward reversal, in that the suggestion is not that husbands generally 'rebel against' their wives.

such interpretations. 'That is not *jenda*,' he insisted. 'If you tell your husband, "You cook the *nsima*, [these days] there is *jenda*," then you have not been listening to me.' However, the messages conveyed were not entirely consistent. During the same training session, another facilitator told the women that they take on too much domestic work, and that this inequitable division of labour meant that they aged more quickly than their husbands. The refrain that men and women are capable of carrying out the same tasks[4] reinforced calls to understand that gendered divisions of labour are culturally and geographically relative, and can, therefore, shift over time. 'Does not this constituency have a female MP?' one facilitator asked, rhetorically, comparing the contemporary situation with the political 'culture' (*chikhalidwe*) of Kamuzu Banda's reign, during which women were expected merely to praise their leader through dance, rather than offering substantive contributions to political debates.[5]

The close association of *jenda* with the physical tasks of daily life – cooking and domestic labour – has led Malawian socio-legal scholar Ngeyi Kanyongolo to suggest that the discourse of *jenda*, 'which is arguably as "foreign" as human rights', has had greater purchase because, '[i]n the majority of cases, *jenda* seems more practical than rhetorical. It identifies with not only the idea but also the activities and the persons and their social relationships' (2007: 231). Thus, villagers would remark, in tones combining incredulity, mockery, and admiration, that 'there is *jenda*' (*kuli jenda*) when I responded to their questions about the possibility of men taking on household chores in the UK. They were also keen observers of my partner's behaviour on his visits to the village, noticing that he often took responsibility for cooking in the evenings; enjoyed playing with young children, who were most forgiving of his inability to communicate in Chichewa; and would accompany me on trips to the borehole. His feeble attempts to carry a basin on his head, and the resounding success of his culinary efforts, served to confirm that there really was *jenda* in Europe. All the same, any suggestion that such *jenda* might be possible in Chiradzulu too tended to be met with raucous laughter.

Jenda encodes a particular vision of just gender relations, one that focuses on the desirability of the fundamental similarity of men's and women's roles within marriage. Chiradzulu villagers' laughter when confronted with the possibility of gender equality on these terms alerts us to the fact that it is not the only – or even the most common – vision of

---

The implication is that the discourse of *jenda* encourages women to display disrespect towards their husbands and to usurp their position at the 'head' of the family (*mutu wa banja*).

[4] *Abambo ndi amayi angathe kugwira ntchito chimodzimodzi.*

[5] As Vera Chirwa (2007: 159–61, 182–3) makes clear, this practice continued into the era of multiparty politics. See also Chirwa (2001).

how marital relationships ought to be conducted. I turn now to two cases heard by different magistrates in Chiradzulu District in order to shed light on alternative understandings of gender roles within marriage in this context. The first court was the domain of an old, male magistrate, and we can detect a determination to preserve 'traditional' gender roles; the second was presided over by a slightly younger, female magistrate, who exhibited greater sympathy towards women. In both cases, women addressed the courts as complainants, claiming that their husbands had divorced them 'without valid reasons'.

Case 1: 'Women cannot be compensated because that would encourage them to misbehave'

The following judgment was handed down in the first-grade magistrate's court at Chiradzulu in October 2009. Unusually, this judgment was delivered 'on the spot' following the conclusion of witness testimonies and cross-examination, rather than being read out at a later date, following an adjournment, as was the standard practice.[6] The case was dealt with expeditiously because the magistrate felt it to be a simple matter.[7] Immediately before the judgment was delivered, the magistrate asked each party in turn whether they favoured divorce or reconciliation. The husband replied that he wanted divorce (*banja lithe*); the wife that she wanted the marriage to continue (*ndikufuna ukwati*). He then proceeded with the judgment:

> The complainant is [name and village], her claim is that the defendant has divorced her without valid reasons. The defendant is [name and village], he said that they just deserted each other because of disagreements. The complainant said that they married in 2001 and have borne three children. She has a house at her home [village] but it needs mending on the roof. She said it was this year that the defendant declared divorce in the presence of both advocates [*ankhoswe*].[8] She said that when they discussed, the defendant said he did so because the complainant [had] chased him from the matrimonial home. She said that it is not true because the truth is that the defendant had married another lady. Efforts to reconcile the two failed and the defendant's advocate admitted that the defendant did not record to him that the complainant had chased him from the matrimonial home nor did he complain to the complainant's advocate, he just said [it] at the time they discussed, when the complainant found the defendant at another village.

---

[6] The case was heard in several sittings over a period of three weeks. I was present at the first hearing and for the judgment.

[7] The magistrate delivered the judgment in English and the clerk translated it into Chichewa. The transcription is from my notes of the magistrate's English. On this occasion, I was unable to record the Chichewa translation.

[8] 'Advocates' is a common translation for the Chichewa *ankhoswe*. Elsewhere I have rendered *ankhoswe* as 'marriage guardians'.

Case 1:   (*cont.*)

Findings are as follows: although the defendant failed to tell both advocates that the complainant was chasing him at least on two or three occasions using [abusive] words to tell him he should go away, the court has believed [that] the complainant said those words. It was just an issue of procedure that he failed ... The defendant convinced the court that on all occasions he was trying to reconcile with the complainant he did not want every piece of [the] dispute to be reported. That is why he went away to find a [labour] contract building a house, where the complainant followed him. He was surprised that the complainant was insulting him although he was not found with a woman because she was not justified in insulting him based only on rumours.

The defendant's advocate said that it was true that the defendant was found with another lady. However, the issue of being found with another lady is not connected to this case.

The complainant had begun doing business ordering and selling dried maize. She found that the defendant was somebody to look after in marriage and started to insult him. At custom, anything which pains the mind is good grounds for divorce, so that is a good ground. The court grants divorce in favour of the defendant without compensating anything at all.

The problem with marriage when people stay at the wife's home is that if the wife sees the husband not doing anything, she has [had] a house built for her by the husband and he has not paid *lobola* [bridewealth], so if he is sent away there is nothing that the uncle will refund. She makes anything so that he will go away. That is at a high rate in Chiradzulu and women cannot be compensated because that would encourage them to misbehave.

I urge the defendant to fix the roof of the complainant's house. The defendant remains responsible to [help] look after the children.[9]

There are many grounds on which this judgment might be critiqued, not least its hasty delivery. More interesting for my purposes here, however, is a consideration of the way in which the magistrate introduced

[9] The judgment followed the convention of delivering a single narrative in which replies to direct questions and responses to cross-examination are absorbed in a coherent account of each witness's testimony. (Although some magistrates did report what was said under cross-examination more transparently, they did not record the questions, only the responses.) Because of the impromptu style of delivery, there was no written judgment in the case file when I consulted it. The magistrate had simply written: 'Divorce is granted without any compensation as defendant has a valid reason for divorce. Defendant to repair the roof of complainant's house and continue maintaining his children.' His notes taken during the case hearings contained the wife's denial of having used insulting language – 'I did not say you should go away just because you were just being fed' – and the husband's accusations: 'After some days, complainant followed me and called me a whore who had sexual looseness' and 'Complainant said that my piece is too small to fit her demand'.

'custom' to support his finding that the wife was at fault, firmly embed-
ding his assessment in the local matrilineal and matrilocal context, as
well as gesturing to certain patriarchal 'traditions'. Thus, in his judgment, 'custom' was both preserved and condemned. The 'custom' of
tolerance for male infidelity was upheld by the magistrate's decision to
define the husband's reported infidelity as peripheral to the claim before
the court, which was that the defendant had divorced his wife 'without
valid reasons'. The phrasing of the claim was such that the defendant was
required to provide evidence that he did have valid reasons for leaving his
wife, and so it was those things that had pained *his* mind that became
relevant. In this regard, his wife was held to account for insulting him on
the basis of mere rumour, the suggestion being that she was not justified
in doing so by 'custom', which requires 'evidence' of infidelity before a
woman can broach the issue.[10] The magistrate's judgment leaves the
issue of whether the wife had in fact caught her husband with another
woman ambiguous. He reports the defendant's denial and his *nkhoswe*'s
confirmation but ultimately states that the matter is 'not connected to
this case'. On this issue, it is clear that the scope of what is relevant is
more restricted in relation to the wife than to the husband, for whom
'*anything* which pains the mind' is considered 'good evidence'.

Custom was overlooked, however, when it came to the husband's
dereliction of his customary responsibility to inform the *ankhoswe* of any
marital difficulties and to attempt reconciliation through them. Here, the
magistrate's relative inattention to proper customary procedure contrasts
sharply with the approach taken in the victim support unit (VSU), as we
saw in Chapter 3. Of course, there is nothing new, or even particularly
remarkable, about the patriarchal proclivity to define 'custom' to the
advantage of men (Chanock 1985; McClendon 1995; Schmidt 1990).
What seemed to irk the magistrate was the wife's apparent financial
independence, achieved through her engagement in the business of
ordering and selling maize, combined with his assessment that she had
come to consider her husband a material burden. The implicit suggestion
is that the wife had violated the ideal gender balance by taking on the role
of breadwinner, which the magistrate viewed negatively regardless of
whether she saw her husband 'not doing anything'.

Tellingly, the magistrate also seized the opportunity to opine on the
general ills of matrilineal kinship. This particular magistrate hailed from
the Northern Region, where patrilineal kinship norms are more common
and patrilocal residence predominant. He clearly believed patriliny to be
superior to the matrilineal practices he found in Chiradzulu, where he
considered women to have fewer incentives to remain married once their

[10] The quintessential evidence is an item of clothing belonging to the husband and one
from his partner, seized at the moment of discovery.

husbands had fulfilled their duty to build houses in their wives' home compounds. Yet he did not ignore this customary requirement altogether, for he found it necessary for the husband to mend his wife's roof even after divorce, combining this requirement with the constitutionally aligned, but un-'customary', reminder that parental responsibility is shared between mothers and fathers and does not end with the dissolution of marriage. Of course, a father's ongoing interest in the welfare of his children accords not only with the constitution, and with human rights provisions, but also with the patrilineal practices this magistrate favoured.

Contrast this, then, with the following judgment delivered by a female magistrate in the second-grade magistrate's (SGM's) court at Mbulumbuzi (in the same district, within a few hours' walking distance of Chiradzulu court) in March 2010.[11] The female complainant in this case was also suing her husband for divorcing her 'without valid reasons'.

Case 2: 'The truth is that he was not chased but he chose to leave and get married to this other woman'

This case concerned a couple who had married in 1997 and, from the statements they gave in court, it was clear that their difficulties had begun almost immediately. In her testimony, the complainant stressed her husband's frequent absence from their home and his regular misappropriation of household resources. Early in their marriage he had won a building contract in Mitengo village and he subsequently established a relationship with a woman there and fathered a child. His wife's attempts to discuss their problems, first at church and later with a number of traditional authorities, proved futile, and the couple were eventually referred to court in 2008.

The original court case ended when the defendant requested reconciliation. However, their relationship continued to be marred by disagreements over household resources and the defendant's ongoing relationship with the woman at Mitengo. The complainant's efforts to resolve matters through their *ankhoswe* did not succeed. One particularly dramatic row featured in the evidence of both parties and involved physical violence towards the complainant and her mother, as well as damage to household property. The defendant testified that the row had begun when he returned home late one night and his wife threw the food that she had prepared for him into water, forcing him to sleep on an empty stomach. In her judgment, the magistrate explained:

---

[11] I was present when the evidence was given in this case but was unable to attend court when the judgment was delivered; the transcript of the judgment is copied from the magistrate's handwritten records (kept in English). As with the first case, the magistrate delivered the judgment in English, and the clerk provided a translation for the benefit of all present. My account of the case summarises the magistrate's lengthy judgment.

Case 2:   *(cont.)*

The defendant said he damaged the items because the complainant criticised him that he had nothing when he went to marry her. The defendant is all the same surprised as to why he was summoned to court because it was the complainant who packed [his belongings] for him.

The police attended the incident but no action was taken and the complainant went again to consult the village head.

It later emerged that the defendant was continuing to visit the woman in Mitengo, but when his wife asked him why:

he said he had no time to entertain questions. Adding that he had now found himself a perfect woman, who carries him to and from [the] bathroom. Later he started packing. The complainant called her parents to see what was happening. They were told that he had no time to entertain stupid questions from anyone.

The complainant informed the village head and her *nkhoswe* again and, eventually, the village head referred them back to court.

The magistrate concluded as follows:

In the very beginning of the issue the court has learnt that the defendant married at Mitengo. He for so many times cheated that he went to work yet he was there [with] this woman. The complainant came to court and the defendant decided to withdraw the case and promised to leave this woman and go back to the matrimonial home. He did but the situation now grew worse. It was this same woman who caused all the problems in this family. The defendant is very unable to divorce this woman ... However, the defendant does not even indicate that it is polygamy. Then it is good that he chooses one partner other than finding unfounded faults in the complainant.

The two have worked together in the fields and the complainant also worked hard to sell their produce but disappointingly the defendant used the same sources to keep the other woman's life going.

It's sad that the defendant could not state exactly what made him leave the home. His reason was that he was chased by the complainant. The truth is that he was not chased but he chose to leave and get married to this other woman. As of now the defendant is settled with this woman. What he had been denying all along has now become a reality. The defendant can no longer deny the fact that he is back to his lover.

What he did when this matter was first presented before the court by withdrawing the matter was just a way of cheating both the complainant and the court.

Going by the evidence in the first case and the evidence after the reconciliation, the court is satisfied that the complainant had all the reasons to come to court to lodge her claim. It has been proven by the court that indeed the complainant was divorced without reasons. The reason as per what the court has discovered is that the defendant did not want to continue with the marriage but go for his lover at Mitengo.

Case 2: *(cont.)*

It therefore satisfies the court that the defendant is liable to the claim by the complainant and will be ordered as per the claim.

Delivered in open court this 17th Day of March 2010 at Mbulumbuzi SGM Court.

Signed, 17/03/2010

Submissions:

Complainant: I want him to divorce me
Defendant: I am ready to divorce her.

Order:

The complainant has asked for divorce due to the problems she has gone through. The defendant is very ready to divorce her. The court will not go further than dissolving the marriage today the 17th day of March 2010 at Mbulumbuzi SGM Court in favour of the complainant. Defendant is then ordered to pay into court as follows:

K55,000 compensation to complainant
K3,500 child maintenance
K450 court expenses

Today the defendant pays into court the sum of K7,950 then a monthly instalment of K7,500. ROA [Right of Appeal] explained.
Signed, 17/03/2010.

The couple at the centre of this case was relatively well off by rural standards, as was made clear in the course of the hearing by references to material possessions, including televisions and DVD players, which were beyond the reach of the majority of villagers. The impression created was of industrious and successful agriculturalists (mention was made of large maize harvests and tobacco and tomato sales), whose income from the sale of their produce had at times been supplemented by the husband's occasional building work. The complainant's grievances were numerous and included, but were not limited to, her husband's infidelity and dishonesty; his physical violence; his failure to attend hearings with *ankhoswe* and traditional authorities; the fact that he damaged their property; his unjust division of the proceeds of their joint labour; and his failure to provide for the household which meant that she had to sell maize intended for their consumption to replace household items that he had taken to Mitengo. Her reported criticism of her husband – that he 'had nothing' at the time of their marriage – speaks to her belief that his current wealth and status, which facilitated his infidelity, was a product of their relationship. He was reaping, but not sharing, the rewards of having established a successful household in her matrilineal compound and of their joint labour on land accessed through her kin.

For his part, the defendant accused his wife of undue surveillance of his movements; accosting him when he returned home late at night; uncontrolled jealousy and anger; damaging property; and insulting him. He claimed that his second wife in Mitengo showed him much greater respect, going so far as to carry him between the house and the bathroom so that he did not have to dirty his feet. This statement, combined with his account of the complainant's insults about his financial situation at the time of their marriage, serves to build a picture of his wife's comparative lack of respect for him as the head of their household. Both parties presented substantial accounts of the other's misdemeanours, and the magistrate's findings could hardly have been more different from those of her male colleague in Chiradzulu.

Whereas, in the first case, the magistrate described wives' propensity to 'make anything so that [their husbands] will go away', the second magistrate ruled that the husband was 'finding unfounded faults' in his wife. Far from being 'unconnected', the defendant's infidelity was viewed as integral to the case, providing his wife with 'all the reasons to come to court'. The defendant's failure to formalise polygamy meant that this second relationship was deemed illicit (signalled by the magistrate's use of the English terms 'lover' and 'other woman' rather than 'wife'). As in the first case, the magistrate diagnosed an illegitimate attempt by one party to shift the responsibility for the breakdown of the marriage onto their counterpart. Although strikingly different, the words of both magistrates bring to mind Gluckman's description of Lozi judgments as 'sermons on filial, parental, and brotherly love' (1973 [1955]: 22).

In the second case, the fact that the defendant's *nkhoswe* did not testify reduced the likelihood that the magistrate would find in his favour. In the magistrates' courts, as in the VSU, failure to produce a member of the extended matrilineal family willing to serve as witness was generally taken to signal that the person in question was troublesome, and that their relatives had tired of their antics. As at the village court (*bwalo*), *ankhoswe* were 'expected to speak on behalf of the relationships in which the litigant[s were] embedded' (Englund 2011: 185). In most cases they were the only witnesses called; as such, their silence spoke volumes.[12]

---

[12] In this case, it may also be relevant that the defendant hailed from Balaka District, which lies a significant distance to the north of Chiradzulu, making it more difficult for his relatives to attend the case. When the magistrate questioned the defendant about the whereabouts of his *nkhoswe*, he answered that the latter had vacated his post (*anatuluka*), attempting to explain that he had been frustrated by his fellow *nkhoswe*'s conduct. However, the magistrate responded: 'Let us not beat around the bush ... I'm sure your advocate has not come because of your bad behaviour ... Let us take it that he

It is also worth noting that the female magistrate employed the moral language of disappointment in her account of the dispute. The magistrate diagnosed a failure to acknowledge mutual dependence: the fact that the husband had not shared the proceeds of the couple's combined labour with his spouse constituted a denial of his wife's contribution and a rejection of his moral and material obligations as husband. Disappointment is 'the flip side of dependence' (Englund 2011: 112); this is a theme to which I will have cause to return below.

Misbehaving women or irresponsible men?

I chose to cite at length from two particular judgments, but I could have offered any number of cases heard by the same magistrates to the same effect. They were remarkably consistent in their attitudes towards the disputing spouses who came before them. For one, the problem with contemporary marriage was women's propensity to flee at the slightest provocation; the other frequently found men to be dishonest and unfaithful. The individual magistrates' own gender and biographies are surely not irrelevant here, nor is the fact that the male magistrate had begun his career in the traditional courts under Kamuzu Banda, while his female colleague was trained after the transition to multiparty politics, in the era of human rights.[13] We have here contrasting understandings of gender roles and matrilineal 'custom', as well as differing conceptions of the legal system's role, and its potential flexibility, in relation to marital disputes.

In both cases, the claim brought by the female complainants was that of having been divorced 'without valid reasons'. This claim was extremely common, and seems to have carried over from the former traditional courts.[14] The claim is rather different from a simple request

hasn't come because of your bad behaviour and you did not try to contact him because you knew he wouldn't come because of your bad behaviour.' I encountered similar interactions at the Chiradzulu court. For example, in a case concerning a claim by a male complainant that his wife had deserted him without good reason, the male third-grade magistrate explained: '[I]t has been mentioned by defendant in cross-examination that two advocates from [complainant]'s side stopped handling their disputes because of his behaviour. It is my view that [complainant] chose not to call his advocate [to testify in court] because he was aware that the evidence could not be in his favour. I'm saying this because in matrimonial cases each party is obliged to call his or her advocate to testify. [Complainant] was given the chance but exercised his right to testify alone. I therefore make a finding that his evidence lacks credibility.'

[13] The male magistrate was taken seriously ill in late 2009 and was not expected to return to work. The female magistrate passed away in early 2010. These respective tragedies limited my ability to discuss their personal histories with them or to explore their reflections on their work and judgments. See Chapter 2 for more on the historical development of magistrates' courts in Malawi.

[14] Elizabeth Schmidt cites the similar charge brought against Shona women in colonial Southern Rhodesia: that they had left their husbands 'without just cause or reason'

for divorce, for, in theory, it allows complainants to avoid responsibility for the breakdown of their marriages. If the case ends favourably, their spouse will have been found to have already activated a divorce through neglect, perhaps, or through absence from the marital home. In the first case, the husband was successful in stressing his wife's disrespectful behaviour, convincing the magistrate that she had given him ample cause to leave her. In the second, descriptions of the complainant's anger and aggression, and her failure to provide food for her husband, were either overlooked or understood in the context of the defendant's maintenance of a second, clandestine relationship.

Thus, as we have seen, the claim 'divorced without valid reasons' can have the peculiar consequence of putting the complainant on trial in place of the defendant, for it falls to defendants either to prove that they have not divorced their spouses, or, more commonly, that they *did* in fact have valid reasons, and thus that their spouses were not good wives or husbands. Recognising this, one younger male magistrate I observed would sometimes rewrite the claim at the beginning of a case (see Chapter 5), and the female magistrate cited above clearly strove to maintain a focus on the defendant as the accused. The male magistrate above, on the other hand, appeared to welcome the opportunity to scrutinise women's behaviour, in this instance as in others, and generally found them wanting.

The parties to these disputes, much like their counterparts at the VSU and village *bwalo*, put great weight on who had been the first to say that they wanted to separate. This was always brought up in evidence and a certain amount of pragmatic strategising occurred during the course of disputes (both before they reached a resolution forum and as they moved between them) to avoid declaring a desire for divorce too early in the proceedings; to generate evidence of having sought redress through appropriate channels; and to position one's spouse so that he or she would bear responsibility for the end of the marriage (see Chapter 5). Thus, the defendant in the second case described his 'surprise' at being summoned to court, because, he said, his wife had thrown *him* out ('packed for'/'chased' him), and, therefore, she ought to take responsibility for their separation. For her part, his wife stressed her forbearance and conformity with the expected procedures: the many times she had reported her travails to their *ankhoswe* and the relevant traditional authorities; the various points at which she had hoped in vain to see a change in his behaviour; her compliance with efforts towards reconciliation; her physical pursuit of him when he was absent from the marital home, and so on. Between the complainant and her *ankhoswe*, three occasions were

(1992: 105). It seems likely that this claim has colonial roots in Malawi, too, although men's susceptibility to the charge may be a more recent innovation.

mentioned on which the defendant had reportedly stated that he wanted their marriage to end. However, while the complainant in the first case insisted that she wanted the marriage to continue and was condemned all the same, when the complainant in the second case asserted that she wanted a divorce, the magistrate emphasised that this was 'due to the problems she has gone through'.

The outcome of such strategising had consequences when it came to the question of compensation, as well as implications for the parties' reputations and their ability to gain the support and sympathy of the relevant authorities, kin, and neighbours. As we have seen, while little, if any, shame attaches to divorce, a woman would not wish to be perceived as having desired a divorce in order to pursue other relationships; this would almost certainly fuel village gossip, and might invite the derogatory label *hule* (whore). Similarly, a reputation for mistreating women would be unlikely to enhance a man's prospects of establishing future relationships. It was thus necessary to demonstrate perseverance and adherence to the appropriate procedures for seeking reconciliation, by means of hearings with *ankhoswe* at the very least. The importance of seeking support from *ankhoswe* and keeping them informed of any marital difficulties is evident in the testimonies cited in both judgments, where parties describe informing *ankhoswe* and traditional authorities at various points, or explain their failure to do so. For this reason, the absence of the second defendant's *nkhoswe* was pregnant with meaning. The ease with which the first magistrate forgave the defendant his lapses in this regard was unusual but consistent with his moral condemnation of the wife, and of women in matrilineal areas of the country more broadly. That such contrary approaches to gender justice can coexist in Chiradzulu magistrates' courts is indicative of the degree to which gender norms, matrilineal custom, rights, and justice are contested in contemporary Malawi.

Achieving respectable adulthood

When Jennifer Cole states that '[g]etting married, forming a household, and raising children epitomize respectable adulthood in Tamatave' (2010: 71), she could just as well be referring to contemporary rural Malawi as to twenty-first-century urban Madagascar. As in Tamatave, where many men and women do not attain respectable adulthood in this way, in Malawi, too, *not* marrying does not rule out the attainment of respectable adulthood, regardless of the strength of the rhetoric and image of married respectability. If marriage is not necessarily critical, however, motherhood is more closely associated with the transition to female adulthood (although this may be achieved through means other than the experience of pregnancy and childbirth), linked as it is with the ability to care for others. As we saw in Chapter 1, the perspectives of those who have not achieved married respectability or who have rejected remarriage following divorce or widowhood shed an interesting light on understandings of the institution of marriage and gender roles within it (and see Chapter 6).

Take Mercy, for example. A mother of four in her mid-thirties, she had entered into marriage twice, but neither relationship had lasted more than a few months. Mercy had thus never managed to achieve the status that might accrue to a woman who had been married for many years and who had raised children within an expansive household with the support of their father, sustained through joint agricultural endeavours and the cash income supplied by a (perhaps intermittently) employed spouse. While she could be referred to as the mother of her children (*Mayi wake wa Triza*), 'Wife of X' (*Mkazi wa X*) or 'Mrs X' (*Mayi X*) had never become regular substitutes for the clan name she had inherited from her father.

In contrast to several other unmarried women in the village, Mercy described a frustrated desire to marry rather than a deliberate decision to remain single. She believed herself to have been thwarted by a combination of a generalised shortage of marriageable men and the machinations of her elderly grandmother, whom she looked after and who, Mercy believed, deliberately frightened off her suitors for fear of losing her carer. Yet despite these difficulties in attaining the status of married woman, there was no suggestion that Mercy had somehow failed to achieve respectable adulthood. As a mother, farmer, carer, and household head, she was an active participant in an array of local groups, from the Catholic church choir to a number of NGO committees on which she held positions of authority and through which she gained access to training sessions, like those described at the beginning of this chapter, and the highly valued cash allowances that sometimes accompanied them (which she put towards the cost of her eldest daughter's secondary school fees). Mercy was neither marginalised in village affairs nor overlooked by the village head when it came to opportunities to participate in 'development' activities (*za chitukuko*).

Whether or not unmarried women aspired to married life, they tended to explain their positions in relation to their perceptions of men's abilities to contribute materially to their households. Thus, Mercy bemoaned the fact that, without a husband, she would have to find the resources to pay other men to rebuild her decrepit toilet and washroom, and she did not know how to stop her young son from stealing from her because she could not provide him with the lunchtime snacks and new school exercise books that he coveted. The good thing about marriage, she mused, would be the increased support (*chithandizo*), in terms of both material resources and the sharing of the agricultural and domestic workload.[15] That said, she was realistic about the potential downside of marriage, recognising that husbands could be more of an encumbrance than a blessing, that some prevented their wives from doing business (*bizinesi*), and that others beat them (*kumenya*). In discussing the relative merits and drawbacks of marriage, Mercy moved firmly into the language of morality – of good and bad husbands, admirable and pitiable unions.

'These days there are no marriages'

Mercy's remarks chimed strongly with those of Aida, a 39-year-old woman who had remained unmarried since her husband passed away in 2002. Unlike Mercy, Aida told me that she had no intention of remarrying; it was enough simply to take lovers (*zibwenzi*) from time to time for the physical pleasure they brought (*kungosangalatsa thupi*). Following her husband's death, Aida had become pregnant with her fifth child, and it was largely a result of her married lover's disappointing reaction to her pregnancy that she had opted for sterilisation after the birth of her youngest daughter. In this way, she could enjoy the benefits of relationships with men without risking pregnancy, which, she argued, would only serve to limit her ability to care for the five children she already had, and make it difficult for her to look after the two dairy cows she had received from a local NGO.

Like Mercy, Aida spoke of the advantages of marriage in relation to the sharing of the domestic and agricultural workload. In particular, a husband would be able to carry out those tasks she currently had to pay others to do: fixing the cow shelter, mending the roof of her house, perhaps even building her a new house with the bricks that her brothers had helped her produce the previous year:

For instance, there is work to do around the house, right? Can a woman here in Malawi climb up to fix the house? It's problematic; people will take you for someone who doesn't understand properly. That kind of work is thought to be men's work, right? Work like on the roof, to arrange the thatched roof, to make bricks, to build houses, that's men's work.

Nevertheless, Aida was under no illusion that marriage would bring an end to all her problems. Her own marriage had started well, but her late husband had become unfaithful and she believed he had spent much of

---

[15] The reference to the domestic workload is not intended to imply a sharing of the daily tasks of fetching water, cooking, sweeping, warming bath water, cleaning dishes and utensils, washing clothes, collecting firewood, and so on. Rather, the allusion is to such tasks as erecting fences, repairing leaky roofs, building bathing shelters and enclosures for livestock, digging pit latrines, constructing drying racks for dishes, cutting roofing grass, etc.

his money on other women. Her husband was not a drinker, but Aida also spoke with disdain of men who squandered their earnings on beer and failed to contribute sufficiently to the running of the household, and she feared entering a relationship with such a man. 'While I'm on my own,' she said, 'I am in control of the budget.' Towards the end of our conversation, in a statement of defiant independence, Aida cited the NGO slogan '*Amayi angathe*' (women are able), explaining to me that it meant that men and women could do the same work. While this directly contradicted her earlier musings on the disadvantages of single life, it helped make sense of her decision to remain unmarried and articulated a degree of pride in her achievements as a single mother, household head, farmer, and livestock owner.

There is a sense in some of the recent literature on Africa that increased gender tensions have led to a dramatic decline in the institution of marriage across much of the continent (Cornwall 2002; Griffiths 1997; Hunter 2010; James 1999a; 1999b).[16] The argument in many of these works would not surprise the male magistrate cited above: women are finding means of surviving and providing for their children through engagement with the market economy in ways that make husbands appear unnecessary or burdensome (see, e.g., Talle 1998).[17] However, as Mark Hunter demonstrates in his discussion of gender relations in post-apartheid South Africa, 'plummeting marriage rates' (2010: 139) there do not signal the '"breakdown" of the heterosexual family' (ibid.: 6), but rather index the reconfiguration of intimate relationships in the context of rising unemployment, rampant social inequality, and increased female mobility.

I suspect Aida would have agreed with a diagnosis of social change with respect to gender relations in rural Malawi. She expressed a powerful moral critique of contemporary marriages, which she contrasted with those of times gone by: 'These days people don't have love [*chikondi*],' she said. 'It's not like it was with our parents/ancestors [*makolo*] long ago ... Now, today, love is lacking ... there is no mutual trust, no mutual dependence in marriages.' She continued:

Because before, if a person was married – take Mr Mboma [one of the oldest men in the village] – he reached the point that his wife died, he was staying here, his wife died and he left here to go and live at his place. But his contemporaries, some of them are still around, they are still married, although they struggle to walk, they're so old. It means that their love was something united at that time. But today, there is no love. I mean to say that young men just seek a wife, they just

---

[16] There is an interesting echo here, albeit with significant differences in tone, with the concerns of colonialists and missionaries during the mid-twentieth century (see, e.g., Mbilinyi 1988; Moore and Vaughan 1994; Schmidt 1992: 96).

[17] Much of this work relates to urban contexts, however, and to non-agricultural modes of subsistence (cf. Gulbrandsen 1986).

ruin her, right? As soon as they've given the girl a child they start to see her as ugly. Rather than buying her the things she needs so that she can wash her clothes, dress smartly, and look good, they just see her as ugly and they want another woman. And that's where conflicts enter the marriage. If the husband is leaving the house to look for another marriage somewhere else, is that going to please his wife? That can't please her and the marriage has come into difficulties; it turns out that the marriage has ended. The woman is struggling, maybe they have borne two children, she is struggling with them and because of poverty with those children another man will come along and say, 'I'll look after you, I want to marry you,' and she will accept because of those problems. They'll stay with those problems and when something happens you'll hear the new husband say 'enough' and look for another wife somewhere else. They only want to play games, it's not that they want marriage. No, these days there are no marriages.[18]

When Aida said that 'there are no marriages', she did not mean that people were no longer entering into marital relationships. Rather, she was referring to a perceived weakening of the bonds that bind spouses together. She suggests that, as a result, contemporary marriages are shorter-lived than was the case in the past and that men and women frequently contract multiple, consecutive marriages. It is evident from Aida's words that the 'love' she considers no longer to exist is not simply an emotional phenomenon; it incorporates material elements – the provision of soap, for example – and requires a cooperative unity, mutual trust and dependence (*kukhulupirana, kudalirana*), and a serious commitment to an ongoing relationship, as opposed to simply playing around (*masewero*). Aida was not alone in holding such views, and the instability of marriage in matrilineal areas of Malawi has long been a source of disquiet for officials and ethnographers, no less than for rural Malawians themselves (Kaler 2001; Mitchell 1956; Reniers 2003). The enduring nature of such concerns, however, suggests that a diagnosis of a present shift towards enhanced marital fragility is misplaced. Rather, we might understand the discourse of 'breakdown' in relation to the institution of marriage as a form of ongoing moral commentary on the impermanence of marriage in this setting.

Morality

An excursion into anthropological theory suggests an analytical vocabulary for a discussion of morality with respect to intimate relationships in Africa. While Janice Boddy talks of 'embodied morality' in the context of

---

[18] Having said this, Aida painted a less than rosy picture of her own parents' marriage, which ended after she and her three siblings were born. Aida's words thus provide support for Kaler's (2001) finding that a 'golden era' of marital stability in this region is impossible to locate as generation after generation has found cause to compare their peers unfavourably with their forebears.

debates surrounding female circumcision in South Sudan (2007: 422), Englund evokes 'the materiality of morality' in relation to rural poverty in Malawi (2008). In both cases, the autonomous individual is eschewed as the foundation for moral sensibilities and moral practice, which are understood in the context of the kind of relational personhood discussed in Chapter 3. Crucially, then, material morality is distinct from the ethics of self-formation, which may entail 'a certain aversion to the human condition of dependence' (ibid.: 45).[19] Rather, relationships of mutual dependence are a necessary condition of full moral personhood. Englund finds support for the concept of material morality in the work of mid-twentieth-century anthropologists, particularly that of Max Gluckman, who, as we have seen, approached morality 'less as a set of rules than as being predicated on the materiality of obligations' (ibid.: 43).[20] In Gluckman's work, Englund reminds us, 'moral obligation is inseparable from the material and affective practices that constitute persons' (ibid.: 34).

Pertinent here is the apparent individuation of household production and consumption in Malawi (see, e.g., Davison 1993; 1997: 172–7; Peters 1997a: 204–5; Vaughan 1987: 133–47): the fact that, among matrilineal groups of sisters living in adjacent houses with their respective husbands and children, each woman maintains her own maize store, and each household unit farms its own gardens and cooks its own meals on its own fire. In this way, households are made visible as separate units. Following Vaughan (1983: 277–8), Englund argues that this ought not to be interpreted as evidence of a 'desire for self-sufficiency' (2008: 41; and see Peters 1997a: 205). Rather, individuation enables the expression, or enactment, of the relationships on which social reproduction depends, not least those relationships of matrilineal membership through which access to land and resources is obtained. It is through the separation of households that the existential obligations that run between them are revealed, as labour, agricultural products, and cooked food are given and received in ritualised and mundane exchanges that serve to acknowledge and produce attachments beyond particular households, and to establish those who give as adults 'capable of meeting the obligations that [their] relationships entail' (Englund 2008: 41).[21]

---

[19] See Laidlaw (2002; 2014) for an influential perspective on the value of Foucauldian theories of ethical self-formation for anthropological analysis. See Lambek (2010) for an attempt to temper debates between those who maintain a sharp distinction between 'ethics' and 'morality'. Lambek's preference is for the term 'ethics' over 'morality', partly because of its greater 'prominence in philosophy' (ibid.: 9). My use of the term 'morality' reflects a concern to enter debates in the regional literature.

[20] Further support for the idea that it is necessary to look beyond Foucauldian perspectives on ethics as self-formation is found in Paul Anderson's (2011) work on the Egyptian piety movement.

[21] For an alternative approach to morality, see Zigon (2007).

Just as Gluckman's understanding of moral compulsion did not assume that social relations were harmonious or static, so too in contemporary Malawi 'the scope of relationships and the extent of material contributions they deserve are never so rigidly stipulated as to prevent dispute and conflict' (Englund 2008: 41). This is as relevant in the context of marriage as it is to inter-household exchange, and this view of morality is entirely consistent with a form of love (*chikondi*) that combines the affective and the material (see Chapter 1). Indeed, we might fruitfully extend the concept of material morality to the realm of marital relationships to argue that the divergent, yet complementary, roles that men and women take on as husbands and wives both make visible and enact their existential moral obligations to one another. The differential contributions of husbands and wives establish the household unit at the same time as they constitute themselves, and each other, as adult spouses, mothers and fathers, sons- and daughters-in-law. In this sense, 'complementarity' can be understood as inherent in the material morality of marriage. Perhaps it ought not to come as a surprise, then, that women do not seek justice as 'equality', in the straightforward sense of autonomous sameness, in magistrates' courts or VSUs. Rather, when they bring complaints to these forums they seek the rebalancing of relationships built on the moral obligations of mutual and complementary labour, care, and provision – or, where that is not possible, separation.

Complementarity

'Complementarity' is a word that has appeared in a variety of guises in reference to gender relations in Africa.[22] It is thus worth clarifying my argument in relation to some of these other usages. One important example is the way in which complementarity has been seen to characterise feminism on the African continent. In the words of Obioma Nnaemeka: 'Power-sharing, complementarity, accommodation, compromise, negotiation, and inclusiveness form the foundation of African feminism' (2005 [1998]: 32). She contrasts this to Euro-American feminists' emphasis on confrontation and struggle.[23] However, Nnaemeka highlights the 'danger' of an uncritical overemphasis on gender complementarity that risks masking 'real and insidious gender inequalities and conflicts particularly in racist and imperialist contexts' (ibid.: 37). It is far

[22] Complementarity also has a fraught history within Euro-American feminist politics and scholarship. I hope that readers familiar with these debates will recognise the very different context and intent of my argument.
[23] As is clear from Nnaemeka's writing, however, disagreements among African feminists as to how 'African feminism' ought to be defined and how it might position itself in relation to 'Western feminism' are plentiful.

from my intention to evoke the kind of patriarchal nostalgia for a supposedly 'harmonious, albeit unequal, society of the past' (Mbilinyi 1988:
20), in which women knew their place and male authority was assured,
and which has been variously employed to justify the 'stifling' of women's
dissent in relation to the colonial and postcolonial regulation of marriage
(ibid.: 21–5). On the contrary, complementarity in rural Malawi is both
contemporary and contested.

'Complementarity' has also been deployed to characterise a form of
'African' marriage that is said to be consonant with so-called African
'communalism' – 'a marriage rooted in complementary spheres of action
rather than passion and emotional fulfilment' (Thomas and Cole 2009:
15).[24] However, other observers of African gender relations have
inveighed against a deficit of complementarity, the presence of which is
taken as emblematic of 'Western' marriage. Thus, Ilsa Schuster argued
that, in 1960s Lusaka, the institution of marriage was 'defective': 'instead
of harmonious cooperation, complementary role playing, constructive
sharing and mutual fulfilment, there is deep hostility, antagonism, and
violence' (Schuster 1979: 139, cited in Ferguson 1999: 190; see also
Chanock 1985: 151). Such constructions have long been employed to
establish racial and generational differences both within Africa and
beyond, and it ought to be clear by now that I do not employ the concept
of gender complementarity in opposition to 'love'; nor do I find it useful
to decide in advance what love might (or should) look like in any
particular social setting.[25]

In the West African context, Christine Oppong's influential collection
stresses the intrinsic complementarity, interconnection, and mutual
dependence of men and women: 'in the activities of production and
consumption, in the exercise of power and control, in artistic, ritual
and symbolic expression, in sexual relations and procreation ... Neither
can exist alone' (1983: 72–3). This literature largely depicts complementarity through the separation of parallel institutions of male and
female authority: for instance, the so-called precolonial 'dual-sex'
systems described by Kamene Okonjo (1976) for the Igbo of Nigeria
(see also Nnaemeka 2005 [1998]; Nzegwu 2006). There is also a strong
sense that the 'interlocking complementarity of female and male roles'
(Oppong 1983: 367) has been radically transformed by colonial and
postcolonial political economic forces, which have precipitated a decline
in the 'need of one sex for the other to play conjugal and co-parental roles

---

[24] For example, see Murray (1981) for an insight into how a view of African conjugal roles
as complementary underpinned the economic logic of apartheid policies.
[25] See contributions to Cole and Thomas (2009) for discussions of the patchy success of
women in Africa who have embraced ideals of romantic love as a means of realigning
gender relations (especially Smith 2009; see also Abu-Lughod 1990; cf. Mann 1982).

for the achievement of economic and social status' (ibid.: 373). Oppong is not alone in suggesting that colonial rule precipitated significant shifts in gender relations, eroding the position of women vis-à-vis men in sites across the continent (see, e.g., Goheen 1996; Leacock 1977; Okonjo 1976; Oyěwùmí 1997; Schmidt 1992; Sudarkasa 2005 [1986]; cf. Mutongi 2005 [1999]).[26] As a result, gender complementarity is often viewed with notable nostalgia in African feminist writing.

We might take heed, however, of Oyèrónké Oyěwùmí's (1997) criticism of studies that take 'gender' for granted as a meaningful category in precolonial Nigeria (see also Walker 1991: 26–9 on South Africa). For Oyěwùmí, seniority is a more significant distinction, and the lives of male and female members of Yoruba society are misunderstood if they are viewed simply as husbands and wives, without recognising, for example, their different roles and locations in relation to their marital and natal lineages. She thus argues against 'a simple notion of complementarity between the role of fathers and the role of mothers', positing that a more 'complex notion of complementarity' is necessary. Such a conception would 'transcend the individuality of mothers and fathers'; allow for transformations over time; recognise the significance of multigenerational compounds for the division of labour and childcare responsibilities; and better account for relationships between siblings, with all that they entail, as well as those between parents and their adult children (Oyěwùmí 1997: 74–5).[27] This is of clear relevance to the Malawian case, where marriage is widely understood to concern networks of kin beyond the husband and wife, and the answer to the rhetorical question 'Do two people make a marriage?' (*Nanga banja ndi anthu awiri?*), is a resounding 'no'.

One limitation of several of these approaches to complementarity is the way in which 'gender equality' and 'complementarity' tend to be treated as an indivisible pair, as if the latter term were merely a restatement of the former. However, if gender equality is taken to imply sameness – expressed, for example, through references to an absence of 'ritual and economic differentiation' (Errington 1990: 1) – then equality and complementarity require separate treatment. Complementarity is explicitly *not* sameness. Indeed, it is only possible in the presence of difference and,

---

[26] Missionaries, too, have been charged with promoting forms of marriage that 'undermined women's value within the home' (Cole 2009: 119).

[27] Rather than a complementarity between mother and father in relation to parenthood, for instance, Oyěwùmí argues that 'it was more a division of labour between the idi-aya (maternal kin – the mother's house) and the idi-baba (paternal kin – the father's house). An ana[tomical] female belonging to the paternal kin, for example, would play the role of the father as she enacted the obligations of the father's side' (Oyěwùmí 1997: 74). Much of Oyěwùmí's argument is reminiscent of earlier anthropological work highlighting the cultural construction of gender (see, e.g., MacCormack and Strathern 1980).

I would add, mutual dependence. This is at the core of the disjuncture between *jenda* as taught to Malawian women by NGO facilitators and gender relations as they are lived, critiqued, and aspired to by the rural poor. Interestingly, a tacit recognition of connections between complementarity and a form of inequality appears in studies from elsewhere in the region, including Corinne Kratz's (2010 [1994]) work on Okiek initiation rites in Kenya, where pairings such as 'complementarity and control' (ibid.: 53), 'complementarity and hierarchy' (ibid.: 330), and 'complementarity and interdependence' (ibid.: 317, 334) enter the analysis, without explicit theorisation of complementarity per se.

In relation to contemporary Malawi, Ngeyi Kanyongolo (2007: 222–47) has argued that *jenda* and women's rights constitute one particular discourse, while a nascent alternative employs idioms of what she calls 'substantive complementarity', in which 'women and men play complementary roles which are equally important in not only rhetorical, but substantial terms' (ibid.: 229). While *jenda* refers to the reversal of gender roles and can also be applied to 'people who advocate for increased economic independence for women' (ibid.: 230):

> in the discourse of substantive complementarity, women take pride in their role as care givers in the family and society, in general, but at the same time, demand respect for, and recognition of, their caring roles by having a share of other economic resources. (Kanyongolo 2007: 231)

According to Kanyongolo, the discourse of substantive complementarity is less common than that of *jenda* (ibid.: 237), but she compares it favourably because women's caregiving is neither 'externalised' nor 'casually glossed over' (ibid.: 240). In other words, the validity of women's differential roles in household reproduction is explicitly recognised in a way that it is often not in 'Western' feminist scholarship (Arnfred 2011).

What I posit here is close to Kanyongolo's description of substantive complementarity, except that it is not merely a discourse primarily expressed in urban centres. Nor does it inevitably follow that a complementary division of labour between husbands and wives will necessarily entail predominantly female caregiving (see below). Rather, I propose a conception of complementarity as a function of a form of material morality that requires individuation in order to make visible the existential obligations involved in particular relationships characterised by mutual dependence. While there are differences between the various uses of complementarity discussed above – between those suggesting a form of structural complementarity, the most basic of which is a formal division of labour, and those that entail an affective complementarity of fellow feeling – the form of complementarity that, I argue, people strive for in marital relationships in this context is both structural and affective, relying as it does on mutual acknowledgement or recognition. This is precisely what was denied to the complainant whose husband disposed of the products of their shared labour alone. Such complementarity need not imply specific content, and it is certainly not a harmonious end state: it cannot be taken for granted as the fail-safe outcome of moral rules or social norms. On the contrary, it is a dynamic achievement that can always be contested, and may never be realised, but nonetheless informs women and men in their daily interactions.

Conclusion: from morality to justice

Saba Mahmood has pointed out the ways in which 'liberal presuppositions have become naturalized in the scholarship on gender' (2005: 13): in particular, the 'universality of the desire – central to liberal and progressive thought, and presupposed by the concept of resistance it authorizes – to be free from relations of subordination and, for women, from structures of male domination' (ibid.: 10; see also Walker 1991: 30–1). But while, for Mahmood, such observations prompt a study of the ways in which Egyptian women might exercise agency through inhabiting norms, rather than resisting them, others have been led in different directions by comparable dissatisfactions with the ways in which liberal assumptions have shaped scholars' questions and analyses. Drawing on his examination of the production and reception of a popular radio programme in Malawi (*Nkhani Zam'maboma*, or 'News from the Districts'), Englund (2011) argues that 'equality' is poorly understood if it is pitched in necessary opposition to dependence. Instead, he suggests that equality can inhere in claims to dependence. He thus asks his readers to consider 'how equality as a condition of claim-making differs from equality as a utopian goal pursued under the auspices of human rights activists and democratic politicians' (ibid.: 4). It is a question that is rarely asked among the governing classes, but such an understanding of equality is useful in elucidating the concepts of justice that animate the kinds of disputes we have seen in this chapter and in Chapter 3. The language of 'obligations' favoured by Englund has much in common with that of justice, if both are seen to entail a constitutive complementarity and mutual dependence – particularly if we consider that thinking about obligations provides a window onto the intersections of law and morality.

The two magistrates cited above differed in the extent to which they embraced messages of gender equality or sought to enforce 'customary' norms (however they might be defined), and neither could be said to have engaged exclusively with either one of these approaches. In each case, 'equality' as sameness was distant from view, and their concerns are better understood as relating to the extent to which spouses could be seen to have fulfilled or deviated from gender-specific roles, and the degree to which any such deviance could be considered reasonable (cf. Griffiths 1997: 134–5). Their opposing perspectives are indicative of the wide scope for contestation with respect to contemporary gender relations in Malawi. Contestable yet unifying, the spectre of justice shimmering in their courtrooms was intimately connected to ideas about appropriate behaviour in relationships and thus to gender roles as they are lived, aspired to, and assessed.

Aida made the same connection when she told me that her own marriage had not been 'just' (*silinali banja la chilungamo*). The reasons she gave for this lack of justice related to her late husband's failure to live up to her expectations of material support. He had spent much of his time and money on other women, and, as a consequence, her experience of marriage had been characterised by perseverance (*timangokhala mopilira*). Following her husband's death, she decided that marriage was not for her. With respect to marital relations, then, I suggest that justice is inherent in the complementarity intrinsic to material morality. It is through the complementary roles of husbands and wives that their households are constituted as units of production and consumption, while the spouses themselves achieve recognition through their relationship to one another and in subsequent exchanges beyond the household. When women bring claims to the VSU or magistrates' courts, they do not necessarily challenge the legitimacy, or desirability, of these complementary roles; rather, they point to their spouses' failure to meet their expectations in fulfilling their part.

The ethnography of this region has long characterised marital relationships through a form of gendered division of labour that seems to foreshadow the contemporary concerns of women such as Mercy and Aida. In 1951, Lucy Mair, writing of the Chewa and Ngoni of Dedza District in central Malawi, described the obligations of marriage as discerned from claims brought before the native courts:

The husband must provide his wife with sleeping-mats and clothes, must clear a field for her to plant, and keep her house and grainstore in repair; if he is at work, sending money is regarded as the equivalent of these duties ... A wife must fetch firewood and water, keep the fire going, cook for her husband and care for him if he is ill.[28] (Mair 1951: 113–14; see also Richards 1940: 85–7)

To this day, there remain tasks that are closely associated with men and women respectively in their roles as husbands and wives. But these are

[28] In matrilineal areas of the country, wives are expected to take care of their husbands when they are unwell, but when illnesses are severe, and death a clear possibility, men are usually taken 'home' (*kwawo*) to be cared for by female members of their own matrilineage.

not immutable, and they tend to be less clear-cut in practice than they are in the imagination. As we saw above in the magistrates' judgments and Mercy's musings, women's engagements with the market economy as traders, as well as the joint commercial endeavours of married couples, are common features of twenty-first-century life. We have also seen how positively villagers value girls' education and their optimism for young women's future lives and relationships (see Chapter 1). On the other hand, men regularly struggle to access the cash economy, and many are absent for long periods of time through labour migration. As fathers, brothers, and maternal uncles, they may also be more involved in the welfare and care of children than gender stereotypes allow. It is also clear that matrilineal norms of female land ownership and matrilocal residence patterns play a significant part in shaping gender roles and aspirations as well as configuring networks of relationships within and between households. The forms that complementarity might take, and the context in which it is sought, are infused with matrilineal norms and practices that guide (without fixing) the conditions of possibility.

Moreover, it is important to remember that temporal shifts in the size and shape of households, even over relatively short periods of time, can have a profound impact on the negotiation of gender relations and the gendered division of labour. As Henrietta Moore and Megan Vaughan have written in reference to matrilineal Bemba in Zambia:

The cooperation implied in conjugality and evidenced in the sexual division of labour is something to which individuals aspire, but it is often a feature of a particular stage in an individual's life and in the developmental cycle of the household rather than a fact of life or of social organisation. (Moore and Vaughan 1994: 225)

Gender roles are fluid, varied, and subject to ongoing negotiation. While particular content is not essential to achieving the moral and material ideal of complementarity, individuation and mutual recognition are.

Crucial in this regard is the statement of the female magistrate: 'The two have worked together in the fields and the complainant also worked hard to sell their produce but disappointingly the defendant used the same sources to keep the other woman's life going.' As I mentioned above, in describing the evident breakdown of complementarity, the magistrate employed the morally freighted language of disappointment. In so doing, she signalled the ideal of mutual dependence and suggested a moral failing on the part of the defendant. 'Gender justice' in this context, then, does not necessarily entail formal equality as envisaged by NGO facilitators in their *jenda* training sessions. Rather, justice might be achieved through the recognition of mutual dependence and complementarity. Such complementarity has to be achieved continually and is always open to contestation. While the idea of a 'just marriage' (*banja la chilungamo*) has the potential to unite people across difference, its content in relation to particular relationships, and competing interpretations of 'custom' in a given social setting, cannot be known in advance and can be defined and contested only through practice. Indeed, it is in their success and failure in achieving complementarity that women and men in rural Malawi come to know justice.

5   Handling violence

How does the ideal of moral-material reciprocity, or complementarity, in marital relationships influence understandings of gender violence (*nkhanza*)? Although the spectre of violence played a part in several of the cases discussed, so far we have considered marital disputes without directly addressing questions of gender-based violence, despite the fact that the victim support unit (VSU) in particular was specifically designed to deal with domestic abuse. Against the expectations of many, however, violence tends not to be the central concern of men and women seeking resolution to their disputes. This chapter asks what, if not violence, is foregrounded by disputants and those working to assist them, and how incidents of violence are incorporated into the wide-ranging narratives told in these settings. Posing questions of this kind reveals a great deal about expectations of gender relations and aspirations for just marriages in this matrilineal context, while simultaneously drawing our attention to certain strategies employed by disputants to demonstrate moral person-hood. Moreover, it enables an examination of the broader meaning of *nkhanza*, the Chichewa term routinely used to translate gender-based violence, which is more accurately rendered in English as 'cruelty'. *Nkhanza* includes, but is not limited to, physical abuse. As we shall see, accusations of *nkhanza* invite assessments of behaviour within marriage in relation to the ideal of moral-material reciprocity; indeed, they often signal the breakdown of complementarity.

Assuming violence

It is commonly assumed that Africa is rife with violence. War, famine, and rape dominate media representations of the continent and occupy a considerable number of academics. It is similarly well known that women and children bear the brunt of African violence. The African woman-as-victim needs no introduction (Hodgson 2017; Kratz 2010 [1994]: 341–7; Scully 2011); she is a familiar sight and merely a particular rendering of the well-worn master trope of the 'Third World' woman-as-victim (Spivak 1993 [1988]). From the earliest accounts of travellers, missionaries, and colonial administrators, the need for sustained interventions to 'civilise' far-flung corners of the earth was established with the aid of images of women as 'oppressed beasts of burden, subject to drudgery and degrading marriage practices' (Cornwall 2005: 2). Western feminist writers also offered representations of African women in this vein (e.g. Cutrufelli 1983), partly as a foil to their own relative 'liberation' (Mohanty 1988). Unsurprisingly, African women writers have often found such depictions to be of little relevance to their lives (Nnaemeka 2005 [1998]; Oyĕwùmí 1997; 2002; Tamale 2005; and see Arnfred 2011).

Women's agency has come and gone as a central concern of main-stream anthropological debates, transforming understandings of gender relations in Africa in the process (see, e.g., Hodgson and McCurdy 2001). Nevertheless, beyond the academy, the image of the African woman-as-victim – or, in today's parlance, 'vulnerable' women – main-tains its power to generate and justify interventions, raise funds, and influence public opinion. Such representations not only fill the news-reels and copy of the international press; the Malawian media, too, shares an interest in women's suffering, as is attested by countless stories and features in the national newspapers (e.g. Masina 2010; Mzungu 2009; Sekeleza 2009; Tayanjah-Phiri 2009). Intense media interest does not come from nowhere; it is born out of a broader discourse, incorpor-ating voices from national and international NGOs, parliaments, devel-opment agencies, policy think tanks, and so on.[1] That women's rights and gender violence have gained prominence as issues of concern in the multiparty era is evident in the designation of the Ministry of Gender, Children, and Community Development, the passing of the much-heralded (yet little used) Prevention of Domestic Violence Act in 2006, and the strong governmental and civil society support for the police VSU programme.[2]

In accordance with this emphasis, a key element of civic education since 1994 has been 'gender sensitisation', which is aimed at educating the Malawian populace about gender equality and gender violence. Radio programmes, news items, training sessions (such as those described in Chapter 4), NGO activities, and political rallies have all been deployed to this end, and their reach has been extensive. Chiradzulu District is not untypical in playing host to branch offices of a number of national NGOs, large-scale projects funded by international

[1] For examples from media sources, advocacy and donor representations, and NGO literature, see, for example, Care Malawi (2010), Human Rights Watch (2003), Nyondo (2012), Scottish Government (2012), and UNICEF (n.d.a; n.d.b).
[2] The ministry has since been renamed the Ministry of Gender, Children, Disability, and Social Welfare.

organisations (including ActionAid, Oxfam, and World Vision), and visits by incumbent and aspiring politicians. Nor is it unique in terms of the popularity of radio broadcasts (television ownership, on the other hand, is negligible), many of which explicitly serve the purposes of civic education (Englund 2011: 40–4). Print media reaches a more restricted audience, newspapers being both costly and unintelligible to the vast majority of rural Malawians, who are not well versed in English. But journalists occasionally accompanied NGOs or the odd visiting politician, and stories reporting the successes of NGO or development activities in Chiradzulu, or the need for intensified efforts to combat gender violence, were not uncommon in the major national newspapers (Chimpweya 2010; Ngwira 2009).

The following news story, which appeared in *The Nation* in January 2010, draws on a tried and tested formula (Chavula 2010). An individual victim is identified and her story is narrated in order to provide an opportunity for gender 'experts' to expound upon the 'gloomy picture'. In this case, the woman featured was a resident of the rural compound in which I lived. When Anagama told me that she had been photographed for a news feature about gender violence (*nkhanza*), I was surprised. I was aware that her second marriage had not been a happy one, I had heard her former husband described variously as lazy and tight-fisted, and I knew that she was an active member of the Women's Forum committee, but I had never thought of Anagama as a victim. Feisty and independent, an industrious farmer, mother of seven, and carer for her own disabled mother, she was a regular stand-in for the group village head (her brother) and a prominent and popular villager – all of which was obscured, together with her very real struggles against poverty, when her life story was aligned with the meta-narrative of the African woman-as-victim.

In the story, Anagama is described as a 'survivor of gender-based violence', a 'defenceless' 'mother of five' who lives in a 'mud hut'. It is explained that her 'walk out of misery' began when she joined the Women's Forum group, which is 'determined to bring change through peer sensitisation and income-generating activities'. The description of Anagama as both victim and survivor follows a brief reminder of the extremes to which gender-based violence can extend, accomplished through reference to the widely publicised case of Marietta Samuel, who, in 2004, had her hands chopped off by her husband in an act of unspeakable brutality that captured the national imagination. Marietta had become the quintessential poster girl for gender violence, her image adorning countless news stories like this one, whether or not the specifics of her case were under discussion. The author of this particular story was quick to map Anagama's experience on to a generic matrix, paying little attention to particularities. Juxtaposing her misery with that of Marietta served both to introduce the presumed likelihood of physical abuse, and to reinforce the image of women's universal victimhood.

Rights (*maufulu*), gender (*jenda*), and gender-based violence (*nkhanza*) tend to be treated as kindred concepts in Malawi, all of which arrived with the onset of multiparty democracy. In the training session discussed at the beginning of Chapter 4, a female police officer from the VSU led a session on *nkhanza* to teach the assembled villagers about the many forms that violence can take: physical, emotional, economic, sexual, 'traditional', and against children.[3] By the time of my fieldwork, these were more or less familiar teachings and it was not uncommon for divorcees or widows, such as Anachisale (see Introduction), to explain to me that their marriages had been characterised by *nkhanza* in ways that they would not tolerate nowadays. Nor did they think that they would have to, given the widening of options for redress in the form of VSUs, NGOs, and so on, and the more diffuse understanding among their fellow villagers that *nkhanza* had no place in contemporary Malawi.

However, despite the strong focus on gender-based violence and the broad sensitisation campaigns that have left few persons and places in Malawi untouched, violence played a minimal role in the narratives produced in the course of marital disputes heard at the *bwalo*, the VSU, and the magistrates' courts. Regardless of whether they were reported in a setting whose *raison d'être* was to address domestic violence, the kinds of stories that women told were framed around accounts of the quotidian fabric of marital life, in which episodes of cruelty or violence jostled for space alongside such mundane activities as the picking of pumpkins. In this chapter, I explore the ways in which cases progressed in these venues, asking what, if not violence, *was* prioritised by narrators and those charged with resolving disputes, and how outcomes were shaped. My principal focus is on cases heard in the magistrates' courts, but I introduce examples from the VSU for comparative purposes. In certain respects, these forums were very different: procedures were less formalised in the VSU; police officers did not pronounce judgement, nor award compensation; cases were conducted in relative privacy and entirely in the vernacular. As we shall see, however, there were important similarities, not least with respect to how violence was approached when it was a feature of the disputes under discussion. Police officers and magistrates shared disputants' reluctance to consider violent incidents outside of the relational context in which they occurred, assessing them in the light of ideals of complementary give and take in marriage.

---

[3] *Nkhanza zokhudza: thupi, m'malingaliro, chuma, kugonana, miyambo, ndi ana.*

Gender violence in the magistrates' courts

During 2009–10, I attended all or part of 93 civil cases heard by four magistrates. At Chiradzulu Court, I observed 23 cases handled by the older male first-grade magistrate (FGM) we encountered in Chapter 4; 12 handled by his younger male colleague, a second-grade magistrate (SGM); and 48 by the latter's subsequent replacement, a young male third-grade magistrate (TGM) whose judgment in a criminal case will be discussed in Chapter 6.[4] At Mbulumbuzi, I witnessed nine cases heard by the female SGM whom we met in Chapter 4. Following her untimely death, some of these cases were concluded by her eventual successor, a male TGM.[5] I obtained copies of these judgments but I did not attend live sessions in his court.

As we saw in Chapter 4, there was significant variation in the ways in which different magistrates approached the cases that came before them. However, certain aspects of the cases were extremely consistent. The claim 'divorced without valid reasons' was common in all of the courts, accounting for almost 40 per cent of the cases I witnessed (36 out of 93); by comparison, three claims were lodged for 'divorce because of cruelty [nkhanza]'. Altogether, 61 per cent of the civil cases I attended concerned marital breakdown, with another 4 per cent dealing with marriage (not breakdown), and 12 per cent pregnancy and child maintenance; 67 of the complainants were women (72 per cent) and 21 men (23 per cent).[6]

The 2006 Prevention of Domestic Violence Act provides for three different orders: protection, occupation, and tenancy. These are civil remedies that can be issued to prevent the respondent from making contact, or sharing a home, with the applicant for a specified period.[7] Although magistrates were aware of the Act and had received training on it, I saw it employed only once, by the TGM at Chiradzulu in a situation in which a woman had been assaulted by her husband while they awaited judgment on their marital dispute. This was the most extreme case of gender violence I encountered at any point during fieldwork and it was recognised as severe by all involved. The husband was eventually found liable for the breakdown of their marriage on

---

[4] Also included in the 93 cases is a single case heard by the elder male replacement for the sick FGM, another FGM whose court I had scant opportunity to observe.

[5] As mentioned in Chapter 2, the differences in magistrates' grades are ambiguous and of little practical relevance, particularly in civil cases.

[6] These final figures relate to 95 per cent of the cases: in deceased estate cases, the complainant is recorded as the District Commissioner, and I did not record the gender of the complainants in one debt case and one case of damage to crops.

[7] The emphasis of the Act is on protection, rather than punishment.

the grounds of adultery and violence and ordered to pay K30,000 compensation and to build his wife a house. Criminal proceedings for assault culminated in a six-month jail sentence, suspended for 12 months.[8] This was one of only two instances in which the TGM had utilised the Prevention of Domestic Violence Act in his career. On another occasion, he told me, he had issued a protection order to a pregnant woman who had been referred to him from the VSU. His predecessor, the SGM, had never formally employed the Act, although he recalled a case in which he had told a man not to go to his wife's home until after the conclusion of their case and advised the wife to contact the police if her husband caused any further disturbance, recognising this as structurally equivalent to issuing a protection order. Separately, both the SGM and TGM suggested that the main factor affecting their limited use of the Act was the dearth of people coming forward to apply for orders, which they considered to be a result of limited awareness of the Act among Malawian citizens. Be that as it may, they acknowledged that they were not bound to await an application for an order: where they recognised the need for intervention during the course of a dispute hearing, they were at liberty to act.

Across all of the cases I observed, it was extremely uncommon to hear disputants employ human rights and anti-domestic violence rhetoric to frame the issues at stake. For the most part, instances of violence were described in a matter-of-fact style, as single episodes in long narrative accounts of relationships. Statements such as 'he hit me' (*anandimenya*) were given no more stress than accounts of a husband's nocturnal absence (*sanagone ku nyumba*), or his failure to attend discussions with *ankhoswe* (*sanabwere*). Nor did accounts of such violence mentioned in passing become a focus for subsequent cross-examination, or attract particular attention in magistrates' judgments.

A rare exception occurred in the TGM's court at Chiradzulu, in a case brought by a male complainant against his wife for deserting him and the matrimonial home. In the course of her evidence, the female defendant described her husband's violent conduct, including vicious threats and insults, beatings, destruction of property, and denial of access to the home so that she had to sleep in the kitchen outhouse.

---

[8] The exceptionality of this case is further underlined by the fact that it was the only instance I was aware of during my fieldwork in which criminal charges accompanied a civil hearing. See Thornberry (2010) on the bifurcation of criminal and civil law in South Africa's Eastern Cape during the colonial period and the subsequent classification of all customary law as civil law.

The magistrate noted that her evidence was corroborated by that of her *nkhoswe* and ruled that:

According to the evidence produced by defence, a counter-accusation has been made to justify why she deserted and the defendant has testified that the [complainant]⁹ is a violent man and that he has been assaulting her severely whenever a quarrel ensued between them ... I make a finding that the [complainant] was indeed perpetuating violence against the defendant in the form of beatings, threats and alleging baseless accusations against her that she is a prostitute and loves money ... *The time has come for men to realise that wife battering is no longer part of the democratic era, whereby human rights issues, especially women's rights, are included in the laws of this country* ... The [complainant] was not successful with the claim he brought before the court. That is to say he is the one that was at fault for the marriage to end. I make an order that he should pay K30,000 compensation to the defendant and build her a house.¹⁰

This was the most direct reference to human or women's rights that I encountered in the courts. The case was also notable for the procedural flexibility displayed by the magistrate in identifying a 'counter-accus-ation' in the defendant's narrative testimony, and allowing that to over-ride the original claim.

Human rights and violence against women were not the only terms in which violence could be addressed, however. In another case, where the claim was for divorce on the grounds of cruelty, the same magistrate based a finding of cruelty/violence (*nkhanza*) on 'custom', making no reference to 'rights':

According to customary law, marriage can come to an end where a spouse has been mistreating another. Going by the evidence adduced by the [complainant], the defendant had a habit of beating her up and could lock her outside the matrimonial home. The [complainant] became afraid to the extent that she would not even ask why he was coming [home] late. Whenever the [complainant] reported to advocates [*ankhoswe*], the [defendant] could promise to change but in no time, he could start assaulting her again. At one time she complained at the VSU that the defendant had beaten her up; the defendant refused to attend when summoned ... On cross-examination, the defendant did not challenge on [the] issue of beatings and did not dispute that he has married another woman. The [complainant's advocate's] testimony did corroborate that the defendant was fond of assaulting the [complainant] ... The defendant is liable on [the] ground of cruelty towards the [complainant] and the marriage between the two has irretrievably broken down ... The defendant should compensate the [complainant] with the sum of K80,000 and construct a house.¹¹

---

⁹ Magistrates differed in their choice of terms. While some talked of 'complainants', others referred to 'plaintiffs'. For the sake of consistency, I employ the term 'complainant' throughout.

¹⁰ Emphasis added.

¹¹ Emphasis added. The higher level of compensation awarded in this case was related to the declared earnings of the defendant, which, at K8,000 per month, were above average for rural workers.

Such cases were unusual, however. More typical, even where violence was mentioned in testimony, was a response that maintained a view of violence as one aspect of a complex dispute, which did not demand separate treatment and which had to be understood in the context of the relationship as a whole. In this, magistrates shared a great deal with police officers in the VSU and traditional authorities at the *bwalo*. To an extent, this reflects a reality of more limited domestic violence than media reports and awareness-raising campaigns imply. It also evidences a degree of tolerance towards violence within marriage that many find unacceptable. Beyond this, however, it suggests that the priorities of those bringing cases, and those hearing them, are not entirely aligned with those of gender and women's rights activists who have placed combating gender violence at the centre of their agenda.[12]

'But how are things in general?'

At the VSU, too, violence tended to be approached as something that had to be contextualised and understood in relation to particular relationships and the history of a dispute. In one case, a husband brought a complaint against his wife, making a direct appeal to the police to arrest her for wounding him (*kukhapa*).[13] The husband produced a medical report from the hospital, confirming that he had a scalp injury and a human bite wound on his finger. On the reverse of the report was the original referral letter from the VSU, which explained that he had reported an assault by his wife. When I first saw the husband in the police station, he had a plaster on his head and was wearing a blood-splattered T-shirt. That day, the case was quickly adjourned because police officers did not want to proceed in the absence of the couple's *ankhoswe*. Two days later, the parties reconvened in front of a sub-inspector, a sergeant, and the sheikh, and the husband explained that his wife had injured him because he had taken a chicken from their yard and sold it. His wife insisted that their dispute (*nkhani*) predated the incident with the chicken, and related an earlier episode involving a damaged hoe, which she had promised to replace by selling maize worth

---

[12] It is worth remembering that this is a context marked by widespread social acceptance of divorce and female-headed households, uxorilocal residence, female inheritance of land, and the absence of bridewealth. The experiences of women abused by their partners is clearly qualitatively distinct from those of women elsewhere, such as those Merry describes in India, who 'needed to stay with their husbands in order to have a respectable place to live' (2006b: 142). One effect of the universalising discourse of violence against women is the obfuscation of social and cultural particularities with their attendant implications for understandings and experiences of gender violence.

[13] It was not unheard of for men to complain that their wives had behaved violently towards them, and in many cases it was impossible to say categorically that one party was the aggressor and the other the victim.

K700. The hoe had belonged to her husband and had been broken when her brother borrowed it to prepare soil for making bricks. She then recounted how a chicken had coughed during the night and the next morning her husband had chased it, caught it, and tied it up, ignoring her attempts to ascertain what he was up to. Concerned, she had followed him to the district headquarters (*boma*), where she saw him sell the chicken to her *mlamu* (brother- or sister-in-law) for K400. She had protested that it was not his chicken to sell, and, eventually, the money and the chicken had been restored to their original owners.

When she had finished telling her side of the story, the sub-inspector summed up and asked an initial question: 'So, there's the story of the hoe, and the story of the chicken, but how are things in general?' She replied that they often disagreed (*timakhala motsutsana*). The sergeant asked the husband's *nkhoswe* what he had to say about the matter and he responded that, as *nkhoswe*, he had dealt with similar disputes between the pair five times. The sub-inspector then turned to the husband and asked if there were no peaceful means of dealing with such issues. In reply, the husband explained that, as newlyweds, they had lived among his kin and they used to fight a lot, often ending up with cases at the *bwalo*. Later, after they had borne two children, they had moved to live alongside his wife's relatives and he had told her: 'Starting from today, I won't hit you.' He did not elaborate upon this point, but his words appeared to reflect a sense that his actions would be under greater scrutiny once they were living with his wife's matrilineal kin. As he continued, it became clear that he felt more vulnerable in their new surroundings. His wife 'gets angry', he said, and beats him. He stressed that he did not return her blows but simply apologised. By contrast, he asserted that there had never been a single occasion on which his wife had apologised to him, and she had stopped warming bathing water for him, so that he had to wash in the river.

His wife assured the officers that she did not want to end the marriage (*kuthetsa banja*): 'He is my husband,' she said, 'and we have three children together.' At this point, the sheikh returned the discussion to the issue of the hoe, asking for the husband's take on the matter. The husband insisted that he was not satisfied with the solution of selling maize to pay for the replacement because the maize was his, he had cultivated it: 'So she'd sell *my* maize to return *my* hoe?'[14] He explained that it had been a special hoe that had cost him K750 and he had not wanted it to be lent out. The sheikh then moved on to the issue of the chicken, asking if the husband had sat down with his wife to discuss the

---

[14] This maize was likely grown on his wife's land and she would have a greater stake in its distribution. Her husband's claim to rights in its disposal reflects his contribution in terms of labour.

idea of selling the chicken to raise money for the hoe. However, the husband was quick to dismiss this possibility. Making reference to her violent temper, he explained that between himself and his wife, it was as if she were the husband in their relationship. Undeterred, the sheikh responded by asking him whether their dispute would have reached the VSU if he had told his wife he wanted to sell the chicken to buy a new hoe. 'Yes,' he replied. 'I know my wife; you can't sit down and talk about issues with her, you'd have *phokoso* [discord, conflict] until the next morning.' The sheikh posited that the situation need not have reached this stage: 'Is there really an issue here? You said your wife could take back the chicken and you returned the money. What was the problem?'

When the officers enquired about whether he had been drinking, the husband admitted that he had, but countered that he had shared just one Coca-Cola bottle of *kachasu* (locally distilled spirit) between three people, so he was not drunk. His wife interjected that that was a lie. Continuing, her husband accused her of hitting him while she was trying to retrieve the chicken. He said he had told her he was taking the chicken home, but she interrupted again to say that he was lying. The sub-inspector's frustration was audible as he intervened: 'You both wanted the chicken. The chicken was now being taken home. What was the problem?' Answering his own question, he hypothesised that the entire affair was a consequence of the husband's drinking, which the husband promptly denied, suggesting instead that it was the work of the devil (*Satana*) and a result of their failure to count on each other or to discuss things together (*kusawerengerana kapena kusakambirana*). His wife spoke again, saying that things were better when her husband was not drunk, but that when he drank they had problems all week long. She explained that, because her husband was drunk, she had been concerned that he would sell the chicken again, rather than taking it home, and she insisted that he had been the one who started the fight.

Summarising the case so far, the sub-inspector explained: 'He came here yesterday [sic] and said that his wife had wounded him and asked us to arrest her, but we want to know why this happened.' The sheikh joined in, saying that the problems were marital issues (*za banja*) and required discussion. Eventually, the husband relented, conceding that he had erred (*ndinalakwitsa*). Asked who had been the source of the problems, he said 'the one who took the chicken' and assured everyone that he would not really have allowed the police to arrest his wife. Turning to the wife, the sheikh asked how *she* had erred. She responded that her mistake had been to hit her husband with an unburnt brick (*chidina*). Her male *nkhoswe* interrupted to add that she had made her husband bleed. Echoing this reproach, the sub-inspector also reminded her of her failure to warm bathing water for her husband, thus relating the apparent breakdown in the routine division of household labour to the more spectacular incidents under discussion. At this point the wife apologised, asking for forgiveness and promising that she would not repeat her mistakes. 'How will you avoid this in the future?' the sub-inspector enquired. By 'avoiding each other' (*kupewana*), she replied. With some prompting, she added that they would 'listen to one another' (*kumvetsetsana*) and 'discuss things together' (*kukambirana*).

Not untypically, this case hearing was marked by an immediate concern to understand the wife's violent behaviour in the context of their relationship and the dispute as it had unfolded ('How are things in general?', 'We want to know why this happened'). There was a strong focus on the propriety of each spouse's behaviour, but not in the abstract. Drinking, failing to communicate, and the non-fulfilment of gender roles were all relevant factors as the discussion circled around the ebb and flow of mundane reciprocities. The effort to comprehend the wife's violence in relation to her husband's conduct led to a more rounded understanding of the texture of their relationship and raised the possibility that the case would not have escalated to such an extent had the husband communicated openly (and soberly) about his intention to sell the chicken. The officers were explicit that they did not want to address violence in isolation, despite the husband's original request for his wife to be arrested and the medical evidence of the harm she had inflicted upon his body. Recognising this violence as an element of a marital dispute (*za banja*), they asserted the need for broad discussion rather than direct intervention. This attitude was consistent with an understanding of gender violence as both a reaction to circumstances and as changeable, an aspect of behaviour that could be repudiated following advice and open dialogue.

The view of those working in the VSU seemed to be that gender violence could be left behind in more ways than one. Not only could perpetrators – male or female – alter their behaviour, but there was also a sense of the historical transformation of social mores. As one female officer put it during another case hearing, 'hitting women is a thing of the past' (*zomenya akazi zinatha*), out of sync with the times, both politically, in the democratic era, and religiously, given that, as far as the police were concerned, 'there is no church that says to hit your wife – they all advocate love [*chikondi*]'. Their faith in counselling as an effective remedy for marital discord relied on an understanding of violent or disruptive behaviour as malleable and amenable to reason.

Shifting attitudes to violence within intimate relationships were also suggested by the contrast between the older FGM and his younger colleagues. Of all the magistrates I observed, the FGM evinced the least sympathy for female complainants, and he was the only one not to award any compensation in the cases I observed. Not only was he the eldest of the magistrates discussed here, but he was also the only one whose home village was in a patrilineal area of the country. His approach no doubt bore the imprint of his geographic and generational provenance.

Establishing moral personhood: procedure, strategy, and claim-making

While violence was generally not drawn out of narrative accounts of marital breakdown or given prominence in the process of dispute resolution, we have seen that moral credentials were. In seeking to demonstrate morality, disputants emphasised their efforts to live up to complementary ideals and highlighted the other party's failure to fulfil moral-material obligations. They achieved this in three key ways: by stressing adherence to procedure; by strategising, linguistically and extra-linguistically, in the course of the dispute; and through the framing of claims.

Procedure

A great deal of emphasis was placed on procedure, with magistrates and police officers seeking to establish whether disputants had followed the appropriate course of action in dealing with their difficulties before reaching them. For example, the FGM would castigate parties for taking their dispute to the wrong forum:

The complainant made a mistake by taking the issue of pregnancy to church before it was discussed with the defendant's relatives. The issue of pregnancy first involves customs because after one has admitted [paternity], whether they get married or not, a child will be born and that child will be a relative of both parties.

He drew similarly negative conclusions when he considered a party to have avoided attempts to deal with a dispute through their *ankhoswe*:

It is true that ... the complainant and her mother ... were not happy with this marriage. This is why instead of bringing the complainant's advocate [*nkhoswe*], uncle, and other relatives to discuss their disputes, they just [took] her and [her] goods away. Denying discussions is a strong sign of lack of interest in the marriage.

In order to establish credibility and elicit adjudicators' sympathies, it was important that parties show they had adhered to the correct procedures throughout. In the first instance, this meant involving matrilineal kin; the right people needed to have been informed at the right times and through the proper channels. Who knew what, when, and how were vital pieces of evidence, attesting to the parties' positions in webs of relationships that served to bear witness to their efforts to live well and to resolve their disputes as they arose (cf. Comaroff and Roberts 1981: 113).

One interpretation of this emphasis on proper procedure would be that those handling cases were upholding 'custom' by encouraging people to value traditional institutions, such as *unkhoswe* and chieftaincy (*ufumu*), as in the following judgment by the FGM:

There is enough evidence that the defendant chose to desert the complainant because he did not want to formalise his marriage [i.e. conduct *chinkhoswe*] with the complainant. Court finds the defendant to be a crook and a bad person as he wants to end our customs of following proper ways of marriage formalities.

As we saw in Chapter 3, however, 'customary law' in contemporary Malawi has to be understood beyond models of a fossilised product of male collusion (cf. Chanock 1985; Hay and Wright 1982a). Indeed, magistrates themselves recognised the extent to which they were tasked with administering a flexible instrument. In the words of the SGM, 'It boils down to one thing: the magistrate has discretion.' When I asked him about the potential for customary law to shift over time, he replied:

As of now I could say it is changing. Because I don't think things are as they used to be five years ago ... things they always get changing every now and then, so don't expect that they will be the same all the time.

To be sure, one catalyst for such change, as the SGM identified, has been the introduction of ideas about human and women's rights following the democratic transition: 'Because as of now, we hear about "gender" and all that, people have to move away from this customary law to adapt to the new way of thinking,' he continued. The magistrate did not mean to suggest that there was cause to abandon customary law; he was confident that customary law was responsive enough to accommodate incremental shifts in attitude and the new language of rights.

An emphasis on following procedure, then, did not simply reflect a concern with the enforcement of 'custom', or a conservative faith in static 'tradition'. Rather, it related to the need to evince moral personhood. Demonstrating adherence to customary means of resolving disputes and customary rites for formalising relationships was often key to establishing personal credibility. At times, in addition to administering customary law, and with no sense of contradiction, magistrates seemingly embraced the role of 'educator', alluding to the discourse of rights, perhaps, to set examples of acceptable behaviour in the contemporary era (see Chapters 3 and 6). Such attitudes tended to be revealed towards the climax of their judgments, in phrases such as 'My advice to women in Chiradzulu: it is high time they started following proper procedures when they want to get married' (TGM), or 'I hope this will act as a wake-up call to men and boys who take pride in impregnating girls' (TGM). In this way, magistrates broke down the distinctions between custom, law, and morality much like the Lozi judges observed by Gluckman in the mid-twentieth century. Drawing on the instruments available to them – including rights discourse, knowledge of custom, the flexibility of customary law, and conceptions of moral norms – they sought simultaneously to 'satisfy the demands of morality and justice' (Gluckman 1973 [1955]: 190).

Strategy

As the legal anthropological literature suggests, an emphasis on procedure provided leeway for a certain amount of discursive strategising as parties attempted to position themselves in such a way that they would be looked upon favourably (Comaroff and Roberts 1981; Conley and O'Barr 1990; Hirsch 1998). This was particularly striking when it came to answering the question of whether or not they wanted a divorce. The majority of men and women who were asked this question in court answered, at least in the first instance, that they wanted to remain married. As we saw in Chapter 4, there was a widely held assumption that a case would not end well for a person, especially a woman, who stated directly that she or he wanted a divorce. Indeed, in the FGM's court, there was some truth to this, as shown in the following example from a case brought by a female complainant who claimed to have been divorced without valid reasons:

MAGISTRATE [to defendant]:	Do you have two wives?
DEFENDANT:	I do.
MAGISTRATE [to complainant]:	Do you want divorce or reconciliation?
COMPLAINANT:	The marriage shouldn't end.
MAGISTRATE:	You'll have a polygamist?
COMPLAINANT:	No.
MAGISTRATE:	He has another wife. It means it is you who wants a divorce because you do not want polygamy. So it means you want a divorce. I have written that you want a divorce because you do not want polygamy.

In his final judgment, the magistrate concluded: 'Divorce is granted without compensation to complainant as she is the one who chose divorce.' On another occasion, the same magistrate made his views explicit concerning the impossibility of awarding compensation to a woman who had declared a desire for divorce by asking the male defendant the rhetorical question: 'Is it correct to compensate someone who does not want to be married?' Other magistrates did not feel so constrained by a woman's desire for divorce, however, paying attention instead to whether that inclination was justified by the evidence adduced. The SGM was clear when he explained to me that:

One of the problems is that these guys are afraid in most cases, especially the women. They would think that if they come to court to seek divorce then they are not going to get compensation. I keep on telling them you can come to court to seek divorce and get compensation as long as you have good grounds for your case.

Disputants' reluctance to voice a preference for divorce related to their desire to avoid appearing to take marital breakdown too lightly. A serious commitment to marriage was thought to reflect well on their character. In some instances, parties to disputes were frank with me about their strategies in this regard. One male defendant, for example, accused of divorcing his wife without valid reasons, insisted in court that he wanted his marriage to continue to such an extent that the male SGM adjourned the case for a month so that they might perform a formal *chinkhoswe* ceremony. After the hearing, the defendant told me in no uncertain terms that he had lied in court because he thought that if he said he did not want his wife, the magistrate would rule against him. Instead, his bluff was called. Indeed, magistrates were alert to strategic attempts to mislead them and were not shy about voicing their suspicions, as in the following statement from a judgment delivered by the TGM:

I find that the defendant's submission that he did not want to divorce the [complainant] because their children need them to stay together as a family is baseless and his conduct in this courtroom, everything that he was saying claiming that he had not left the [complainant], he was just saying this in bad faith.

Assessments of the strategic nature of certain claims made in the course of disputes thus fed into magistrates' perceptions of the disputants' integrity and, consequently, of the value of their testimony.

Claim-making

A further discursive factor, which cannot be reduced simply to the strategising efforts of the parties concerned, was the framing of claims. As has already been stated, the most common claim was 'divorce without valid reasons'. This claim frustrated several of the magistrates, who found it to be, in the words of the TGM, 'defective or perhaps incomplete' (*imakhala kuti defective kapena ili incomplete*).

The phrasing of claims was important because it was in relation to particular claims that magistrates were required to weigh the evidence and witnesses were invited to testify (see, e.g., Moore 1986: 303). Claims set the limits of what would be considered relevant evidence in a particular case. The potential consequences of an ill-conceived claim were well illustrated by a case that came to court as a claim for child maintenance. The couple had been married and the wife, who was the complainant, had recently left the marital home at her husband's workplace. The TGM began by explaining to the complainant that she must give evidence in relation to the specific claim:

You have come to this court for child affiliation . . . we want you to tell us why you are suing the defendant for this claim. Is he the putative father of this child? We want to hear that, we don't want to hear anything concerning marriage because the claim is about child affiliation.

He soon interrupted her evidence when it became clear that she was covering wider issues, reminding her: 'This is not an issue to do with [a] marriage claim, it is about child maintenance. You started well, but it appears you're now going somewhere [else].' Throughout the hearing, the magistrate urged witnesses for both parties to remember that: 'We are not discussing [an] issue concerning marriage here but child maintenance.' The complainant's *nkhoswe* voiced his concern that 'she didn't complain well' (*sanadandaule bwino*), because she should really have complained about the fact that her husband had divorced her (*kuwasiyira banja*). The magistrate did not appreciate this intervention, however, and admonished the witness: 'It is not your case; you are not required to amend the claim.' As the defendant began giving evidence, the magistrate interjected again:

Before you proceed, it would appear from the way you are testifying, it is like the [complainant] sued you on [a] claim concerning marriage. But the claim before me is . . . a simple matter concerning child maintenance. I do not know what was the problem at the registry . . . OK, since we had directed the [complainant] only to testify on the claim she brought before this court, your defence should also concentrate on the claim.

In his judgment, the magistrate focused resolutely on the issue of child maintenance before finally advising the couple that, if they wanted residual disputes over marital property to be dealt with, they should pursue a separate claim relating to the breakdown of their marriage:

it seems both [parties] gave evidence as if the case before me was that of matrimony . . . It has to be noted that in a case of child affiliation or maintenance what is important is that it is proved that the defendant is the putative father of the child . . . In the present case, the defendant has not disputed that he is the father of the child . . . I find that the [complainant] has proved her claim . . . The court only acts on matters that have been pleaded by the parties. What I can advise both parties is that for the issue of household property to be resolved, you must first of all commence proceedings concerning matrimony. That is, you can either go to court or to the marriage advocates, or the village head, so that there should be a formality that the marriage has ended.

Suzulo kaye, ndiyeno zikatelo ndi m'mene timakambirana za katundu ... [Divorce first, once that is done that is when we discuss issues of property ...].

As we saw above, when the same magistrate registered a counter-accusation of cruelty in a case brought to him under a claim of desertion, magistrates were capable of greater flexibility than was displayed in this instance. Reflecting on a case of 'divorce without valid reasons', for example, the male SGM explained:

[The complainant] was at fault because she was rude to her husband and the problem was discussed with their advocates but she didn't change. She said she was dumped for no reasons but she was rude, she didn't cook, and her husband was doing his own laundry. I told her she had not come to court with clean hands. The right claim was for maintenance of the child; there were reasons enough for the divorce so the original claim was dismissed.

In that case, the magistrate disregarded the marital dispute, but awarded child maintenance instead, signalling a less rigid approach. We might thus speculate that, in the case above, the TGM also thought a child maintenance claim more likely to serve the complainant's need for financial support than a claim that would have placed the focus on her comportment within the marriage. It was evident in court, however, that those testifying would have appreciated the opportunity to narrate the breakdown of the relationship and their sense of the injustice it had entailed. The framing of claims was of signal importance because the listed claims set limits to the kinds of testimony that would be considered relevant to the case, and thus the extent to which the details of a relationship would come under scrutiny.

For the SGM, the 'main challenge [was] to isolate or to identify the problems', because:

the kind of claims which appear ... on the court file are framed by the clerks ... So the challenge is for you to really identify the problems between the parties. That is why you have even to find out from the parties what is it they want, from the beginning. Because if you just base yourself on what is written on the file, then I think you'll be misled because when you hear the case you will find out that what comes out during the course of the hearing is something different than what is on the file.

Here, the SGM gestured towards the fact that he had adapted the format of hearings in his court to allow for an extended discussion of the claim before he invited complainants to begin their testimony under oath. This modification was a response to his perception of shortcomings in the definition of claims. His remarks on the problem of 'what is written on the file' echo the TGM's reference to the registry, or court office, where complaints were first received. It was during bureaucratic interactions between complainants and clerks in these administrative spaces that claims were defined and recorded. Indeed, several magistrates identified clerks as the principal source of inadequate or repetitive claims. The SGM associated this with the fact that many contemporary clerks had previously been employed in the traditional courts, until the two court systems were merged in 1995 (see Chapter 2): 'So, it's like we have a lot of under-qualified guys from the traditional courts,' he explained. The TGM, too, traced the abundance of 'divorce without valid reasons' cases to the clerks' familiarity with the former traditional courts. Both men had worked as clerks before undergoing lay magistracy training. They remembered being corrected themselves, as they now tried to correct their own clerks, to encourage claims that were specific about the remedy the complainant was seeking, and the grounds for their complaint.

At the same time that they heaped responsibility for the overabundance of claims of 'divorce without valid reasons' on their clerks, magistrates also bemoaned the seeming incapacity of officers working in the VSU to advise those whom they referred to court on how to frame their claims. This was something they occasionally raised at Court Users Association meetings, with limited success. Although hearings in the VSU were not restricted by the need to articulate a formal claim, complainants were routinely asked to summarise their complaints succinctly at the end of their narrative accounts. However, questions such as 'So, what is it you're really complaining about?' often proved difficult to answer for people who had just described their grievances at length.

Alongside clerks and VSU officers, complainants themselves did not escape blame. Magistrates lamented their apparent inability to formulate appropriate claims and express desired remedies, but most of all they exhibited frustration and impatience with the generalised failure of witnesses, male and female, whether complainants, defendants, or *ankhoswe*, to streamline their narrative testimonies. In the courtroom, their exasperation was often revealed in what were at times bad-tempered requests for brevity: 'I'm a busy man, can you shorten your stories?' (FGM); 'Why can't you just come to the point instead of discussing each and every detail that are irrelevant?' (TGM). Clerks, too, encouraged parties to be brief, and might, for instance, intervene in the course of testimony to remind a witness to 'answer the question' (*yankhani funso*).[15] Nevertheless, as we shall see, the same magistrates could also be highly attentive to the mundane details they heard in their courts, and the inclusion of such details sheds important light on the moral-material dimensions of the relationships in dispute.

---

[15] It was not uncommon in the VSU, too, to hear police officers request that complainants focus on the immediate issues that had brought them to their office, 'rather than things that occurred in 2001'.

Extra-linguistic factors

A great deal of attention has been paid to discourses of disputation within legal anthropology. A number of studies have highlighted the importance of language and linguistic strategies to success in legal arenas, noting, too, how gender, race, and class can shape access to linguistic resources and affect the ways in which words are uttered and statements heard (see, e.g., Conley and O'Barr 1990; Hirsch 1998).[16] Important insights are to be gained from the analysis of language and linguistic strategies, but this approach does not take us far enough in our efforts to understand the various factors influencing the outcomes of marital disputes in rural Malawi. Authors who focus on linguistic strategising work from the premise that:

There is no concrete set of social facts 'out there' against which the truth value of words or propositions can readily be measured; veracity subsists, rather, in the extent to which events and interactions are persuasively construed and coherently interpreted. (Comaroff and Roberts 1981: 238)

Thus, emphasis is placed on the 'strategic negotiation' (Comaroff and Roberts 1981: 239) of 'elements of a rhetorical order' (ibid.: 151).

Accordingly, for Comaroff and Roberts, the fact that the 'conjugal process' among the Tswana consists of a series of events, rather than a singular moment of status transition, makes sense only in light of the fact that the 'incidents' that mark the transition to full marriage can be 'deployed rhetorically as normative referents in the context of dispute' (1981: 150). Events such as the transfer of bridewealth, or the coming together of affines, may be strategically reinterpreted so as to insist upon, or deny, marital relationships, and the 'interests, rights, liabilities and statuses' (ibid.: 156) that they entail. Be that as it may, and I do not refute the significance of their insight, nor that of Conley and O'Barr, that 'at any particular point in time the dispute *is* the account being given at that time' (1990: x), there is clearly more to the disputes under discussion here than linguistic manipulation.

Strategising in these cases also has important extra-linguistic dimensions. What people do, have done, and are reported to have done provides necessary evidence of their intentions and moral status, as well as the veracity of their oral testimony. The TGM's judgment in the following case of 'divorce without valid reasons' illustrates the concomitant importance of linguistic and extra-linguistic positioning:

The [complainant's advocate's] testimony corroborated the [complainant's] testimony and this court believed his evidence because he was not cross-examined by the defendant and this clearly indicates that he agrees with what

---

[16] Such studies marked a clear departure from more positivist social scientific approaches to the study of law, rightly insisting that law is constructed rather than a simple matter of applying rules to facts.

he had said. I'm saying this because the defendant has not disputed the fact that he had told the [complainant] to go home first and that he would follow her later with the matrimonial property. He has also not disputed that since sending the [complainant] home he has not gone to her home to stay as he has been promising ... the defendant has not explained why he decided to dump the [complainant]. When he was cross-examined, the defendant stated that when he came back from Lilongwe, he did not go to the [complainant's] home. This is a clear indication that he is not interested in the marriage with the [complainant]. I am saying this because almost a year and four months have elapsed without the defendant showing any sign that he still loves his wife. It has been stated that the [complainant] went to complain at the victim support unit at PIM police [station].[17] When he was summoned there the defendant stated that he still loved the [complainant] and that he would go and stay with her at her home. He did not do this [and] the [complainant] decided to complain to this court.

According to the totality of evidence in this case, it is clear that the defendant had already made up his mind that he should get rid of the [complainant] ... Had the defendant acted in good faith, I am sure he could have joined the [complainant] in no time. I therefore find him liable for the marriage to break down because he just left the [complainant] in suspense. He did not bother to take their matter to the marriage advocates so that if there was any problem it could be resolved.

The defendant's failure to cross-examine his wife's *nkhoswe* hindered his attempts to defend himself against the claim, as did the discrepancy between his words and deeds throughout the course of the dispute: he had made promises that had not been fulfilled and it was his behaviour, as much as his commentary on it, that eventually exposed his lack of 'interest' in the marriage. Crucial in this regard was his failure to consult the *ankhoswe*, which would have served to demonstrate his willingness to remedy any difficulties between himself and his wife. The complainant's actions, on the other hand, were exemplary: she had initiated a hearing at the VSU, and, when the defendant failed to meet his commitment to return to her home, she had taken her complaint to court.

In both the VSU and the magistrates' courts, considerable emphasis was placed on the actions of the parties, what they had done, to whom they had spoken, and the extent to which they had been able to recruit the support of their matrilineal kin, as represented by their *ankhoswe*. Notwithstanding coordinated perjury, these things cannot be achieved through rhetorical skill alone.[18] There is no doubt that linguistic mastery

---

[17] PIM (Providence Industrial Mission) is a trading centre and the location of the independence hero John Chilembwe's church, from which it takes its name.

[18] It cannot be denied that parties occasionally lie under oath. It is also likely that some *ankhoswe* connive in attempts to mislead the courts. Cross-examination and the removal of witnesses from the courtroom until it is time for their testimony limit the effectiveness of such strategies. In general, the institution of *ankhoswe* was held in high regard by police officers and magistrates, who expected them to provide truthful, non-partisan accounts. Speaking of the importance of the presence of *ankhoswe* at the VSU, one police

and oral strategy played a role, but strategising in this context also had an important physical and material aspect.[19] Parties to a dispute, anticipating the prospective need to narrate their troubles and describe their physical, emotional, and moral responses, took seriously the practical decisions about where to go, whom to tell, and how to react to the words and deeds of their fellow disputant(s). These were pragmatic concerns as much as – if not more than – issues of rhetoric. They were also more than merely rational, maximising strategic choices, for, as we have seen, they were matters of moral propriety: moral personhood was simultaneously demonstrated and constituted through compliance with proper procedure in the course of a dispute. Evidence of having desired to resolve a dispute through *ankhoswe*, traditional leaders, police officers, and the courts, and of having maintained the support and cooperation of matrilineal kin along the way, shed light on a person's moral and social standing and could not be reduced to a matter of linguistic strategy alone.

This relates to the ways in which 'cases' are understood as events. It would be a mistake to approach hearings – whether with *ankhoswe*, chiefs, police officers, or magistrates – as the final destination of a dispute. Disputes originated beyond these forums, continued alongside them, and, more often than not, persisted after their close (see also Moore 1986). This was evident in the fact that disputes moved with relative ease between venues, and they could subsequently return, even to the magistrates' court, which was widely perceived as the forum of last resort. We saw this in Chapter 4, where the case heard by the female magistrate had come to court for the second time, and the same was true of a number of the cases I observed. Case hearings were very often not the end of the story, not least because of the important role that dispute-resolution processes themselves could play in terms of reputation management and the recruitment of support from kin and neighbours. The fact that a dispute might be discussed again in another forum adds a further strategic dimension to the ways in which disputants proceeded; consulting *ankhoswe* and attending a hearing at the *bwalo* or VSU might hold the key to resolving a dispute, but even if it did not, attempts to discuss matters in such venues could become powerful future evidence of a person's relative good faith, moral standing, and position within webs of social relations. As Griffiths puts it, dispute hearings allow people to

officer explained: 'Without *ankhoswe* things don't go well; they are *our* witnesses.' In the absence of compelling evidence to the contrary, I proceed on the assumption that the majority of those who testify do so in good faith.

[19] The line between what I refer to as the 'linguistic' and the 'extra-linguistic' defies clear demarcation, but this does not negate the utility of the kind of loose differentiation I make here. The ethnographic method is ideally suited to unmasking false dichotomies between assumed linguistic and non- or pre-linguistic registers (Navaro-Yashin 2009).

'put their position on record' and establish 'prospective credibility' (1997: 136), which might be mobilised at a later stage, by demonstrating compliance with particular social roles and thereby establishing their status as morally upright members of the community. Thus, while oral testimony was critical, its value for those concerned lay in its ability to speak to social actions and the extra-discursive texture of human relationships.

Beyond violence: *nkhanza* as a failure of complementarity

The very real, and potentially moral, significance of actions and the co-implication of discursive and extra-discursive factors in determining the outcome of disputes are also evident when we consider that, although magistrates frequently complained about witnesses who gave a lot of 'irrelevant information', they did not always dismiss such information as who had offered whom a chair, and who had eaten with whom in the course of a dispute. The following example comes from the judgment delivered by the TGM at Chiradzulu, cited above in relation to the direct use of the language of human rights. The magistrate was ruling on a claim brought by a male complainant against his wife, accusing her of deserting him:

That night she slept in the kitchen with the children because he had locked her out of the house. She put back the things in the house the following morning for the sake of the marriage. *She picked and cooked pumpkins and served him when he came back.* After eating, the [complainant] asked who she was with at the garden. He suspected she was with a man. He beat her up severely; she slept in the kitchen again.[20]

In the course of her quite matter-of-fact description of the cruelty (*nkhanza*) she had suffered, the female defendant had described picking, cooking, and serving a meal of boiled pumpkins. The magistrate, recognising the significance of her reported actions and the attempt she had made to persevere in fulfilling her role as wife despite her husband's behaviour, incorporated this information into his judgment. The effect was to highlight the imbalance in the relationship, making plain the husband's moral-material failings. Even where violence was central to the magistrate's interpretation of a case, and human rights were recognised as relevant, 'justice' as complementarity and the materiality of morality in marital relationships remained prominent.

The influence of the ideal of moral-material reciprocity or complementarity on understandings of cruelty within marriage was

---

[20] Emphasis added.

perhaps best encapsulated by the SGM, when he made the following pronouncement during a case of 'divorce without valid reasons':

At times, a man can make a woman or make someone what you want him or her to be, a spouse can make their spouse what they want him or her to be. If you want her to be rude, you can make her to be rude. The wife can also make the husband to behave in a particular way because of how she behaves. So whenever a spouse complains about the behaviour of the other, or a husband complains about the behaviour of his wife, then we do not just look at the complaints but look at both sides and try to strike a balance. There's a saying, 'When something moves it is moved by another,' so sometimes you can make her behave in a strange way because of how you conduct yourself, because if you don't fulfil your obligations as a husband, if you fail in your obligations as a husband, it is unlikely that someone is going to respect you as a husband. At times we have ourselves to blame when some things happen in a family because we tend not to behave as is expected of us.

The magistrate's words take us directly back to the structural and affective complementarity of gender relations discussed in Chapter 4. They are also reminiscent of a comment made by a friend of mine in a Chiradzulu village as she meditated on her husband's shortcomings. I expressed surprise at the disrespectful tone she had employed in reference to her spouse, and she replied, simply, '*Ulemu umayamba wekha*,' which is perhaps best translated along the lines of 'respect begins with yourself'. Her words, in turn, resonate with Gluckman's suggestion that, where rights are concerned, Lozi 'tend to stress that the defaulter should render the right, rather than that the abused shall receive it' (1965: 173).

We are simultaneously approaching a broader understanding of the ways in which linguistic and extra-linguistic factors (loosely defined) affect the reception of complaints made in the VSU and magistrates' courts, and a clearer formulation of how violence is conceived in the context of marital strife. What has emerged is an understanding of violence that takes little from internationally dominant, universalising models of 'batterers' and their 'victims' (Merry 2006b; 2006c).[21] Rather, physical violence, as understood in these settings, is a matter of cause and effect, amenable to rational analysis, logical argument, and moral dissuasion, and preventable through mutual understanding and open communication. Violence is not condoned, and nor is it redefined as 'discipline', but it is largely interpreted outside 'North American theories of domestic violence as learned behaviour' governable through 'therapeutic intervention' (Merry 2006c: 46). In this regard, magistrates and police officers,

---

[21] The rapid multiplication of indicators 'as tools for assessing and promoting a variety of social justice and reform strategies around the world' (Merry 2011: S83), including violence against women, can only enhance the currency of standardised, quantifiable framings of gender-based violence and its governance.

whose statements have provided the basis for this analysis, share a great deal with those whose disputes they strive to resolve.

As noted above, *nkhanza*, the Chichewa term regularly employed to translate the English 'violence', is more accurately rendered as 'cruelty' and is a wider concept than its routine translation suggests (Saur, Semu, and Ndau 2005).[22] Unacceptable according to customary law, *nkhanza* incorporates physical acts of violence but it can also convey a sense of cruelty that is entirely intangible, as well as describing neglectful behaviour, verbal abuse, and so on. In fact, it covers well the dimensions of violence that NGO facilitators draw out in their courses on gender-based violence (physical, sexual, emotional, economic, 'traditional', and against children). This wide-ranging vernacular term makes a mockery of distinctions between violence and the material dimensions of marital life. As a female constable in the VSU expounded to an errant husband: '*Nkhanza* is not just hitting; if you run off and eat at [a trading centre] while your wife and children are hungry at home, that is *nkhanza*.' Cruelty allows more readily than violence for a broad focus on the texture of relationships, recognising the potential severity of infractions that leave the skin untouched.

When magistrates and police officers listen to the quotidian details of narrative testimony – to claims about the picking of pumpkins or the warming of bathing water – which attest to the moral-material dimensions of married life, they are listening to accounts of the achievement or otherwise of reciprocal and complementary gender roles. Cruelty, including physical violence, may be a key element of these accounts, forming part of a larger story about the moral personhood of those before them. But the handling of the cases discussed here illustrates that there is much more to justice in marriage than the absence of violence.

Justice versus law

If direct appeals to the language of human rights and gender-based violence were rare in these venues, so too was any explicit mention of law. The following judgment, delivered by the male replacement for the female magistrate at Mbulumbuzi as he concluded a case originally heard by his late predecessor, was a rare exception: 'By marrying another woman, the defendant committed adultery. He could not have married another woman before the matter was exhausted. That in itself shows that the defendant acted against the law.' It is not clear which law he considered the defendant to have infringed, but his use of the language of

---

[22] According to Merry, the English term 'cruelty' was used instead of the term 'domestic violence' in India until recently. There, she says, as the latter term becomes 'more widespread ... the number of complaints is increasing dramatically' (2006b: 139–40).

law serves as a reminder that, for the most part, my discussion of legal disputes has proceeded in terms of 'justice' rather than 'law'.

The distinction between justice and law has perhaps been most influentially theorised by the philosopher Jacques Derrida, who argues that the two are distinguishable by their relative calculability (1990). *Droit* – law or right – he posits, is 'stabilizable and statutory, calculable, a system of regulated and coded prescriptions', as opposed to justice, which is 'infinite, incalculable, rebellious to rule and foreign to symmetry, heterogeneous and heterotropic' (ibid.: 959).

> Every time that something comes to pass or turns out well, every time that we placidly apply a good rule to a particular case, to a correctly subsumed example, according to a determinant judgment, we can be sure that law (*droit*) may find itself accounted for, but certainly not justice. Law (*droit*) is not justice. Law is the element of calculation, and it is just that there be law, but justice is incalculable. (Derrida 1990: 947)

Justice, in Derrida's analysis, is 'an experience of the impossible' (Derrida 1990: 974). To be 'just', a decision must be neither strictly calculated nor arbitrary; it must 'be both regulated and without regulation: it must conserve the law and also destroy it or suspend it enough to have to reinvent it in each case' (ibid.: 961). Derrida concludes that 'there is never a moment that we can say *in the present* that a decision is *just*' (ibid.: 961, emphasis in the original). For this reason, justice, like hope (see Chapter 6), has a prospective orientation or, as Butler puts it, 'as an ideal, it is that towards which we strive, without end' (2004: 32). To return to Derrida: 'Justice remains, is yet, to come, *à venir*' (1990: 969).

This distinction is useful with respect to the forms of justice under discussion in this book. I have approached justice as a motivational ideal, towards which disputants and legal authorities orient themselves, and I have described 'gender justice' as a matter of contested morality that takes shape through the negotiation of complementary gender roles. In neither case does justice approximate 'law', if that is to be understood as a calculable force, prescriptive and proscribed. Yet, as Derrida perceived, 'everything would still be simple if this distinction between justice and *droit* were a true distinction' (1990: 959). In practice, law 'claims to exercise itself in the name of justice', and justice, in turn, 'is required to establish itself in the name of ... law' (ibid.: 959–61). If the distinction between law and justice were 'logically regulated' (ibid.: 969), perhaps complainants would not seek justice through the institutions of law at all.

That justice is not equal to law is hardly a surprising claim. That justice is greater than law helps explain why the various institutions of law available in rural Chiradzulu were resorted to serially by those seeking justice, as what was sought and what was administered failed to coalesce. It is also suggestive of why those charged with delivering justice availed themselves of diverse resources and registers in their efforts to resolve disputes in a just fashion. 'Law' as state law, as constitutional human rights, as custom, and as morality might all come into play in the course of a single case. The fluid multiplicity of law in Malawi, and particularly the acknowledged flexibility of customary law, suggests the need either to temper Derrida's vision of legal calculability, or to reconsider whether the courts described here administer 'law' in the strict sense. More compelling is Derrida's attention to the elusive character of justice, its *à venir* qualities, which mean that the search for justice is always a losing battle. Justice may never be realised; there is invariably room for contestation, for dissatisfaction, and for appeal. It may well be that the divergent personal styles of the magistrates described in this chapter, and their ready acceptance of customary law's shifting contours, reflect a tacit recognition of this dissonance between law and justice. In which case, manipulations of the Derridean 'law-ness' of 'law' are demonstrative of conscious efforts to approximate justice.

When HIV and antiretroviral therapies (ARVs) enter the courtroom, they do so as emblems of modernity; unlike marital difficulties, these are not recognised as 'customary' concerns. Nevertheless, HIV remains something that is managed and experienced in gendered ways and in the context of conjugal and familial relationships. By focusing on the efforts of magistrates and police officers to address new challenges presented by the HIV epidemic in matrilineal Malawi – namely, widespread concerns about the stigmatisation of HIV-positive Malawians – this chapter seeks ethnographic purchase on the unfinished, out-of-reach quality of justice. Approaching 'stigma' as a relatively new moral category, I examine the ways in which existing legal resources are brought to bear on this topic.[1] However, a sense that the vernacular expression *kutsalidwa*, 'to be left behind', which is how stigma is best expressed in Chichewa, has more to teach us about the lived experience of HIV-positive villagers leads the discussion out of the courtroom and into matrilineal compounds. It is precisely this relational context that falls from view when disputes relating to HIV are approached through the lens of stigma. Through ethnographic engagement with HIV-positive women's tentative expressions of hope, I argue that legal responses to the challenges of life with HIV share an orientation towards the future with women's more quotidian strategies of 'vigilance' (*kuyang'anitsa*) in relation to marital and reproductive decision making.[2] The 'prospective orientation' (Miyazaki 2004: 10) of hope

---

[1] Henceforth, I omit the quotation marks around the word 'stigma'; it remains, however, a contentious term.

[2] This chapter focuses on the experiences of HIV-positive women as a result of both my greater access to women during fieldwork and the local landscape of disclosure. Not all of the HIV-positive women I came to know were as open about their status as Catherine (discussed below). While some attended local support groups and were widely known to be HIV-positive, others occupied a variety of positions along a continuum stretching to almost total secrecy. Mandatory prenatal screening was one context in which women had little choice but to confront HIV. The local support group I attended had only two regular male attendees, and other men, several of whom I had been told were HIV-positive, did not speak to me directly about their illness, although I became quite close to some of them. It was my decision to respect the privacy they guarded so closely, and

parallels the temporality of efforts to bring about justice through the magistrates' courts, illustrating the shared experiential terrain of justice and hope, as well as highlighting the 'cut' performed when the administration of law serves up its final word, at least temporarily halting justice's onward momentum.

There is no denying the severity of the HIV epidemic in Malawi: estimates of prevalence range from 10 to 15 per cent of the adult population. Nevertheless, much has changed since the introduction of free ARVs in 2004.[3] The availability of ARVs has radically altered the prognosis for hundreds of thousands of HIV-positive Malawians, opening the doors of hope for people who, until very recently, faced a terrible death sentence.[4] For anthropologists, the altered landscape of HIV treatment allows, and even requires, a shift in analytical focus away from death and towards the ways in which HIV-positive people are living with the disease (Johnson 2012; Winchester et al. 2016). For police officers and magistrates, the transformed prognosis for HIV-positive citizens also presents new challenges, not least that of determining how best to intervene in disputes shaped by the epidemic. Stigma has emerged as a prominent category for understanding the experiences of people living with HIV: it is a category with moral overtones, and it introduces a novel impetus for the delivery of justice. Invocations of stigma tend to individualise the experience of HIV-positive persons, however, removing them from their gendered and relational contexts. As a result, the contrast between legal responses to stigma and the ways in which *nkhanza* (cruelty, violence) was treated in Chapter 5 is striking. Whereas a focus on *nkhanza* often served to open up discussion, a turn to stigma has the opposite effect.

it is my hope that future research will provide rich insights into the perspectives of rural men. Existing studies of men and HIV/AIDS include Kaler (2004a), Niehaus (2012), and Simpson (2009).

[3] Figures indicate that, by June 2010, more than 225,000 Malawians were receiving ARV treatment (The Global Fund 2011); in the same year, Malawi topped a Médecins Sans Frontières (MSF) comparison of eight sub-Saharan countries for 'People on [ARVs] as a percentage of country needs' (MSF 2010: 11). Chiradzulu District hospital is home to one of MSF's largest programmes and treatment became available there earlier than in many parts of Malawi (MSF Malawi 2004); MSF support has reduced the impact of erratic ARV supplies reported elsewhere in the country. The view from the villages close to Chiradzulu hospital is thus not quite the view from 'the margins' (Biehl 2006).

[4] I do not mean to imply that ARVs are the first, or only, source of hope for HIV-positive villagers. Other sources of hope, which predate and persist alongside ARVs, include 'traditional' medicines and divine intervention (see, e.g., Doran 2007; Probst 1999). However, ARVs have instigated the most dramatic and widely acknowledged transformations in the health of HIV-positive people.

'Stigma': moral category and legal challenge

I first met Catherine in late July 2010 at the Chiradzulu magistrates' court. She was there to give evidence against her brother, Mayeso, who had been charged with 'use of insulting language'. The case, heard by the third-grade magistrate (TGM), centred on Mayeso's verbal abuse of Catherine, which had occurred in public and included references to her HIV status and the fact that she was taking ARV medication. The judgment went against Mayeso, with the magistrate concluding:

> It is very unfortunate to note that [Mayeso] committed this offence against his relative; instead of protecting his sister he was in the forefront to degrade and humiliate her in such a manner [in] public ... at the Village Headman's forum ... What should be known is that the status of a person in terms of health is a private matter ... People are afraid to come in the open ... about their status just because of the behaviour like the one you did. Since my duty is to protect the citizens of this country, I am of the view that a meaningful sentence ought to be imposed so that the accused should be prevented or deterred from repeating or committing a similar offence in future. [The] sentence that I am going to impose for the convict will act as a warning to others who might be thinking of doing the same. I am of the view that a sentence of 5,000 Kwacha,[5] [or] in default two months imprisonment with hard labour, is appropriate.

Mayeso was unable to pay the fine and went to prison for two months.

The magistrate did not refer directly to stigma in his judgment. However, by invoking the fear of disclosure, the need for protection, and his duty to deter behaviour like Mayeso's, he voiced widespread assumptions about stigma as a defining feature of the HIV/AIDS epidemic. By referring to health as a 'private matter' he also signalled his affinity with human rights-based approaches to healthcare as a freedom or right (*ufulu*) that accrues to the individual. The magistrate's focus on individual behaviour as the engine of stigma, and individual fear as its consequence, chimed with the emphasis of much research and a great many policy statements on HIV risk, prevention, and treatment (see, e.g., Bryceson and Fonseca 2006; Kaler 2004b; Poulin 2007; Rankin et al. 2005).[6] That stigma is dominant in contemporary understandings of the HIV epidemic is a given, but that it characterises the experiences of HIV-positive Malawians in matrilineal areas of the country cannot be taken for granted. John Lwanda notes that, during the early years of the epidemic, 'the initial "segregationist" discourse' (2002: 154) encountered

---

[5] Approximately £23.

[6] Sociologist Erving Goffman, the widely acknowledged pioneer of work on stigma in the social sciences, stated that to theorise stigma, 'a language of relationships, not attributes is really needed' (1963: 13). Nevertheless, many have bemoaned the fact that Goffman's work has inspired understandings of stigma as something that takes its form and has its effects at the level of the individual (see, e.g., Yang et al. 2007).

in urban areas was not apparent in rural Malawi; among kin in the villages, those suffering from HIV/AIDS were well cared for. As the epidemic has progressed, scholars have continued to raise doubts about the relevance of ideas about stigma to rural sufferers of HIV in Malawi. In their extensive research in Zomba District, which borders Chiradzulu to the north, Peters, Kambewa, and Walker 'found little evidence of stigma in people's multiple reactions to HIV/AIDS' (2010: 283). They argue that the term 'does injustice to the complex ways in which many Malawians are seeking to come to terms with the accelerating rates of illness and death' (ibid.).

A closer look at Catherine's case reveals significant disjunctures between the understanding of stigma that guided the magistrate's intervention and the lived experiences of HIV-positive women in rural Chiradzulu. As the magistrate acknowledged, Catherine and Mayeso were siblings in a matrilineal setting, and were thus expected to play important and supportive roles in each other's lives. However, his invocation of stigma served to close down rather than open up an examination of the relational context in which their dispute took place. The magistrate's efforts to combat stigma highlight the influence of broader social transformations on law and morality, while simultaneously signalling the temporal distinctions between the practice of law and the pursuit of justice.

Catherine's immediate response to Mayeso's sentence was positive: '*Azikaphunzira*,' she said, 'he must go and learn [a lesson].' A few weeks later, I visited her at the rural home she shared with her husband and son and she remained hopeful that her brother would be reformed. If not, she said, it would be 'the result of his own inability to understand' (*kukhala kosamva kwake*). From our four brief encounters at court, I had developed a great admiration for Catherine: she was young, determined, and spoke with a strength that belied her fragile body; she had always seemed interested in talking to me, and she did not hesitate that morning when I called to ask if we could meet.

When I arrived, Catherine showed me around her small compound, which bordered a busy, untarred road leading to a major market. I commented on the thousands of bricks that had been moulded and stacked in her yard and she explained that she and her husband would eventually use them to build a new house; she also showed me the pen where she kept a pig. Catherine then led me inside her relatively spacious, although patched and weathered, thatched house and we sat facing each other across a low table, on small wooden chairs.

As we spoke, Catherine described her difficulties with her brother at greater length than she had in court, and I began to see that the charge 'use of insulting language' was only one way in which her complaint against Mayeso could have been framed. Catherine's account of their dispute was chronological, beginning earlier in the day when the village head had come to the compound to discuss a land sale that Mayeso had initiated and for which he needed the consent of his matrilineal relatives, principally Catherine and their grandmothers.[7] Catherine, who farmed the land Mayeso wished to sell, refused on the basis that 'it is not a good thing to sell land. I have a child, and there's my younger sister too; she will also want a garden.'

Later the same day, as Catherine and the younger of her two grand-mothers were leaving the village head's court (*bwalo*) where they had been listening to cases, Catherine began to explain Mayeso's plan to sell the land. It was at this point that Mayeso appeared:

He arrived shouting, wanting to hit me. I just said, 'Don't be rash, calm down first' ... Then, because I had spoken like that, he wanted to grab me and hit me ... right there at the chief's court. He was shouting, then he said: 'You should think about yourself and the medicine you take. The graveyard is open, the grave is dug, it's waiting for you.' My grandmother was right there. Me, I didn't respond at all. I set off ... He continued to say those words, those insulting words, that I take medicine: 'Your units[8] that you take, you should think about yourself, how many days are left until you die?' I didn't react until I reached here; I entered the house and began to cry.

That afternoon, Catherine went to harvest sweet potatoes in her garden with her husband and a young matrilineal kinsman. But she was agitated – 'I still hadn't calmed my heart' (*mtimabe sindinaugwire*) – so she decided to call her senior maternal uncle on her mobile phone and ask him to come to see her. Her uncle had just started a new job in town but he sent his younger brother in his place; he arrived the next day to find that Mayeso had demolished part of the front wall of Catherine's house during the night. The village head came to the compound to talk to him and told the uncle that his nephew was 'a bad person' (*munthu woipa*). He also explained that Mayeso had another case pending against him concerning the group village head (GVH), whom he had also insulted and threatened. According to Catherine, the village head suggested to her uncle that it would be difficult to pursue this new case with the other still unresolved, adding:

'When you see her, your niece, and the way her body is, do you realise that the way she is, she could die from her thoughts? When we say that there's a person at this house, to whom do we refer? We refer to your niece ... yesterday she was nearly beaten up, today she's had her house knocked down, are these things

---

[7] Their mother and maternal grandmother had passed away; their two surviving grandmothers would be maternal great aunts in English kinship terminology.

[8] *Maunitsi* (units) is a reference to mobile phone credit and slang for ARVs (Peters, Kambewa, and Walker 2010: 284). Mayeso likens Catherine to a phone that is running out of credit.

good? I want you to answer me as the head of the matrilineage [*mbumba*].' And my uncle replied: 'These are not good things, to have a house knocked down or to be threatened with being beaten up with the way she is; these things are not good.'

The village head counselled Catherine's uncle to report Mayeso's behaviour to the police. However, the uncle did not pursue the matter and Catherine understood this to be the result of Mayeso's threat to beat him up if he did.[9] Before long, Mayeso resumed insulting her:

He started again. If I met him on the road, maybe I was going to the grocery store and he was coming towards me from that direction, he would say things like 'You'll feel it; you're in the shit with your AIDS.'

Eventually, on the village head's advice, Catherine went alone to the police station, about 90 minutes' walk from her home. There, she was issued with a letter summoning her brother, which she was to leave with the village head. The following day, Catherine repeated her complaint at the police station, this time in the presence of Mayeso, who told the police that Catherine had made the story up. Catherine described how her brother provoked the police when they asked him how he and Catherine were related by responding: 'I don't know her, she is not my relative.' The police then asked Catherine if she had witnesses, and when she replied that she did, she was told: 'We are arresting him because he is denying the complaint. If he had admitted the truth of the matter it would have been different – we usually resolve issues between relatives by simply discussing them.'

Following Mayeso's arrest, Catherine gave a statement explaining 'everything' (*ndinalongosola zonse*), and she returned to the station the same day with her grandmother, who also recorded a statement. Catherine recalled her grandmother's reaction when the police suggested that Mayeso might go to prison: 'He should go to prison,' she had said, 'because even me, there was no part of my body left that he did not insult; his sister too, he insulted every part of her body.' Asked the same question by another police officer outside court on the first day of the trial, she replied: 'He should go. We want him to learn; he should know how to live with people.'

Although the court case was drawn out, Catherine and her grandmother were in the witness stand for a combined total of just 15 minutes, during which time they answered questions posed by a police prosecutor. Both told the court that Mayeso had insulted Catherine by referring to her ARV drugs, explaining that he had been angered by her refusal to agree to a land sale. Catherine confirmed that

---

[9] Catherine made the same accusation in court.

she received ARV treatment. When asked if she had anything to add, Catherine's grandmother described how she had gone to check on Catherine the following morning only to find that the front wall of her house had been knocked down. Catherine had carefully responded only to the questions put to her by the police officer and had not mentioned the demolition. In the second court session, a police investigator testified, reading out Mayeso's caution statement, in which he described first a disagreement with his sister over some bricks and then an altercation on the road after she refused to remove her dog. He did not mention the land sale, or the village head's court, and he made no reference to HIV or ARVs.

At the third hearing, Mayeso elected neither to give evidence nor to call witnesses, and the case was adjourned for judgment. As we saw above, Mayeso was found guilty of insulting his sister and sentenced to two months in prison. The question remains, however: why was Catherine's complaint framed by the charge 'use of insulting language'? Her story – as she described it to me, at least – was one of threatened physical violence, intimidation, and the destruction of property, for which a range of alternative charges would have been available to the police. It was also a dispute between close matrilineal kin over the disposal of customary land. Although Catherine told me that she considered her case to have been handled well because it had not been suppressed (*sanaipondereze*), she was nevertheless surprised, and somewhat disgruntled, that only some of what she had complained about had been taken up in court. In the account of her story she gave to me, we heard her uncle and the village head discussing Catherine's predicament: Catherine's illness, 'the way her body is', and the violence against her were the key elements, rather than the verbal abuse. Catherine's grandmother, too, attempted to bring the damage to Catherine's house into her evidence in court. The issue of the land sale and Mayeso's counter-accusations concerning bricks and Catherine's dog also suggest a broader, more complicated set of disputes. One puzzle, then, is why the police chose to concentrate on this aspect of Catherine's complaint, rather than on other, more obviously 'criminal', components of Mayeso's behaviour or on the domestic basis of their dispute, and at the expense of a more comprehensive investigation.

The police officers I worked with in the victim support unit (VSU) were aware of Mayeso's case, and they told me that they were keeping an eye on it to see how it fared in court. For them, Catherine's HIV status and Mayeso's references to her ARV treatment were key, making it something of a 'test case' from which they hoped to learn in order to better advise complainants in their office when HIV or ARVs were relevant to proceedings. Catherine had not passed through the VSU, but disputes between relatives were the mainstay of VSU work and it was not uncommon for HIV or ARVs to feature in these complaints.[10] At the court, a clerk explained what he perceived to be the benefit of the 'use of insulting language' claim: in a case like Catherine's, it would be possible to employ the similar charge of 'defamation', he said, but that would have to be dealt with by the High Court, which requires lawyers, and then 'people from the villages don't get proper access to justice [*chilungamo*]'. He added that if someone came to their office with a case like this one, he would advise them to go to the police station and open a file with the complaint 'use of insulting language' or 'conduct likely to cause a breach of the peace' so that the case would be dealt with at the magistrates' court.[11] From Catherine's account of their encounter with the police, we may also deduce that Mayeso's defiant, uncooperative attitude hardened officers towards him, inviting formal charges where 'simply discussing' might have sufficed. Indeed, it is possible to speculate that, in other circumstances, this case would have been referred to the VSU rather than entering the magistrates' court as a criminal proceeding.

The police focus on the insults concerning HIV and ARVs, and the solemnity with which the magistrate dealt with the case, must also be understood in the context of the official discourse surrounding HIV/AIDS, vulnerability, and stigma. Such ideas certainly guided the magistrate, who explained to me that this was the first such case he had encountered as they were rare in the courts, but that 'stigma' (his term) is a problem in society at large, and it prevents people from being open about their status. Indeed, stigma has attained such prominence in understandings of HIV/AIDS that its existence can be declared without recourse to evidence; it is simply assumed to characterise the experience of HIV-positive people in Malawi, as in sub-Saharan Africa more generally. In invocations of stigma by government, donor, and NGO representatives, as well as in media coverage, the concept is rarely given any content and the impression is of a static condition or attribute (see, e.g., *Nyasa Times* 2010b). Thus, Nicola Ndovi, acting Programme Manager of the Centre for Human Rights and Rehabilitation, expressed her organisation's 'concern that attitudes that stigmatise and discriminate against people living with HIV and AIDS continue to remain high' (Kateta 2008); and a spokesperson for the National Association of People Living with HIV/AIDS in Malawi recently stated that its members

[10] Cases involving references to HIV or ARVs tended to be disputes between spouses.
[11] It is relatively inexpensive to pursue cases in the magistrates' courts. It was not clear whether this rationale affected the police's decision to charge Mayeso as they did. Unfortunately, I did not have the opportunity to ask them directly. What I can say, however, is that not all police officers at the station were aware of this distinction. It is unlikely that the decision was influenced by knowledge of my research as I came across Catherine's case by chance when it reached the court.

'perpetually face mounting stigma' (Chipalasa 2010).[12] Although it was certainly not the case that the professionals I observed always found themselves in agreement with the media, NGOs, or government policies and priorities, such representations nevertheless coloured the landscape in which they operated.[13] Having thus identified stigma as relevant to the case, the charge 'use of insulting language' brought existing legal tools to bear upon Mayeso's stigmatising behaviour, focusing directly on those aspects of Catherine's complaint that touched on her HIV status. By handing down a sentence intended to act as a deterrent to others, the magistrate also made explicit his wider contribution to efforts to curb the stigmatisation of HIV-positive citizens. He issued a clear message that insulting someone on the basis of their HIV status, and making public reference to the fact that they take ARV medication, is not acceptable.

Kutsala, to leave behind

To what extent, though, did stigma, as invoked by legal professionals in their efforts to administer justice, serve to illuminate or address the relational context of Catherine's case, which was, after all, a dispute between siblings in a matrilineal setting? The Chichewa verb most commonly called upon to describe negative attitudes and behaviour towards people with HIV, and the one that comes closest to capturing the meaning of the English 'stigmatise', is *kutsala*, 'to leave behind'. When she talked about being left behind (*kutsalidwa*), Catherine located her experiences firmly within her matrilineal family group, and in this she was not unique. In addition to her brother, she named her younger sister and the elder of her two grandmothers, all of whom, she said, failed to take proper care of her when she fell ill, did not like to share food with her, and would tell her not to sit and chat with them because she was HIV-positive.

---

[12] For comparable representations by international organisations, see, for example, Avert (2011).

[13] During the well-publicised case of Steven Monjeza and Tiwonge Chimbalanga, a so-called same-sex couple who were arrested after holding a *chinkhoswe* engagement ceremony, for example, magistrates and police officers expressed vehement opposition to NGO calls for leniency towards the accused and reform of the law, and were outspoken, in private, in their disapproval of the president's decision to pardon the two after they had been sentenced to 14 years' imprisonment (for an overview of the case as reported in the media, see, e.g., BBC 2009; Bearak 2010; Mapondera and Smith 2010a; 2010b; and see Biruk 2014 for an anthropological discussion). The difference between the two examples may lie in the fact that arguments in support of Monjeza and Chimbalanga were widely regarded as foreign and imposed. By contrast, the discourse on stigma seems to have been incorporated more readily into national conversations about HIV/AIDS and is generally accepted as relevant to the Malawian context.

It was not the case that Catherine felt left behind by all members of her family; she told me that she could rely on her husband, her younger grandmother, and her two maternal uncles. She also described how a young male matrilineal kinsman, who had formerly allied himself with Mayeso, had recently become more sympathetic towards her, extending his public support by accompanying her to court on the first day of Mayeso's trial. In addition, Catherine contrasted the way in which certain of her relatives treated her with a cast of local non-kin (*anthu a pa dera*) who were kind to her and came to her defence when they saw or heard her family members mistreating her. She spoke with particular affection of a female friend who visited her at home to encourage her when she was having a difficult time and who had come to support her during the night when Mayeso was shouting insults and demolishing the wall of her house.

As suggested by Catherine's reference to the village head's assessment that Mayeso was 'a bad person', and the pending case for threatening the GVH, Mayeso had long been known as troublesome in the area. Indeed, his reputation traversed several villages to reach the compound in which I was living in the area of a different GVH. Catherine's latest difficulties with Mayeso surprised nobody there. Whether we interpret his behaviour as symptomatic of a 'crisis of masculinity' in a context of high unemployment, acute poverty, and female custodianship of land (McNeill and Niehaus 2009; Ngwani 2001), or frame his intention to sell Catherine's garden as an episode in the as yet incomplete rupturing of a matrilineage, the effect of which would be to transform kin into 'strangers' with no claim to family land (Peters 2002), what is certain is that Catherine's relationship with Mayeso was more complicated, more long-standing, and more particular than simple invocations of stigma imply. It was also clearly shaped in important ways by the matrilineal context, which restricted Mayeso's control over land, bolstered Catherine's authority with respect to its disposal, and rendered Catherine's husband largely invisible in the siblings' wrangling over lineage resources.

While Catherine's situation was extreme, resulting as it had done in violent intimidation and a criminal prosecution, my point about stigma's embeddedness in matrilineal family relations is a general one. For another HIV-positive woman I knew, it was her relationship with her mother that was most strained. 'These days,' she explained, 'there is no one else whom I can say leaves me behind in any way.' Another woman described how her elder sister used to gossip about her at the borehole, 'telling people there that I am dying and I'll leave my children for her to raise'. In these cases, and others, such problematic relationships predated the women's HIV tests, and what looked like stigma – or found expression as such – were aspects of ongoing and complex situations. Moreover, these experiences were far from static. A woman named Edith echoed many when she described recent changes in her relatives' behaviour:

I began to notice last year, because if I was at the hospital with one of my children, they used not to follow me there; they didn't help me. But now, if I go to the hospital and I'm admitted overnight, they cook *nsima* and come and see me. It means that leaving each other behind is diminishing; it's coming to an end.

Edith's own attitude had changed, too, partly as a result of her understanding of the extent of the epidemic. Whereas she used to get very upset about the things people said to her, 'These days I don't worry, because they too are in the same group [they are also HIV-positive]; those people who gossip about me, they are in there too.'

For many, the sense of significant temporal shifts in their experiences was compounded by the transformative effects of ARVs, as Edith explained:

I have faith that I will be alive into the future because of the medicine I am taking, it's helping me ... now, with that medicine, I have strength and I farm without problems. I am able to carry out all of my work without difficulty. Of course, I have other problems, but I try hard to acquire clothes and to dress properly, and to feed my children ... if I were not taking the medicines perhaps I would have died, I could have passed away.

Far from dying, Edith had become 'an example to other people ... [They say:] "What about her, she tested [positive] ages ago, how come she's still alive?"' However, Edith acknowledged that some of her fellow villagers who had also tested HIV-positive chose to keep their status secret. She said she had tried to encourage several women who had confided in her after their diagnoses to be open about their illness, but 'they say, "No, I'll die quickly [if I tell my relatives]," and they just carry on as before even though they are taking ARVs'. Edith was not able to explain how it might come about that these women would die sooner if they were open about their HIV status, but it was clear that she was referring to fears that other people might visit misfortune upon them by nefarious means.[14]

Among my HIV-positive informants, even the most outspoken generally found it necessary to impress upon me that there were various routes (*njira zosiyanasiyana*) by which an individual might become infected,

---

[14] The fact that the advent of effective treatment for HIV, and the concomitant shift in the prospects of the HIV-positive, have altered and are continuing to transform attitudes towards and experiences of HIV/AIDS ought not to be interpreted as the triumph of 'science', or the unmediated expansion of biomedical frameworks for understanding the disease. Instead, it seems clear that biomedical understandings have joined a host of other categories and discourses that together help make sense of the often cruel and mysterious vicissitudes of life and death. For more on connections between HIV and witchcraft, see, for example, Ashforth (2005; 2010), Niehaus (2012), and McNeill and Niehaus (2009). For more on witchcraft in Malawi, see, for example, Englund (1996; 2011: 66–89).

principally through tending wounds and caring for the sick. In this way, much like the relatives of the ailing Zomba villagers whom Peters, Kambewa, and Walker describe carefully avoiding mention of AIDS, HIV-positive women distanced themselves from assumptions of sexual impropriety in order to position themselves 'as fully moral, fully social beings just like any other sick person' (2010: 298). It seems probable that this is related to the gendered landscape of disclosure, in which women are more likely than men to be open about their HIV status. While there is greater acceptance of men's extramarital sexual relationships, it is more difficult for them to allude to the tropes of either the innocent victim of a philandering spouse's irresponsible sexual exploits, or the devoted kins-person, infected through the labour of care.

At the same time that dominant discourses emanating from the media, government, donors, and NGOs generate stigma by emphasising the role of illicit sex in the spread of HIV and elicit concern about the effects of stigma, they leave the concept unexamined and, therefore, stable and lacking in content. By contrast, Chiradzulu women's depictions of *kutsalidwa*, being left behind, are inflected by the texture of pre-existing relationships and feed on ongoing antagonisms. There is also a crucial temporal dimension to their experiences. Their own attitudes and behav-iour have shifted, as have those of their kin and fellow villagers. The role of ARV therapies as a catalyst for such transformations ought not to be underestimated, but Catherine's case cautions against a view of ARVs as a simple cure-all for discrimination against HIV-positive villagers.[15] The particularity of Catherine's experience was seemingly lost on the legal professionals who drew on available understandings of stigma in their efforts to assist her. As her dispute travelled from the village through the police station and into the magistrates' court, Catherine's HIV-positive status was simultaneously a resource that helped her find an audience for her complaints, and a burden that served to obscure other aspects of her troubled relationship with her brother. While Mayeso was prosecuted for his stigmatising behaviour, Catherine was left with a sense that only part of her case had reached the court. The contrast with the ways in which VSU officers approached *nkhanza* in Chapter 5, and the efforts of magis-trates to understand marital disputes in all their moral-material complex-ity (see especially Chapter 4), is notable. The moral opprobrium elicited by stigmatising behaviour foreclosed efforts to understand the relational context in which the dispute had unfolded. By contrast, it was precisely these elements that were the focus of HIV-positive women's own accounts of being left behind.

---

[15] Literature from South Africa contradicts the view that stigma is diminishing in the era of ARVs (McNeill and Niehaus 2009; Niehaus 2009).

In relation to Mayeso, it is possible to argue that the individualistic discourse of stigma served to mask his predicament as a young, unmarried man struggling to survive in a context of high unemployment, widespread poverty, and matrilineal access to agricultural land. Mayeso's desire to sell land held by his matrilineal kin ought not to be overlooked. The sale would have freed up much needed capital, albeit at the expense of longer-term security. However, this was not land that Mayeso had an unquestioned right to dispose of. He could not act without the agreement of his sister and grandmothers. As an alternative to selling, they could perhaps have eased Mayeso's need for cash by allocating land for him to farm, but they were not obliged to do so and few women had much to spare. Available evidence also indicates that claims for matrilineal land made by the brothers of female landholders have tended not to find favour among traditional authorities and magistrates (Peters 2010: 192). Young men intending to farm, either to meet their own subsistence needs or for commercial gain, were expected to access land through marriage or by means of rent paid for in cash. We have come to appreciate the degree to which woeful employment prospects, and the associated difficulty of earning a reliable wage, hinder men's efforts to live up to the expectations of their wives and kin. Similar predicaments face young men across much of the African continent, and beyond. The consequent prolongation of youth has been termed 'waithood' (Dhillon and Yousef 2007; Singerman 2007), to capture the sense in which young men in particular find themselves 'stuck' (Hansen 2005; Sommers 2012) between adolescence and social maturity, unable to amass the social and economic capital necessary to establish themselves as adults through marriage and a regular income (Mains 2012; Masquelier 2013; Ralph 2008).

To recognise the constraints encountered by young men in Malawi and beyond is neither to excuse Mayeso's behaviour nor to see it as in any way inevitable. Nevertheless, it goes some way towards explaining his evident anger and frustration, and highlights the particular tensions that can occur between siblings in matrilineal settings. Any assessment of the work that stigma does to narrow the focus of justice in the magistrate's court would thus be incomplete if it did not also take into account the political and economic context in which Mayeso's possibilities for economic advancement were drastically curtailed, making his frustrated desire to sell land held by his sister comprehensible at the very least.[16]

---

[16] It is possible to suggest that the same neoliberal economic conditions that have been said to favour the transmission of HIV (Chirwa 1999; Hirsch et al. 2009; Marsland and Prince 2012) also have an impact on the behaviour of those to whom HIV-positive people might be expected to turn for support.

The magistrate's quick resort to the concept of stigma thus obscured both the wider political and economic background and the particular relational context in which the dispute unfolded. Nevertheless, by expressing disappointment that the offence had occurred between siblings he signalled widely shared expectations that brothers should 'protect' their sisters. A more sustained focus on the relationship between Catherine and Mayeso might have offered further insight into their successes and failures in fulfilling expectations for moral-material reciprocity. Mayeso, as Catherine's brother and maternal uncle to her son, had certain obligations to support her household; in turn, Catherine had obligations to him as custodian of lineage land. The fulfilment of mutual obligations between cross-sex siblings is not the same as the daily achievement of complementarity striven for by cohabiting spouses, but it is another locally acknowledged form of mutual, and gendered, interdependence, and a further yardstick for the measurement of moral personhood and just behaviour.

Tentative hope in a matrilineal setting

Matrilineality and matrilocality profoundly shape the experiences of HIV-positive women in Chiradzulu, as they also affected Mayeso's fortunes. As we have seen, for many, the experience of being left behind has been most keenly felt within their home compounds, at the heart of the matrilineal family (cf. Peters, Walker, and Kambewa 2008: 668). But in the era of ARVs, it is largely through their achievements as farmers, working land they have acquired through matrilineal inheritance in order to feed and provide for themselves and their children, that they are able to reconstitute themselves as confident members of their village communities. Alongside their attempts to unsettle associations between HIV and illicit sex, their invocations of agricultural labour and care for their children can be understood as efforts to demonstrate their moral worth as productive participants in local social and economic processes. Active involvement in agricultural production marks a radical break with their past experiences of AIDS, and their re-establishment as able subsistence farmers sows the seeds of hope, as it were, for the future. The centrality of agriculture to rural sociality (Englund 1999), as well as to survival, further underlines what was at stake for Catherine in her dispute with Mayeso over the sale of her garden.

Unlike Catherine, many of the HIV-positive women I got to know well were not currently married – a situation that, as we have seen, is not uncommon in this part of Malawi (Kaler 2001; and see Chapters 1 and 4).[17]

---

[17] Kaler cites a comparative study that found that women in Chiradzulu 'were not only more likely than women in other regions [of Malawi] to be currently divorced but were

Single women (often divorced or widowed), living separately from the fathers of their children (in female-headed households), constitute a significant minority of households in these villages. They are recognised as legitimate custodians of the gardens they farm and their circumstances are deemed thoroughly unremarkable. The situation in southern Malawi cannot be taken as representative of the country as a whole, just as it is not representative of Africa as a whole. It offers a stark contrast to south-eastern Nigeria, for example, 'where being (and staying) married remains a reputational requirement' (Smith 2009: 178).[18] Understanding the efforts of women in Chiradzulu to live well with HIV, and to contemplate the future, thus requires attending to the texture of their lives as relatively independent subsistence farmers in a matrilineal setting.

In her late forties at the time of my fieldwork, Lucy was twice divorced with one adult daughter and two young grandchildren. She had left her HIV-positive second husband in 2006 when she became ill with an opportunistic infection and he failed to take care of her. Lucy's description of her daily routine as a single woman was characterised by the celebration of 'freedom' (ufulu):

I can set off from here, maybe I'll go to the garden, I can work from maybe seven o'clock [am], maybe six, until ten or eleven, then I knock off maybe at eleven or twelve. If I knock off at twelve, I'll come back here. I won't even think to myself that at home I have a husband. No, when I come here maybe I'll sit like I'm sitting now, maybe I'll go and fetch some water and bring it here. I'll cook my relish, I'll cook nsima and I'll eat. And I go around freely, without anything to trouble me.

Like most villagers, Lucy farmed to feed herself and strove to produce surplus maize and vegetables to generate a small cash income. During the dry season (May – September), she also hired casual workers (ganyu) to mould bricks on her land, which she sold. She hoped eventually to use the revenue to build herself a new house and to roof it with iron sheets, something she had once expected a husband to do for her. Lucy's ambition was to build a house that would remain after her own passing, which her grandchildren would be able to point to with pride and say: 'This is the house my grandmother built.'

Lucy made a direct connection between her ability to farm for herself, to feed herself and produce a surplus, and her decision to remain single, and she evaluated that decision in relation to her health:

---

also less likely to remarry after divorce and, among those who did remarry, more likely to divorce a second time' (2001: 530; referring to Zulu 1996).

[18] See also Frank (2009) on the precarious position of young urban widows in Zambia; Whyte's (2005) depictions of the ambiguities of women's belonging in patrilineal eastern Uganda; and Dilger's work (2008; 2010) in a patrilineal area of rural Tanzania.

I've made the decision myself. I've chosen to be single. I'll see what I can achieve in two or three years by myself. Yes, I'll see what I can do; will I still be the way I was when I was married? I'll compare the way I was then and the way I am now. Will I change or won't I? Then, if I see that I've changed, I won't marry. That'll be it, I'll just remain single … At the moment, I think I've changed.

At other points in our conversations she was more equivocal, expressing a tacit recognition of the sexual advantages of marriage:

I can say that I will marry because, what, can I say that I am elderly? I haven't aged! [laughs] I haven't aged, I'll accept [a proposal], but I'll be very vigilant [*kuyang'anitsa*], asking myself will this help me?

The strategy of remaining single for a number of years before remarrying was not new to Lucy, and nor was it specific to her life with HIV. After ending her marriage to her first husband because 'he was cruel to me – I realised that his behaviour was not helping me', she was single for four or five years before marrying her second husband. As we have seen in the preceding chapters, other divorced or widowed women, HIV-positive or not, sometimes also asserted that they were single by preference and that they may or may not marry again, depending on their assessment of their situation and the suitability of available partners. While single HIV-negative women tended to argue that they were getting by alright alone, with their gardens and livestock, and that pregnancy would limit their ability to provide for the children they already had, other HIV-positive women offered similar reasoning to that of Lucy: their health was more secure while they were unmarried and in full command of their medication, diet, workload, and sexuality. As one woman succinctly put it: 'If I marry, I'll die sooner' (*ndikakwa-tibwa, ndifa mwamsanga*).[19] Another did not rule out remarriage, but was adamant that she could only marry an HIV-positive man: 'As far as I'm concerned, I can't take a man who hasn't tested [positive]. How am I supposed to take my medicine? How can I sleep with him? It's problematic.'[20]

Reflecting on the relatively high rates of divorce and remarriage in matrilineal southern Malawi, which she sees as indicative of 'bad marriages and bad behavior', Amy Kaler concludes that we should 'define

---

[19] In this case, unlike a previous example above, I do not believe the reference to hastened death implies nefarious forces.

[20] Rhine argues that HIV support groups in Nigeria are 'appropriated' by single women 'to facilitate their marriage arrangements' (2009: 370). This was not the case with the local support group I observed, since the two men who attended with any regularity were both married to non-members. As in the Tanzanian case described by Beckmann and Bujra, this support group posed little challenge to authority. Rather, it fed into 'compliance with state and donor agendas' (2010: 1052; see also Marsland 2012).

marriage and heterosexuality as permanently beleaguered, shaky institutions' (2001: 547). However, in the light of all that we have learned
about aspirations for gender justice in matrilineal Malawi, we might
understand somewhat differently the agency these women practised as
they contemplated marriage, initiated divorce, assessed their partners, or
lived independently with their children among their matrilineal kin.
Drawing on long-standing 'traditional' strategies, HIV-positive women
were being vigilant (*kuyang'anitsa*), taking stock of the fact that, with the
help of ARV medication, they were not dying, their bodies were strong,
and they faced new challenges – a situation that had been unimaginable
just five years earlier. The question for these women was how best to live
as HIV-positive women, villagers, wives, and mothers. Their responses
were profoundly shaped by the matrilineal setting, not least by the social
acceptability of female-headed households, the relative independence
afforded by land ownership, and their perceptions of whether a husband
was likely to be a blessing or a burden.

In this context, *kuyang'anitsa*, being vigilant, was a future-oriented
activity that captured well the sense of cautious hope expressed by
HIV-positive women in Chiradzulu. It was best illustrated by an
unmarried woman who described how she had felt the day she brought
her ARVs home for the first time. Terrified, she sat on the edge of her
bed, tossing the tablets up and down gently in her hands. She was
afraid of the effects the pills might have on her body: would her illness
begin to show on her skin? That night she took the medicine as
instructed and the next morning she inspected her skin for signs of
change. She repeated this routine every day for several months before
eventually allowing herself to relax. But, she explained, she would
continue to monitor herself for another three years. If she was still
healthy then, she said, she would try for a child. Although she was
bringing up her late sisters' children, 'It's not the same as having your
own child,' she explained.

While HIV-positive Malawians, their kin, friends, and neighbours
faced new challenges in their efforts to navigate life with HIV, magistrates
and police officers strove to deliver justice in novel situations shaped by
the epidemic. In so doing, they tapped into prevailing discourses about
stigma in order to combat prejudice against HIV-positive citizens. HIV-
positive women, on the other hand, spoke an alternative language, which
more clearly articulated their inevitable immersion in social life. The
vigilance that HIV-positive women in Chiradzulu employed in relation
to sexual and marital relationships was emphatically not a rejection of
sociality, atrophied through stigma. Rather, it was a creative, hopeful
approach to re-establishing themselves in their core relational roles as
mothers, grandmothers, and productive members of their extended
matrilineal families. If being left behind by intimate others is the epitome

of stigma, hope centred on new possibilities for belonging surely constitutes its most profound reversal.[21]

Conclusion: the temporality of justice and hope

With HIV no longer the death sentence it was just a few years ago, police
officers and magistrates find themselves dealing more often with disputes
that touch upon the disease. As they seek to deliver justice in these cases,
they tend to reach for dominant understandings of stigma. In so doing,
however, they import a particular conceptual baggage: principally a
tendency towards depoliticised and ahistorical understandings of HIV,
and a narrow focus on stigmatising behaviour that forecloses investigation of the disputes' broader moral-material and relational contexts and
implications. By contrast, the experience of being left behind is intimately intertwined with personal histories, complex relationships, and
ongoing antagonisms. Moreover, in southern Malawi, matrilineal modes
of land inheritance, and the acceptability of female-headed households,
profoundly shape gender relations and have a strong bearing on the
opportunities available to HIV-positive women as they set about the tasks
of providing for their children and re-establishing themselves as 'fully
moral, fully social beings' (Peters, Kambewa, and Walker 2010: 298). At
the same time, matrilineal norms also affect the lives of their kin and
fellow villagers. Thus, Mayeso's inability to access land, combined with
almost non-existent opportunities for formal employment, likely played a
significant role in his dispute with his sister.

The police officers and magistrate who dealt with Catherine's complaint reached for stigma as a moral category that made possible the
condemnation of Mayeso's behaviour. In so doing, they demonstrated
how new moral and legal challenges can be taken up by those seeking to
administer justice; how they adapt the tools of law, and the goals of
justice and morality, in response to new situations and shifting social
mores. Their efforts to respond to the novel predicaments faced by
Malawian citizens are indicative of the prospective orientation of justice,
and thus its phenomenological proximity to hope. Hope and justice share
a future-oriented temporal horizon; they operate on the same experiential
terrain. Catherine and her grandmother hoped that Mayeso could be

---

[21] Unfortunately, there are very real caveats to this hopeful picture, not least accounts of the
uneven realisation of ARVs' potential to transform HIV into a chronic condition (Biehl
2007; McNeill and Niehaus 2009; Nguyen 2010). Hunger, too, must give us pause.
Poor harvests and a shortage of food would affect those taking ARVs disproportionately
(Kalofonos 2010; Prince 2012). What is more, fears are increasing about the dangers of
drug-resistant strains of HIV. Most worrying of all, financing for HIV programmes is
contingent on donor priorities and serious concerns have been raised about 'donor
retreat' (MSF 2010).

reformed, that he might learn 'how to live with people'; police officers and magistrates hoped to deal with the injustice of stigmatisation and to discourage future instances; Lucy and Edith hoped to continue living well as HIV-positive members of their families and communities; while my friend hoped that one day she might give birth to a healthy child. If justice and hope are both future-oriented, they are also both, of necessity, unfinished: they aim towards an end that has yet to be realised. As we saw above, despite the best efforts of those who sought to assist her, Catherine was not entirely happy with the way in which her case had been handled, feeling that much of the substance of her complaint had fallen by the wayside. While the pursuit of justice by disputants, magistrates, and police officers maintains hopeful forward momentum, the delivery of justice necessarily stops in the present. Seeking justice is an anticipatory activity, and hope is its essential companion; but those charged with its administration are freighted with the requirement to deliver the final word. In Derrida's terms, in striving to deliver justice they inevitably foreclose its essential '*à venir*' quality (1990: 969) [yet to come].

Conclusion

> All women live in a patriarchal world. All women function within an environment that is patriarchal. It is unavoidable, like the air ... [Patriarchy] is an entire world-view, with a million implications and effects, which has structured reality since the prehistory of human existence without any serious objection, challenge, or change until the second half of the twentieth century ... Patriarchy is the systematic subordination of women to men, and this is the experience that all women share. (Smith 2010: 294)

Reading this entry in a recent companion to legal philosophy, I was struck by the apparent disjuncture between Euro-American feminist jurisprudence and decades of work in anthropology that challenges the universality of the assumption of woman as the 'second sex' – downtrodden, subordinated, and abused. To argue that the former vision fails to illuminate particular lives and ways of life is not to deny that some women do indeed occupy miserable positions. Rather, it is to insist upon the need to base understandings, and interventions, on a sound grasp of local realities and a recognition that there is no good reason why those realities ought to match models of gender hierarchy, oppression, and female disempowerment that themselves originate in particular historical contexts (Moore 1988; Rupp 2008). Nor should Euro-American feminists expect the aspirations of women everywhere to fit easily with the goal of formal equality, irrespective of the level of our commitment to this ideal in our own lives (Mahmood 2005: 38).

Much feminist theorising is a great deal more sophisticated than the excerpt cited above. Nevertheless, Marilyn Strathern has perceptively interpreted the relationship between anthropology and feminism as 'awkward', akin to that between neighbours 'whose similarities provoke mutual mockery' (1987: 277). In part, Strathern suggests, this is due to the divergent ethical commitments of feminist scholars and anthropologists to their particular 'others' – men and their informants, respectively. While for feminists, the other is a source of oppression to be overcome, anthropologists strive to establish empathetic relations with, and preserve the 'separate dignity' (ibid.: 290) of, those with whom they work.[1] Anthropology and feminism are not, Strathern argues, competing 'paradigms' that meet as equivalent projects and might succeed one another on the Kuhnian model of 'paradigm shifts' in the natural sciences (Kuhn 1970). Instead, as perennial 'neighbours', their proximity is inevitable, if not always comfortable.

I have grappled with this awkwardness during the course of this research as I presented draft chapters at workshops and conferences. It has tended to be among feminist scholars that my work has received the most uneasy reception, particularly among those whose personal commitment to the feminist cause has involved direct participation in women's activist movements in Europe or North America. It is thus necessary to be absolutely clear that in discussing contemporary gender complementarity and suggesting that it is central to Malawian conceptions of gender justice, I do not mean to imply a universal blueprint, or manifesto, for gender relations. However, I believe it is worth asking what advocacy might look like were it to make room for the perspectives of those whom it seeks to uplift. I thus take seriously the challenge articulated by Saba Mahmood in a very different ethnographic context: that if 'a commitment to the ideal of equality in our own lives' does not 'endow us with the capacity to know that this ideal captures what is or should be fulfilled for everyone else', then 'we need to rethink, with far more humility than we are accustomed to, what feminist politics really means' (Mahmood 2005: 38).

This is not to deny the efforts of feminist theorists to address the unspoken androcentric bias in liberal theory. Although work in this vein is often highly sophisticated and relevant to anthropology, such contributions have rarely entered into mainstream anthropological debates. Nancy Hirschmann (1992; 2003), for example, has focused her critical feminist lens on concepts of freedom, autonomy, equality, and obligations, and the thrust of her theoretical ambition pushes the conversation in a similar direction to the ethnographic argument developed within the pages of this book. In a sense, my project takes up a task proposed by Hirschmann when she argues against standard liberal conceptions of equality and freedom as goals for feminist politics. Hirschmann makes a strong case for ethnographic intervention:

The conception of equality necessary to a feminist vision of freedom must pay attention to the concrete specificities of difference in particular times, cultures,

---

[1] In commenting on Strathern's intervention, Abu-Lughod provides an important reminder that we should not romanticise relationships between anthropologists and their informants, which are invariably unequal (2006 [1991]). See also Moore (1988) for further reflection on the relationship between feminism and anthropology, and see Bennett (2006) for a view from the discipline of history.

and social formations ... Conceiving equality through difference requires considering the material conditions of women's lives in various cultures and classes, the labor that they do, the conditions of power in which they do it; seeing what actually is rather than extrapolating grand theories of human nature from narrow culture- and time-specific samples. Obviously such seeing is never objective, as it occurs through interpretive discursive processes. But a commitment to equality demands that these processes include the perceptions and understandings of participants as well as observers and formulates its picture out of a diversity of voices and experiences ... Only by gaining more complete pictures can we develop and achieve a genuine equality that addresses the lived experiences of different people. (Hirschmann 2003: 224)

Such interventions suggest the potential for productive conversations across disciplinary boundaries between feminist scholars willing to suspend dominant liberal understandings of personhood, agency, and desire.

Of course, Euro-American scholars do not have a monopoly on feminist theorising, and, like anthropologists, African feminists have not always found their 'Western' counterparts the most congenial of neighbours. Drawing on the work of such scholars as Ifi Amadiume (1987; 1997), Oyèrónké Oyěwùmí (1997; 2002), and Sylvia Tamale (2005; 2008), Arnfred observes that motherhood remains a significant 'blank spot' in so-called 'global' feminist thinking, as evinced by the fact that in such documents as the Beijing Platform for Action 'the vision of gender equality has not moved very far from Simone de Beauvoir's visions of "wage work and contraception", i.e. feminine futures on male terrain' (2011: 119). Thus, Nkiru Uwechia Nzegwu has pointed to a peculiar 'convergence of interests' between certain African men and Western feminists that lies in the assumption of male dominance:

Both are engaged in the enterprise of casting their patriarchal view of families as traditional and culturally rooted. Both share the task of representing African women as voiceless and inferior to men. Both have successfully established as true the myth that African women lack agency. (Nzegwu 2006: 18)

The hope expressed in this book is that empirical studies and theoretical works that draw '[i]nspiration and conceptual imagination' (Arnfred 2011: 119) from Africa, and from African women in particular, may offer a means of moving beyond tired tropes of equality as sameness. Indeed, ethnographic engagement in Malawi suggests that, wherever they may be based, feminists would do well to consider the significance of complementarity in gender relations. Complementarity rests on the differentiation of men and women in their relations with one another, insisting on their mutual interdependence. As a concept, it places relationality at the centre of analysis. Thus, without advocating a particular gendered division of labour, I suggest that complementarity and interdependence are values worthy of feminist enquiry and better suited to cross-cultural theorising than individualist notions of 'freedom' and 'equality'. The notion of complementarity foregrounded here is derived from ethnographic analysis of gender relations in matrilineal Malawi, and this study offers an insight into structures of matriliny that have been too readily dismissed by anthropologists and others eager to see patriarchy at every turn.

Matriliny matters

For writers who take as a point of departure the universal denigration of women and femininity, a view of matriliny as little more than an alternative configuration of male authority – one in which uncles reign as opposed to husbands and fathers – promises to expose notions of female authority as 'myths'. They are often aided by the work of celebrated anthropologists, principal among them Claude Lévi-Strauss (1969).[2] This book stands in opposition to traditional anthropological orthodoxy in this regard. Instead, I agree with those such as Peters and Arnfred who insist on the important differences that matrilineal practices can make to gender relations in South-Central Africa's 'matrilineal belt', differences that have tended to be ignored, dismissed, or overlooked by formal authorities, be they colonial officials, post-independence government agencies, or international development organisations.

Indeed, there is little doubt that interventions in Malawi, from Christian mission activity and colonial governance to contemporary development programmes, have favoured men as household heads, master farmers (Kalinga 1993), and traditional authorities. Yet the resilience of the matrilineal extended family, the persistence of uxorilocal marriage and inheritance through the female line, and the ongoing respect for (and responsibilities of) maternal uncles all profoundly shaped the lives of villagers in southern Malawi at the time of my fieldwork. This was clearly demonstrated in Chapter 6, for example, where we saw how matrilineal modes of land inheritance and the acceptability of female-headed households inflected the opportunities available to HIV-positive women as they regained their strength and set about the tasks of providing for their children and re-establishing themselves as capable and responsible members of society in the wake of the roll-out of antiretroviral therapies.

A historical perspective cautions that the fortunes of matriliny are ever changing (Mandala 1990; Phiri 1983; White 1987). It is thus important to bear in mind that the research for this project coincided with good harvests, largely favourable rains, and an agricultural subsidy

---

[2] For an influential feminist critique of Lévi-Strauss's focus on kinship as the exchange of women between men, see Rubin (2006 [1975]).

programme, alongside the declining significance of male-dominated sources of cash income, ARV provision, and prominent talk of human and women's rights. These circumstances may well have favoured the institutions of matriliny, and they certainly affected the ways in which men and women considered their options and opportunities in relation to one another. Moreover, they underline the fact that their rural village location provided Chiradzulu residents with little shelter from the conditions of twenty-first-century life. This was evident, for example, in the advice given to young girls during initiation ceremonies, during which the dangers of HIV and the demands of the neoliberal economy informed the essential message that girls should focus on their education (see Chapter 1). In the context of 'traditional' rites, elder women voiced widely shared aspirations for young girls' future lives that centred on economic and marital security. The ways in which they harnessed customary institutions in order to do this conveyed a powerful argument against a view of 'culture' as somehow in opposition to 'rights' and inimical to women's 'empowerment' (Johnson 2018a; cf. Bennesch 2011; Ribohn 2002).

The material presented here suggests that matriliny, as lived in contemporary Malawi, has much to recommend it as a way of life that fosters a 'greater degree of authority and independence' for women (Peters 1997b: 130). In the context of a book that has deployed concepts such as interdependence and complementarity, the term 'independence' may seem out of place. Nevertheless, we have seen the extent to which women in this matrilineal setting may choose independence from marriage at certain stages of their lives, eschewing conjugal dependence – their own or that of a wayward spouse – while remaining ensconced within webs of relationships with their matrilineal kin. The appearance of independence or self-sufficiency at the household level is a powerful means through which such relationships, and the obligations they entail, may be enacted and fulfilled. This ought to be borne in mind by those who aim to 'empower' Malawian women through generic development schemes, drawing women into the informal economy and away from the fields and granaries over which their control is unquestioned. Recognition of the significance of matrilineal practices for social life in the region would entail rethinking certain assumptions that guide governmental and non-governmental policies in the light of more sophisticated understandings of the life worlds of rural citizens.

This book has asked what gender justice might look like in matrilineal areas of Malawi, engaging with gendered dispute-resolution processes in order to understand how men and women address perceived injustice in the course of their relationships with one another. Focusing on legal forums and disputes has highlighted the broad range of legal resources available in postcolonial Africa and the potential flexibility they provide.

This perspective brings my analysis into conflict with dominant ways of thinking about gender in relation to law.

Towards an anthropology of gender justice

More nuanced feminist legal and political-philosophical scholarship not-withstanding, feminist jurisprudence tends to conceive of law as an androcentric force, 'a paradigm of maleness' (Rifkin 1980: 84), which, behind a cloak of neutrality, safeguards and promotes a masculine privil-ege that is associated with violence and oppression. In the words of Catharine MacKinnon: 'In the liberal state, the rule of law – neutral, abstract, elevated, pervasive – both institutionalizes the power of men over women and institutionalizes power in its male form' (1989: 238; cited in Brown 1995: 129). This view is also echoed in Africanist histori-ography, which posits that, although recourse to the law provided a brief refuge for women in the early colonial period, it was not long before the combined interests of male elders and colonial officials served to redefine 'custom' within more hostile legal regimes (Chanock 1985; Mbilinyi 1988; McClendon 1995; Schmidt 1990; cf. Shadle 1999; 2003). Indeed, women's exclusion from legal arenas, and their inequitable access to legal representation and legal knowledge, is a widespread and serious issue, and not just in Euro-American or international legal forums (see, e.g., Griffiths 2001). From this perspective, feminist scholars seeking to study moral or ethical practice might see greater potential in domains such as 'care', as opposed to 'law' or 'justice'. However, the assumption of universal female disadvantage before the law is questioned by the eth-nography presented in this book. 'Law' in this context is a highly flexible and multifaceted instrument that by no means systematically buttresses male interests. Therefore, in contrast to the Comaroffs' understanding of 'the postcolony' as characterised by 'lawfare' or 'the deployment of legalities to do violence to peoples and their property by indirect means' (Comaroff and Comaroff 2004: 540), this study also suggests the need for caution with respect to the idea that violence necessarily inheres in the law.

Furthermore, we have seen that law and justice are not always as distinct in the vagaries of practice as they may be conceived in philosoph-ical treatises. One of the most striking features of the dispute-resolution cases cited in this book was the fluid multiplicity of legal resources available to formal and traditional authorities as they sought to adminis-ter justice (see especially Chapter 3). State law, constitutional human rights, custom, and morality could all be drawn on in the resolution of a single case, and that flexibility, particularly in relation to customary law, was openly acknowledged. Following Gluckman (1965; 1973 [1955]), I have emphasised the importance of this elasticity for the administration of justice. If, as I have argued (see Chapter 5), manipulations of the Derridean 'law-ness' of 'law' evince conscious efforts to approximate 'justice', the latter's motivational force can also be seen to require considerable ambiguity. As we saw in Chapter 6, however, formal legal judgments of the kind delivered by magistrates sever, at least temporarily, the prospective, hopeful momentum that justice maintains when it is a goal rather than a decision. In these moments, the distinctions between law and justice are more clearly drawn.

The term 'justice', like 'complementarity' or 'equality', is often employed in scholarly writing without reflection, its meaning assumed to be widely shared and understood. Yet, when the question posed asks what might constitute 'just' behaviour or a 'just' decision in a given scenario, the concept's obliqueness becomes apparent. Justice is a challenge, a goal, an ideal, something to which people aspire, for which they strive, argue, and compete. Gender justice is inevitably relational as well as situational, and its particular configurations cannot be known in advance. In the Malawian context, I have argued that a particularly salient ideal of gender justice takes the form of complementarity, where the corollary of complementarity is not equality but interdependence, and the achievement of complementarity is never guaranteed (see especially Chapter 4). As we have seen, love and care are imbricated in this formulation of justice, rather than constituting an alternative source of insight.

'Material morality' (Englund 2008) has been central to the ways in which I have interpreted the ideal complementarity of gender relations in this context. Crucially, material morality entails individuation of the contributions of husbands and wives to household reproduction in order to make visible the existential obligations that characterise relationships of mutual dependence. Complementarity in this sense is both structural and affective, and is based on reciprocal acknowledgement or recognition: it cannot be taken for granted and is often contested. Expectations for gender relations and gender roles are variable, and discourses of *jenda* and women's rights constitute an additional language and a fresh yardstick against which to evaluate situations and aspirations. Indeed, ambivalence characterised the tone of many of my conversations about gender relations with villagers and legal professionals, augmenting the message that gender justice is pursued within particular relationships and is not simply a function of gendered identities. These conversations also reinforced the idea that complementarity does not imply particular content or specified roles; it must always be pursued and contested in practice.

The second-grade magistrate cited in Chapter 5 at times expressed himself in ways that echoed ideals of material morality and gender complementarity, for example when he spoke of the interdependence of

husbands and wives and the effects that the behaviour of each can have
on the other. At other times, however, his reflections conveyed ambiguity
and illustrated the wide scope for contestation with respect to gender
relations. In discussions with me, he revealed considerable misgivings
about 'traditional' gender roles and the contemporary *jenda* agenda:

When you grow up in the villages, people are perceived to have different roles
maybe because of the socialisation process. It is expected that a man will do this
and that and his wife is supposed to do this and that ... When they don't conduct
themselves as expected that is reason enough [for divorce]. As a husband, my wife
is supposed to wash my clothes, cook for me, be polite, respect my parents. It is
always the wife who is somehow on the receiving end ... These days there is
jenda, but it is difficult in the villages to expect a man to wash his wife's clothes
and you cannot think of a man cooking food for a wife unless she is rich;
otherwise it is always the woman cooking for the family. They go to the garden
together in the morning; they come back, the woman carrying a huge pile of
firewood, with a child on her back. And when they get home, the man expects his
wife to cook, and then fetch water for his bath. She only rests when she goes to
sleep and, if she's unfortunate, the man will demand sex the whole night and she
has no time to rest. Women have a lot to do if they are to survive in a family.
Maybe there is a need to change mindsets ... Even in town, you can't expect a
man to cook for the family, unless he's been exposed, maybe at school, and
understood gender issues. If your parents come to your house and find you
cooking and your wife watching TV, they'll cry and ask, '*Chifukwa?*' ['Why?']
They'll think you've had love potion to make you cook for the family – it is not
expected!

The magistrate's words illustrate the extent to which *jenda*, as introduced
by civic educators and NGOs, is understood in relation to gender roles
and is seen as challenging conventional divisions of household labour.
The contrast between this statement and the advice he gave disputants in
his court (see Chapter 5) is also indicative of the level of ambivalence
that surrounds ideas about gender relations in contemporary Malawi.
Through the course of this book, we have come to appreciate the significance of the material aspects of marital relationships, but we have also
witnessed equivocal views about appropriate behaviour with regard to
family provisioning. In Chapter 4, we heard the male first-grade magistrate denigrate a woman who had started conducting business buying
and selling maize and had, the magistrate felt, come to consider her
husband a burden. In another judgment, however, the same magistrate
condemned a wife for not making a more direct material contribution to
her household:

She says she is a local farmer but she doesn't do business; her survival depends on
her husband's wages ... The purpose of being married is not just to bear children
and wait for a husband to do everything else. Every married woman needs to do
something to help the home – business, farming, office work – being lazy is not a
good thing in these economic situations; it does not promote family development.

It is to such ambivalence that I refer when I argue that complementarity is a source of contestation. Gender roles are never so rigidly delineated as to negate negotiation or rule out the possibility of conflict. In practice, in the to and fro of daily lives, it is in their success and failure in achieving complementarity that women and men in rural southern Malawi come to know justice.

A view of justice as an ideal is not devoid of political potential; it might, perhaps, serve as a foundation for feminist critique, despite the seeming incompatibility between the notion of 'complementarity' and mainstream feminist sensibilities. This potential is suggested by Wendy Brown's argument that it is when rights are approached as 'empty signifiers without corresponding entitlements' that 'they function to encourage possibility' (1995: 134). According to this perspective, 'the political potency of rights lies not in their concreteness ... but in their idealism' (ibid.). In Chapter 6, I critiqued the use of the concept of stigma on similar grounds, arguing against its utility precisely because it remained content-less. An analytical concept of justice as widely shared because it is loosely defined and relatively empty of specific content might be subjected to a similar critique. But this is a concept derived from ethnographic attention to the ways in which justice animates disputes, and it is offered not as a universal instrument for analysis but as a stimulus to further questioning. Like rights in Brown's formulation, if justice is an ideal, its contours must always be discovered anew.

Articulating a generalisable feminist theory or politics has not been my concern in this book. I have nevertheless found support for ethnographic exploration in the work of critical feminist scholars, not least in Hirschmann's invocation of the need to 'pay attention to the concrete specificities of difference' (2003: 224). As Strathern makes clear, the awkwardness of the relationship between feminism and anthropology is unlikely to be overcome. 'The tension must be kept going,' she states, 'there can be no relief in substituting the one for the other' (1987: 286). This book cannot pretend to resolve the differences between these intellectual neighbours, but it is my hope that the ongoing negotiations between them, to which it contributes, may be productive in another sense; not, perhaps, by bringing about a reconciliation, but by stimulating dialogue across difference in the best tradition of both.

Shifting the focus from rights to justice, as I have done in this book, enables us to fold ideas about morality, the good life, relational personhood, and complementary gender roles into understandings of gender relations and gendered disputes. In making this analytical move, and in drawing together in a single study a broad range of themes that are often considered to pertain to distinct domains of anthropological analysis, despite their stubborn interrelatedness in social life – including gender, law, kinship, and morality – it has been my intention to demonstrate the fecundity of the category of 'gender justice'. In the process, I hope that I have also produced a sense of possible alternatives to the dominant paradigms of human rights and gender equality.

Bibliography

Abu-Lughod, L. (1990) 'The romance of resistance: tracing transformations of power through Bedouin women', *American Ethnologist* 17 (1): 41–55.

(2006 [1991]) 'Writing against culture' in E. Lewin (ed.), *Feminist Anthropology: a reader*. Oxford: Blackwell.

Allen, L. (2013) *The Rise and Fall of Human Rights: cynicism and politics in occupied Palestine*. Stanford CA: Stanford University Press.

Allman, J. and V. Tashjian (2000) *'I Will Not Eat Stone': a women's history of colonial Asante*. Oxford: James Currey.

Amadiume, I. (1987) *Male Daughters, Female Husbands*. London: Zed Books.

(1997) *Reinventing Africa: matriarchy, religion and culture*. London: Zed Books.

Anders, G. and O. Zenker (2014) 'Transition and justice: an introduction', *Development and Change* 45 (3): 395–414.

Anderson, P. (2011) '"The piety of the gift": selfhood and sociality in the Egyptian Mosque Movement', *Anthropological Theory* 11 (1): 3–21.

Andersson, J. A. (2006) 'Informal moves, informal markets: international migrants and traders from Mzimba District, Malawi', *African Affairs* 105 (420): 375–97.

(2012) 'Southern African migration from the periphery: Malawians to South Africa in numbers and cultures'. Conference paper presented at the Cadbury Workshop 'South Africa: Retrospection, Introspection, Extraversion', Centre of West African Studies, University of Birmingham, 18–19 May.

Apter, A. (2012) 'Matrilineal motives: kinship, witchcraft, and repatriation among Congolese refugees', *Journal of the Royal Anthropological Institute* 18 (1): 22–44.

Archambault, C. S. (2010) 'Women left behind? Migration, spousal separation, and the autonomy of rural women in Ugweno, Tanzania', *Signs* 35 (4): 919–42.

Arnfred, S. (2011) *Sexuality and Gender Politics in Mozambique: rethinking gender in Africa*. Woodbridge: James Currey.

Ashforth, A. (2005) *Witchcraft, Violence, and Democracy in South Africa*. London: University of Chicago Press.

(2010) 'Spiritual insecurity and AIDS in South Africa' in H. Dilger and U. Luig (eds), *Morality, Hope and Grief: anthropologies of AIDS in Africa*. Oxford: Berghahn Books.

Avert (2011) 'HIV and AIDS in Malawi', Avert <www.avert.org/aids-malawi.htm>, accessed 11 January 2011.

Baker, B. (2008) *Multi-choice Policing in Africa*. Uppsala: Nordiska Afrikainstitutet.

Banda, C. C. (2008) 'Gendered patterns of Malawian contemporary migrancy: the case of Zubayumo Makamo area in Mzimba District, 1970s–2005'. MA thesis, Chancellor College, University of Malawi.

Banda, G. C. (2011) 'Local courts: can they be abused by the state?', *Malawi Voice*, 20 April <www.malawivoice.com/politics/local-courts-can-they-be-abused-by-the-state/>, accessed 17 June 2011.

Barber, G. (2001) '"It's only natural!" The views of villagers from Chiradzulu District, southern Malawi on matrilineal inheritance and matrilocal residence' in J. McCracken, T. J. Lovering, and F. J. Chalamanda (eds), *Twentieth Century Malawi: perspectives on history and culture*. Occasional Paper 7. Stirling: Centre of Commonwealth Studies, University of Stirling.

BBC (2009) 'Malawi "gay wedding" couple deny indecency charges', BBC News, 30 December <http://news.bbc.co.uk/1/hi/world/africa/8434743.stm>, accessed 11 January 2011.

Bearak, B. (2010) 'Malawi president pardons gay couple', *New York Times*, 29 May.

Beckmann, N. and J. Bujra (2010) 'The "politics of the queue": the politicization of people living with HIV/AIDS in Tanzania', *Development and Change* 41 (6): 1041–64.

Benda-Beckmann, F. von (2007 [1970]) *Legal Pluralism in Malawi: historical development 1858–1970 and emerging issues*. Zomba, Malawi: Kachere Series.

Benda-Beckmann, K. von (1981) 'Forum shopping and shopping forums: dispute processing in a Minangkabau village in West Sumatra', *Journal of Legal Pluralism* 19: 117–59.

Bennesch, N. H. (2011) 'Unequal partners: sex, money, power, and HIV/AIDS in southern Malawian relationships'. PhD thesis, Boston University.

Bennett, J. M. (2006) *History Matters: patriarchy and the challenge of feminism*. Philadelphia PA: University of Pennsylvania Press.

Biehl, J. (2006) 'Pharmaceutical governance' in A. Petryna, A. Lakoff, and A. Kleinman (eds), *Global Pharmaceuticals: ethics, markets, practices*. Durham NC: Duke University Press.

(2007) *Will to Live: AIDS therapies and the politics of survival*. Princeton NJ: Princeton University Press.

Biruk, C. (2014) '"Aid for gays": the moral and the material in "African homophobia" in post-2009 Malawi', *Journal of Modern African Studies* 52 (3): 447–73.

Boddy, J. (2007) 'Clash of selves: gender, personhood, and human rights discourse in colonial Sudan', *Canadian Journal of African Studies* 41 (3): 402–26.

Boeder, R. (1974) 'The history of labour emigration from Malawi to its neighbours, 1890 to the present'. PhD thesis, Michigan State University.

Bohannan, P. (1957) *Justice and Judgment among the Tiv*. London: Oxford University Press.

Bombeya, S. (2000) 'Asawapatse belo – Muluzi', *Tamvani: Gawo La Chichewa La Weekend Nation*, 29–30 April.

Brantley, C. (1997) 'Through Ngoni eyes: Margaret Read's matrilineal interpretations from Nyasaland', *Critique of Anthropology* 17 (2): 147–69.

Brogden, M. (2004) 'Community policing: a panacea from the West', *African Affairs* 103 (413): 635–49.

Brown, W. (1995) *States of Injury: power and freedom in late modernity.* Princeton NJ: Princeton University Press.

Bruwer, J. P. (1955) 'Unkhoswe: the system of guardianship in Chewa matrilineal society', *African Studies* 14 (3): 113–22.

Bryceson, D. F. (2006) '*Ganyu* casual labour, famine and HIV/AIDS in rural Malawi: causality and casualty', *Journal of Modern African Studies* 44 (2): 173–202.

Bryceson, D. F. and J. Fonseca (2006) 'Risking death for survival: peasant responses to hunger and HIV/AIDS in Malawi', *World Development* 34 (9): 1654–66.

Burrill, E. (2015) *States of Marriage: gender, justice, and rights in colonial Mali.* Athens OH: Ohio University Press.

Butler, J. (2004) 'Jacques Derrida', *London Review of Books* 26 (21): 32 <www.lrb.co.uk/v26/n21/judith-butler/jacques-derrida>.

(2016) 'Afterword to Marilyn Strathern's "Before and after gender"' in S. Franklin (ed.), *Before and after Gender: sexual mythologies in everyday life.* Chicago IL: Hau Books.

Care Malawi (2010) *Supporting Female Headed Households Program.* Lilongwe: Care Malawi <http://p-shift.care2share.wikispaces.net/file/detail/Draft+Program+Strategy+P3+_Female+HHH_+280510.pdf>, accessed 13 June 2012.

Chanock, M. (1985) *Law, Custom and Social Order: the colonial experience in Malawi and Zambia.* Cambridge: Cambridge University Press.

Chapalapata, M. (2000) 'Serial killer in Chiradzulu', *Malawi News*, 19–25 February.

Chavula, J. (2010) 'Gender-based violence: getting the message to the grass roots', *The Nation*, 27 January.

Chesluk, B. (2004) '"Visible signs of a city out of control": community policing in New York City', *Cultural Anthropology* 19 (2): 250–75.

Chikaya-Banda, J. (2012) *Duty of Care: constitutional and law reform, in Malawi.* London: Africa Research Institute <http://africaresearchinstitute.org/news ite/wp-content/uploads/2013/03/Duty-of-Care-Constitutional-and-law-reform-in-Malawi-SYE7G00JZV.pdf>, accessed 20 March 2013.

Chikoko, R. (2000) 'Nkhanza za achiwembu m'boma la Chiradzulu', *Tikambe Supplement to Malawi News*, 1–7 April.

(2010) 'Malawi seeks to ban polygamy', *The Citizen*, 5 May <www.thecitizen .co.tz/News/1840386-1803032-rfnsehz/index.html>, accessed 24 June 2011.

Chimpweya, J. (2010) 'Cavwoc extends its empowerment programme', *The Nation*, 9 March.

Chinsinga, B. (2002) 'The politics of poverty alleviation in Malawi: a critical review' in H. Englund (ed.), *A Democracy of Chameleons: politics and culture in the new Malawi.* Uppsala: Nordiska Afrikainstitutet.

(2011) 'Seeds and subsidies: the political economy of input programmes in Malawi', *IDS Bulletin* 42 (4): 59–68.

(2012) 'The political economy of agricultural policy processes in Malawi: a case study of the fertilizer subsidy programme.' Working Paper 39. Brighton: Future Agricultures Consortium <http://opendocs.ids.ac.uk/opendocs/handle/123456789/2249>, accessed 1 March 2013.

Chipalasa, M. (2010) 'Napham exposes HIV/AIDS policy gaps' <www.bnltimes .com/index.php?option=com_content&task=view&id=4163&Itemid=26>, accessed 11 January 2011.

Chirwa, E. and A. Dorward (2013) *Agricultural Input Subsidies: the recent Malawi experience*. Oxford: Oxford University Press.

Chirwa, V. M. (2007) *Fearless Fighter: an autobiography*. London: Zed Books.

Chirwa, W. C. (1994) 'Alomwe and Mozambican immigrant labor in colonial Malawi, 1890s–1945', *International Journal of African Historical Studies* 27 (3): 525–50.

   (1999) 'Sexually transmitted diseases in colonial Malawi' in P. W. Setel, M. Lewis, and M. Lyons (eds), *Histories of Sexually Transmitted Disease and HIV/AIDS in Sub-Saharan Africa*. London: Greenwood Press.

   (2001) 'Dancing towards dictatorship: political songs and popular culture in Malawi', *Nordic Journal of African Studies* 10 (1): 1–27.

Chiweza, A. L. (2007) 'The ambivalent role of chiefs: rural decentralization initiatives in Malawi' in L. Buur and H. M. Kyed (eds), *State Recognition and Democratization in Sub-Saharan Africa: a new dawn for traditional authorities*. Basingstoke: Palgrave Macmillan.

Clarke, K. M. (2009) *Fictions of Justice: the International Criminal Court and the challenge of legal pluralism in sub-Saharan Africa*. Cambridge: Cambridge University Press.

Clarke, K. M. and M. Goodale (eds) (2010) *Mirrors of Justice: law and power in the post-Cold War era*. Cambridge: Cambridge University Press.

Clarke, M. (2012) 'The judge as tragic hero: judicial ethics in Lebanon's shari'a courts', *American Ethnologist* 39 (1): 106–21.

Cole, J. (2009) 'Love, money, and economies of intimacy in Tamatave, Madagascar' in J. Cole and L. M. Thomas (eds), *Love in Africa*. Chicago IL: University of Chicago Press.

   (2010) *Sex and Salvation: imagining the future in Madagascar*. Chicago IL: University of Chicago Press.

Cole, J. and L. M. Thomas (eds) (2009) *Love in Africa*. Chicago IL: University of Chicago Press.

Comaroff, J. and J. L. Comaroff (2004) 'Policing culture, cultural policing: law and social order in postcolonial South Africa', *Law and Social Inquiry* 29 (3): 513–45.

   (2006a) 'Criminal obsessions, after Foucault: postcoloniality, policing, and the metaphysics of disorder' in J. Comaroff and J. L. Comaroff (eds), *Law and Disorder in the Postcolony*. Chicago IL: University of Chicago Press.

   (2006b) 'Law and disorder in the postcolony: an introduction' in J. Comaroff and J. L. Comaroff (eds), *Law and Disorder in the Postcolony*. Chicago IL: University of Chicago Press.

Comaroff, J. L. and S. Roberts (1981) *Rules and Processes: the cultural logic of dispute in an African context*. Chicago IL: University of Chicago Press.

Conley, J. M. and W. M. O'Barr (1990) *Rules versus Relationships: the ethnography of legal discourse*. Chicago IL: University of Chicago Press.

Cornwall, A. (2002) 'Spending power: love, money, and the reconfiguration of gender relations in Ado-Odo, Southwestern Nigeria', *American Ethnologist* 29 (4): 963–80.

   (2005) 'Introduction: perspectives on gender in Africa' in A. Cornwall (ed.), *Readings in Gender in Africa*. Oxford: James Currey.

Cutrufelli, M. R. (1983) *Women of Africa: roots of oppression*. London: Zed Books.

Daily Times (2000) 'Comment: human rights trap', *Daily Times*, 11 October.

Davison, J. (1993) 'Tenacious women: clinging to *banja* household production in the face of changing gender relations in Malawi', *Journal of Southern African Studies* 19 (3): 405–21.

(1997) *Gender, Lineage, and Ethnicity in Southern Africa*. Boulder CO and Oxford: Westview Press.

Deleuze, G. (1989) *Cinema 2: the time-image*. Minneapolis MN: University of Minnesota Press.

Derrida, J. (1990) 'Force of law: the "mystical foundation of authority"', *Cardozo Law Review* 11: 920–1045.

Devereux, S. (2002) 'The Malawi famine of 2002', *IDS Bulletin* 33 (4): 70–8.

Dhillon, N. and T. Yousef (2007) *Inclusion: meeting the 100 million youth challenge*. Washington DC: Middle East Youth Initiative <www.meyi.org/publication-inclusion-meeting-the-100-million-youth-challenge.html>, accessed 22 July 2018.

Dilger, H. (2008) '"We are all going to die": kinship, belonging, and the morality of HIV/AIDS-related illnesses and deaths in rural Tanzania', *Anthropological Quarterly* 81 (1): 207–32.

(2010) '"My relatives are running away from me!": Kinship and care in the wake of structural adjustment, privatization and HIV/AIDS in Tanzania' in H. Dilger and U. Luig (eds), *Morality, Hope and Grief: anthropologies of AIDS in Africa*. Oxford: Berghahn Books.

Doran, M. (2007) 'Reconstructing *Mchape* '95: AIDS, Billy Chisupe, and the politics of persuasion', *Journal of Eastern African Studies* 1 (3): 397–416.

Douglas, M. (2001 [1969]) 'Is matriliny doomed in Africa?' in M. Douglas and P. M. Kaberry (eds), *Man in Africa*. London: Routledge.

Durham, D. (2002) 'Uncertain citizens: Herero and the new intercalary subject in postcolonial Botswana' in R. Werbner (ed.), *Postcolonial Subjectivities in Africa*. London: Zed Books.

Eggen, Ø. (2011) 'Chiefs and everyday governance: parallel state organisations in Malawi', *Journal of Southern African Studies* 37 (2): 313–31.

Engelke, M. (1999) '"We wondered what human rights he was talking about": human rights, homosexuality and the Zimbabwe international book fair', *Critique of Anthropology* 19 (3): 289–314.

Englund, H. (1996) 'Witchcraft, modernity and the person: the morality of accumulation in central Malawi', *Critique of Anthropology* 16 (3): 257–79.

(1999) 'The self in self-interest: land, labour and temporalities in Malawi's agrarian change', *Africa* 69 (1): 138–59.

(2002) *From War to Peace on the Mozambique–Malawi Borderland*. Edinburgh: Edinburgh University Press.

(2006) *Prisoners of Freedom: human rights and the African poor*. Berkeley CA: University of California Press.

(2008) 'Extreme poverty and existential obligations: beyond morality in the anthropology of Africa?', *Social Analysis* 52 (3): 33–50.

(2011) *Human Rights and African Airwaves: mediating equality on the Chichewa radio*. Bloomington IN: Indiana University Press.

(2012a) 'Human rights and village headmen in Malawi: translation beyond vernacularisation' in J. Eckert, B. Donahoe, C. Strümpell, and Z. Ö. Biner (eds), *Law Against the State: ethnographic forays into law's transformations*. Cambridge: Cambridge University Press.

(2012b) 'Poverty' in D. Fassin (ed.), *A Companion to Moral Anthropology*. Oxford: Wiley-Blackwell.

Epprecht, M. (1998) 'The "unsaying" of indigenous homosexualities in Zimbabwe: mapping a blindspot in an African masculinity', *Journal of Southern African Studies* 24 (4): 631–51.

(2004) *Hungochani: the history of a dissident sexuality in Southern Africa*. Montreal: McGill-Queen's University Press.

(2013) *Sexuality and Social Justice in Africa: rethinking homophobia and forging resistance*. London: Zed Books.

Errington, S. (1990) 'Recasting sex, gender, and power: a theoretical and regional overview' in J. M. Atkinson and S. Errington (eds), *Power and Difference: gender in island Southeast Asia*. Stanford CA: Stanford University Press.

Fallon, A. (2010) 'Malawi frees jailed gay couple', *Guardian*, 29 May <www.guardian.co.uk/world/2010/may/29/malawi-frees-jailed-gay-couple>, accessed 1 August 2011.

Ferguson, J. (1999) *Expectations of Modernity: myths and meanings of urban life on the Zambian Copperbelt*. Berkeley CA: University of California Press.

(2013) 'Declarations of dependence: labour, personhood, and welfare in southern Africa', *Journal of the Royal Anthropological Institute* 19 (2): 223–42.

(2015) *Give a Man a Fish: reflections on the new politics of distribution*. Durham NC: Duke University Press.

Frank, E. (2009) 'Shifting paradigms and the politics of AIDS in Zambia', *African Studies Review* 52 (3): 33–53.

Gloppen, S. and F. E. Kanyongolo (2007) 'Courts and the poor in Malawi: economic marginalization, vulnerability, and the law', *International Journal of Constitutional Law* 5 (2): 258–93.

Gluckman, M. (1965) *The Ideas in Barotse Jurisprudence*. New Haven CT: Yale University Press.

(1973 [1955]) *Judicial Process among the Barotse of Northern Rhodesia (Zambia)*. Manchester: Manchester University Press.

Gluckman, M., J. C. Mitchell, and J. A. Barnes (1949) 'The village headman in British Central Africa', *Africa* 19: 89–106.

Goffman, E. (1963) *Stigma: notes on the management of spoiled identity*. Harmondsworth: Penguin Books.

Goheen, M. (1996) *Men Own the Fields, Women Own the Crops: gender and power in the Cameroon grasslands*. Madison WI: University of Wisconsin Press.

Goodale, M. and K. M. Clarke (2010) 'Introduction: understanding the multiplicity of justice' in K. M. Clarke and M. Goodale (eds), *Mirrors of Justice: law and power in the post-Cold War era*. Cambridge: Cambridge University Press.

Gough, K. (1961) 'The modern disintegration of matrilineal descent groups' in D. M. Schneider and K. Gough (eds), *Matrilineal Kinship*. Berkeley CA: University of California Press.

Government of Malawi (2004 [1994]) *The Constitution of the Republic of Malawi*. Zomba, Malawi: Government Press.

(2011) *Local Courts Bill, 2010*. Zomba, Malawi: Government Press.

Greenhouse, C. J. (2012) 'Law' in D. Fassin (ed.), *A Companion to Moral Anthropology*. Oxford: Wiley-Blackwell.

Griffiths, A. (1997) *In the Shadow of Marriage: gender and justice in an African community*. Chicago IL: University of Chicago Press.

(2001) 'Gendering culture: towards a plural perspective on Kwena women's rights' in J. K. Cowan, M.-B. Dembour, and R. A. Wilson (eds), *Culture and Rights: anthropological perspectives*. Cambridge: Cambridge University Press.

Groes-Green, C. (2013) '"To put men in a bottle": eroticism, kinship, female power, and transactional sex in Maputo, Mozambique', *American Ethnologist* 40 (1): 102–17.

Groves, Z. (2011) 'Malawians in colonial Salisbury: a social history of migration in central Africa, c.1920s–1960s'. PhD thesis, Keele University.

Gulbrandsen, Ø. (1986) 'To marry – or not to marry: marital strategies and sexual relations in a Tswana society', *Ethnos* 51 (1–2): 7–28.

Hansen, K. T. (2005) 'Getting stuck in the compound: some odds against social adulthood in Lusaka, Zambia', *Africa Today* 51 (4): 3–16.

Hay, M. J. and M. Wright (eds) (1982a) *African Women and the Law: historical perspectives*. Boston MA: African Studies Center, Boston University.

(1982b) 'Introduction' in M. J. Hay and M. Wright (eds), *African Women and The Law: historical perspectives*. Boston: African Studies Center, Boston University.

Hirsch, J. S., H. Wardlow, D. J. Smith, H. M. Phinney, S. Parikh, and C. A. Nathanson (2009) 'Conclusion: "world enough and time": navigating opportunities and risks in the landscape of desire' in J. S. Hirsch, H. Wardlow, D. J. Smith, H. M. Phinney, S. Parikh, and C. A. Nathanson (eds), *The Secret: love, marriage, and HIV*. Nashville TN: Vanderbilt University Press.

Hirsch, S. F. (1998) *Pronouncing and Persevering: gender and discourses of disputing in an African Islamic court*. Chicago IL: University of Chicago Press.

(2010) 'The victim deserving of global justice: power, caution, and recovering individuals' in M. Goodale and K. M. Clarke (eds), *Mirrors of Justice: law and power in the post-Cold War era*. Cambridge: Cambridge University Press.

Hirschmann, D. and M. Vaughan (1983) 'Food production and income generation in a matrilineal society: rural women in Zomba, Malawi', *Journal of Southern African Studies* 10 (1): 86–99.

Hirschmann, N. J. (1992) *Rethinking Obligation: a feminist method for political theory*. Ithaca NY: Cornell University Press.

(2003) *The Subject of Liberty: toward a feminist theory of freedom*. Princeton NJ: Princeton University Press.

Hodgson, D. L. (1996) '"My daughter ... belongs to the government now": marriage, Maasai and the Tanzanian state', *Canadian Journal of African Studies* 30 (1): 106–23.

(2002) 'Women's rights as human rights: women in law and development in Africa (WiLDAF)', *Africa Today* 49 (2): 3–26.

(2011) '"These are not our priorities": Maasai women, human rights, and the problem of culture' in D. L. Hodgson (ed.), *Gender and Culture at the Limit of Rights*. Philadelphia PA: University of Pennsylvania Press.

(2017) *Gender, Justice and the Problem of Culture: from customary law to human rights in Tanzania*. Bloomington IN: Indiana University Press.

Hodgson, D. L. and S. McCurdy (2001) *'Wicked' Women and the Reconfiguration of Gender in Africa*. Oxford: James Currey.

Hornberger, J. (2007) '"Don't push this constitution down my throat!" Human rights in everyday practice. An ethnography of police transformation in Johannesburg, South Africa'. PhD thesis, Utrecht University.

(2010) 'Human rights and policing: exigency or incongruence?', *Annual Review of Law and Social Science* 6: 259–83.

Human Rights Watch (2003) *Policy Paralysis: a call for action on HIV/AIDS-related human rights abuses against women and girls in Africa*. New York NY: Human Rights Watch <www.hrw.org/reports/2003/12/01/policy-paralysis>, accessed 13 June 2012.

Hunter, M. (2010) *Love in the Time of AIDS: inequality, gender, and rights in South Africa*. Bloomington IN: Indiana University Press.

Hynd, S. (2011) 'Law, violence and penal reform: state responses to crime and disorder in colonial Malawi, c.1900–1959', *Journal of Southern African Studies* 37 (3): 431–47.

Izzard, W. (1985) 'Migrants and mothers: case-studies from Botswana', *Journal of Southern African Studies* 11 (2): 258–80.

James, D. (1999a) 'Sister, spouse, lazy woman: commentaries on domestic predicaments by Kiba performers from the Northern Province' in D. Brown (ed.), *Oral Literature and Performance in South Africa*. Oxford: James Currey.

(1999b) *Songs of the Women Migrants: performance and identity in South Africa*. Edinburgh: Edinburgh University Press.

Johnson, J. (2012) 'Life with HIV: "stigma" and hope in Malawi's era of ARVs', *Africa* 82 (4): 632–53.

(2013) 'Chilungamo? In search of gender justice in matrilineal Malawi'. PhD thesis, University of Cambridge.

(2017) 'After the mines: the changing social and economic landscape of Malawi–South Africa migration', *Review of African Political Economy* 44 (152): 237–51.

(2018a) 'Feminine futures: female initiation and aspiration in matrilineal Malawi', *Journal of the Royal Anthropological Institute* 24 (4).

(2018b) '"It is better for me to agree when my guardian is here": consent and relational personhood in postcolonial Malawi' in M-C. Foblets, M. Graziadei, & A. D. Renteln (eds) *Personal Autonomy in Plural Societies: A Principle and Its Paradoxes*, Oxford: Routledge

Johnson, J. and G. H. Karekwaivanane (eds) (2018) *Pursuing Justice in Africa: competing imaginaries and contested practices*. Athens OH: Ohio University Press.

Jul-Larsen, E. and P. Mvula (2009) 'Security for many or surplus for the few? Customary tenure and social differentiation in southern Malawi', *Journal of Southern African Studies* 35 (1): 175–90.

Kadzamira, E. and P. Rose (2003) 'Can free primary education meet the needs of the poor? Evidence from Malawi', *International Journal of Educational Development* 23 (5): 501–16.

Kainja, G. (2009) 'Community policing and customer care for Tanzania Police Force'. PowerPoint presentation by the Officer in Charge of Community Policing Services Branch, Malawi Police Service <www.communitypolicing.mw/downloads-reports/community-policing-and-customer-care-for-tanzania-police-force/>, accessed 30 May 2011.

(2010) 'Malawi Police Service: its roles and functions'. PowerPoint presentation by the Officer in Charge of Community Policing Services Branch, Malawi Police Service <www.communitypolicing.mw/downloads-reports/malawi-police-services-roles-functions/>, accessed 1 June 2011.

Kakande, A. (2011) 'Uladi "change goal": Mussa attacks govt over Local Courts Bill', *Malawi* Voice, 8 February <www.malawivoice.com/politics/uladi-change-goal-mussa-attacks-govt-over-local-court-bill/>, accessed 17 June 2011.

Kaler, A. (2001) '"Many divorces and many spinsters": marriage as an invented tradition in southern Malawi, 1946–1999', *Journal of Family History* 26 (4): 529–56.

—— (2004a) 'AIDS-talk in everyday life: the presence of HIV/AIDS in men's informal conversation in southern Malawi', *Social Science and Medicine* 59 (2): 285–97.

—— (2004b) 'The moral lens of population control: condoms and controversies in southern Malawi', *Studies in Family Planning* 35 (2): 105–15.

Kalinga, O. J. M. (1993) 'The master farmers' scheme in Nyasaland, 1950–1962: a study of a failed attempt to create a "yeoman" class', *African Affairs* 92 (368): 367–87.

Kalofonos, I. A. (2010) '"All I eat is ARVs": the paradox of AIDS treatment interventions in central Mozambique', *Medical Anthropology Quarterly* 24 (3): 363–80.

Kamwendo, G. H. (2006) 'Sociolinguistic research and academic freedom in Malawi: past and current trends', *Southern African Review of Education* 12 (1): 5–16.

Kanyongolo, F. E. (2006) *Malawi Justice Sector and the Rule of Law: a review by AfriMAP and Open Society Initiative for Southern Africa*. London: Open Society Initiative for Southern Africa.

—— (2011) 'Local Courts Bill, the baby and the bathwater', *The Nation*, 4 February <www.nationmw.net/index.php?option=com_content&view=article&id=13985:local-courts-bill-the-baby-and-the-bathwater&catid=242:edge-kanyon golo&Itemid=345>, accessed 16 June 2011.

Kanyongolo, N. R. (2007) 'Social security and women in Malawi: a legal discourse on solidarity of care'. PhD thesis, Warwick University.

Kanyongolo, N. R. and Malunga, B. (2018) 'Conflicting Conceptions of Justice and the Legal Treatment of Defilement in Malawi' in J. Johnson and G. H. Karekwaivanane (eds) *Pursuing Justice in Africa: competing imaginaries and contested practices*. Athens OH: Ohio University Press.

Kateta, M. (2008) 'Malawi struggles to fight HIV stigma', Africanews.com, 24 October <www.africanews.com/site/list_messages/21214>, accessed 15 December 2010.

Kishindo, P. (2001) 'Language and the law in Malawi: a case for the use of indigenous languages in the legal system', *Language Matters* 32 (1): 1–27.

—— (2010) 'The marital immigrant. Land, and agriculture: a Malawian case study', *African Sociological Review* 14 (2): 89–97.

Klaits, F. (2005) 'The widow in blue: blood and the morality of remembering in Botswana's time of AIDS', *Africa* 75 (1): 46–62.

—— (2010) *Death in a Church of Life: moral passion during Botswana's time of AIDS*. Berkeley CA: University of California Press.

Kratz, C. A. (2010 [1994]) *Affecting Performance: meaning, movement, and experience in Okiek women's initiation*. Tucson AZ: Wheatmark.

Kringelbach, H. N. (2016) '"Marrying out" for love: women's narratives of polygyny and alternative marriage choices in contemporary Senegal', *African Studies Review* 59 (1): 155–74.

Kuhn, T. (1970) *The Structure of Scientific Revolutions*. Chicago IL: University of Chicago Press.

Kuper, A. (1970) 'Gluckman's village headman', *American Anthropologist* 72 (2): 355–8.

Laidlaw, J. (2002) 'For an anthropology of ethics and freedom', *Journal of the Royal Anthropological Institute* 8 (2): 311–32.

(2014) *The Subject of Virtue: an anthropology of ethics and freedom.* Cambridge: Cambridge University Press.

Laing, A. (2012) 'Malawi to increase legal age of marriage to 21', *The Telegraph*, 7 November <www.telegraph.co.uk/news/worldnews/africaandindianocean/malawi/9662476/Malawi-to-increase-legal-age-of-marriage-to-21.html>, accessed 8 January 2013.

Lambek, M. (2010) 'Introduction' in M. Lambek (ed.), *Ordinary Ethics: anthropology, language and action.* New York NY: Fordham University Press.

Last, M. (1981) 'The importance of knowing about not knowing', *Social Science and Medicine* 15 (3): 387–92.

Lazreg, M. (2005 [1994]) 'Decolonizing feminism' in O. Oyěwùmí (ed.), *African gender studies: a reader.* New York NY: Palgrave Macmillan.

Leach, E. R. (1961) *Rethinking Anthropology.* London: Athlone Press.

Leacock, E. (1977) 'Women in egalitarian societies' in R. Bridenthal and C. Koonz (eds), *Becoming Visible: women in European history.* London: Houghton Mifflin.

Lévi-Strauss, C. (1969) *The Elementary Structures of Kinship.* London: Eyre & Spottiswoode.

Lwanda, J. (2002) 'Tikutha: the political culture of the HIV/AIDS epidemic in Malawi' in H. Englund (ed.), *A Democracy of Chameleons: politics and culture in the new Malawi.* Uppsala: Nordiska Afrikainstitutet.

MacCormack, C. P. and M. Strathern (eds) (1980) *Nature, Culture and Gender.* Cambridge: Cambridge University Press.

MacKinnon, C. (1989) *Toward a Feminist Theory of the State.* Cambridge MA: Harvard University Press.

Mahmood, S. (2005) *Politics of Piety: the Islamic revival and the feminist subject.* Princeton NJ: Princeton University Press.

Mains, D. (2012) *Hope Is Cut: youth, unemployment, and the future in urban Ethiopia.* Philadelphia PA: Temple University Press.

Mair, L. P. (1951) 'Marriage and family in the Dedza District of Nyasaland', *Journal of the Royal Anthropological Institute* 81 (1/2): 103–19.

Makambe, E. P. (1980) 'The Nyasaland African labour *"ulendos"* to Southern Rhodesia and the problem of the African "highwaymen", 1903–1923: a study in the limitations of early independent labour migration', *African Affairs* 79 (317): 548–66.

Malawi Human Rights Commission (2007) *2006 Executive Report on Human Rights Accountability in Malawi By the Three Arms of Government.* Lilongwe: Malawi Human Rights Commission.

Malawi News (2000) 'Chiradzulu serial killers: army urged to move in', *Malawi News*, 8–14 April.

Malawi Police Service and MHRRC (n.d.) *Guidelines for the Support and Care of Victims of Gender-Based Violence, HIV and AIDS Related Abuses, and Other Human Rights Violations.* Lilongwe: Malawi Police Service Community Policing Services Branch and Malawi Human Rights Resource Centre (MHRRC).

Malawi Voice (2015) 'Malawi parliament overwhelmingly passes Marriage, Divorce and Family Relations Bill without amendment', *Malawi Voice*, 13 February <http://malawivoice.com/2015/02/13/malawi-parliament-over

whelmingly-passes-marriage-divorce-and-family-relations-bill-without-amendment/>, accessed 19 March 2015.

Malinowski, B. (1926) *Crime and Custom in Savage Society*. London: Kegan Paul, Trench, Trubner & Co.

(1999 [1922]) *Argonauts of the Western Pacific: an account of native enterprise and adventure in the archipelagos of Melanesian New Guinea*. London: Routledge.

Mamdani, M. (1996) *Citizen and Subject: contemporary Africa and the legacy of late colonialism*. Princeton NJ: Princeton University Press.

Mandala, E. C. (1990) *Work and Control in a Peasant Economy: a history of the Lower Tchiri Valley in Malawi, 1859–1960*. Madison WI: University of Wisconsin Press.

(2005) *The End of Chidyerano: a history of food and everyday life in Malawi, 1860–2004*. Portsmouth NH: Heinemann.

Mangulenje, J. (2009) 'Marriage is for mature people, not 16-yr-olds', *The Nation*, 26 August.

Mann, K. (1982) 'Women's rights in law and practice: marriage and dispute settlement in colonial Lagos' in M. J. Hay and M. Wright (eds), *African Women and the Law: historical perspectives*. Boston MA: African Studies Center, Boston University.

Mapondera, G. and D. Smith (2010a) 'Malawian gay couple jailed for 14 years', *Guardian*, 20 May <www.guardian.co.uk/world/2010/may/20/malawian-gay-couple-jailed-14-years>, accessed 11 January 2011.

(2010b) 'Gay couple freed by Malawi presidential pardon return to home villages', *Guardian*, 30 May <www.theguardian.com/world/2010/may/30/malwi-gay-couple-freed-villages>, accessed 22 July 2018.

Marks, S. (1999) 'Southern Africa' in W. R. Louis and J. M. Brown (eds), *The Oxford History of the British Empire. Volume IV: the twentieth century*. Oxford: Oxford University Press.

Marsland, R. (2012) '(Bio)sociality and HIV in Tanzania: finding a living to support a life', *Medical Anthropology Quarterly* 26 (4): 470–85.

Marsland, R. and R. Prince (2012) 'What is life worth? Exploring biomedical interventions, survival, and the politics of life', *Medical Anthropology Quarterly* 26 (4): 453–69.

Masina, L. (2010) 'Women fight harmful cultural practices', *Daily Times*, 12 January.

(2015) 'Malawi parliament criticized for passing Marriage Bill', Voice of America, 19 February <www.voanews.com/content/malawi-parliament-criticized-for-passing-marriage-bill/2650067.html>, accessed 19 March 2015.

Masquelier, A. (2005) 'The scorpion's sting: youth, marriage and the struggle for social maturity in Niger', *Journal of the Royal Anthropological Institute* 11 (1): 59–83.

(2013) 'Teatime: boredom and the temporalities of young men in Niger', *Africa* 83 (3): 385–402.

Mauss, M. (2002 [1954]) *The Gift: the form and reason for exchange in archaic societies*. London: Routledge.

Mbavi. (2011) 'UDF, MCP got it wrong on traditional courts and are getting it wrong now', *Malawi Voice*, 28 January <www.malawivoice.com/latest-news/udf-mcp-got-it-wrong-on-traditional-courts-are-getting-it-wrong-now/>, accessed 18 June 2011.

Mbilinyi, M. (1988) 'Runaway wives in colonial Tanganyika: forced labour and forced marriage in Rungwe District, 1919–1961', *International Journal of the Sociology of Law* 16 (3): 1–29.

McClendon, T. V. (1995) 'Tradition and domestic struggle in the courtroom: customary law and the control of women in segregation-era Natal', *International Journal of African Historical Studies* 28 (3): 527–61.

McCracken, J. (2012) *A History of Malawi 1859–1966*. Oxford: James Currey.

McNeill, F. G. and I. Niehaus (2009) *Magic: AIDS review 2009*. Pretoria: Centre for the Study of AIDS, University of Pretoria.

Merry, S. E. (1988) 'Legal pluralism', *Law and Society Review* 22 (5): 869–96.

(2006a) 'Anthropology and international law', *Annual Review of Anthropology* 35 (1): 99–116.

(2006b) *Human Rights and Gender Violence: translating international law into local justice*. Chicago IL: University of Chicago Press.

(2006c) 'Transnational human rights and local activism: mapping the middle', *American Anthropologist* 108 (1): 38–51.

(2011) 'Measuring the world: indicators, human rights, and global governance', *Current Anthropology* 52 (S3): S83–S95.

Miers, H. (2011) *Counterpoints: talking gender to Africa*. London: Africa Research Institute.

Mitchell, J. C. (1956) *The Yao Village: a study in the social structure of a Malawian people*. Manchester: Manchester University Press.

(1959 [1951]) 'The Yao of southern Nyasaland' in E. Colson and M. Gluckman (eds), *Seven Tribes of British Central Africa*. Manchester: Manchester University Press.

Miyazaki, H. (2004) *The Method of Hope: anthropology, philosophy, and Fijian knowledge*. Stanford CA: Stanford University Press.

Moffett, H. (2006) '"These women, they force us to rape them": rape as narrative of social control in post-apartheid South Africa', *Journal of Southern African Studies* 32 (1): 129–44.

Mohanty, C. T. (1988) 'Under Western eyes: feminist scholarship and colonial discourses', *Feminist Review* 30: 61–88.

Moore, H. L. (1988) *Feminism and Anthropology*. Cambridge: Polity.

Moore, H. L. and M. Vaughan (1994) *Cutting Down Trees: gender, nutrition, and agricultural change in the Northern Province of Zambia, 1890–1990*. London: James Currey.

Moore, S. F. (1986) *Social Facts and Fabrications: 'customary' law on Kilimanjaro, 1880–1980*. Cambridge: Cambridge University Press.

(2005) 'Certainties undone: fifty turbulent years of legal anthropology, 1949–1999' in S. F. Moore (ed.), *Law and Anthropology: a reader*. Oxford: Blackwell Publishing.

MSF (2010) *No Time to Quit: HIV/AIDS treatment gap widening in Africa*. London: Médecins Sans Frontières (MSF) <www.msf.org.za/about-us/publications/reports/no-time-quit-hivaids-treatment-gap-widening-africa>, accessed 12 August 2011.

MSF Malawi (2004) *Antiretroviral Therapy in Primary Health Care: experience of the Chiradzulu programme in Malawi*. Geneva: World Health Organization and Médecins Sans Frontières (MSF) Malawi <www.who.int/hiv/pub/prev_care/en/chiradzulu.pdf>, accessed 12 August 2011.

Msiska, M.-H. (2017) '*Kujoni*: South Africa in Malawi's national imaginary', *Journal of Southern African Studies* 43 (5): 1011–29.

Murray, C. (1981) *Families Divided: the impact of migrant labour in Lesotho*. Cambridge: Cambridge University Press.

Mutongi, K. (2005 [1999]) '"Worries of the heart": widowed mothers, daughters and masculinities in Maragoli, Western Kenya, 1940–60' in A. Cornwall (ed.), *Readings in Gender in Africa*. Oxford: James Currey.

Mwambene, L. (2007) 'Reconciling African customary law with women's rights in Malawi: the proposed Marriage, Divorce and Family Relations Bill', *Malawi Law Journal* 1 (1): 113–22.

Mwasinga, E. and S. Nkowani (2012) 'Push marriage age to 21', *Daily Times*, 27 November <www.bnltimes.com/index.php/daily-times/headlines/national/12649-push-marriage-age-to-21>, accessed 8 January 2013.

Mzungu, W. (2009) 'Horror of sexual abuse', *The Nation*, 16 July.

Navaro-Yashin, Y. (2009) 'Affective spaces, melancholic objects: ruination and the production of anthropological knowledge', *Journal of the Royal Anthropological Institute* 15 (1): 1–18.

Nduna, A. (2009) 'Zaka 16 zachepadi, koma ...', *Tamvani: Gawo La Chichewa La Weekend Nation*, 29 August.

Nguyen, V.-K. (2010) *The Republic of Therapy: triage and sovereignty in West Africa's time of AIDS*. Durham NC: Duke University Press.

Ngwani, Z. (2001) '"Real men reawaken their fathers' homesteads, the educated leave them in ruins": the politics of domestic reproduction in post-apartheid rural South Africa', *Journal of Religion in Africa* 31 (4): 402–26.

Ngwira, K. (2009) 'The dark, darker, and darkest face of Chiradzulu', *Daily Times*, 16 July.

Niehaus, I. (2009) 'Leprosy of a deadlier kind: Christian conceptions of AIDS in the South African Lowveld' in F. Becker and P. W. Geissler (eds), *AIDS and Religious Practice in Africa*. Leiden: Brill.

———— (2012) *Witchcraft and a Life in the New South Africa*. Cambridge: Cambridge University Press.

Nnaemeka, O. (2005 [1994]) 'Bringing African women into the classroom: rethinking pedagogy and epistemology' in O. Oyěwùmí (ed.), *African Gender Studies: a reader*. New York NY: Palgrave Macmillan.

———— (2005 [1998]) 'Mapping African feminisms' in A. Cornwall (ed.), *Readings in Gender in Africa*. Oxford: James Currey.

NSO (2008a) *2008 Population and Housing Census Preliminary Report*. Zomba, Malawi: National Statistical Office (NSO) <www.nsomalawi.mw/index.php?option=com_content&view=article&id=10:2008-phc-preliminary-results&catid=8&Itemid=6>, accessed 1 May 2012.

———— (2008b) *2008 Population and Housing Census: gender report*. Zomba, Malawi: National Statistical Office (NSO) <www.nsomalawi.mw/images/stories/data_on_line/demography/census_2008/Main%20Report/ThematicReports/Gender.pdf>, accessed 3 May 2012.

———— (2008c) *Population and Housing Census Main Report*. Zomba, Malawi: National Statistical Office (NSO) <www.nsomalawi.mw/images/stories/data_on_line/demography/census_2008/Main%20Report/Census%20Main%20Report.pdf>, accessed 28 October 2011.

———— (2008d) *Population Characteristics*. Zomba, Malawi: National Statistical Office (NSO) <www.nsomalawi.mw/index.php?option=com_content&view=article&id=107%3A2008-population-and-housing-census-results&catid=8&Itemid=3>, accessed 28 October 2011.

———— (2008e) *Table: population size and composition*. Zomba, Malawi: National Statistical Office (NSO) <www.nsomalawi.mw/index.php?option=com_

content&view=article&id=107%3A2008-population-and-housing-census-results&catid=8&Itemid=3>, accessed 28 October 2011.

(2014) *Malawi Labour Force Survey 2013: key findings report*. Zomba, Malawi: National Statistical Office (NSO) <www.nsomalawi.mw/images/stories/data_on_line/demography/Labour Force/Labour Force Survey 2013/Key Finding Report_Labour Force Indicators.pdf>, accessed 8 October 2014.

NSO and ICF Macro (2011) *Malawi Demographic and Health Survey 2010*. Zomba, Malawi and Calverton MD: National Statistical Office (NSO) and ICF Macro <www.nsomalawi.mw/images/stories/data_on_line/demography/MDHS2010/MDHS2010 report.pdf>, accessed 31 October 2010.

Nyasa Times (2009) 'IG commends Britain for Malawi police reform programme', *Nyasa Times*, 23 December <www.nyasatimes.com/national/ig-commends-britain-for-malawi-police-reform-programme.html>, accessed 16 June 2011.

(2010a) 'Malawi reacts to intentions of banning polygamy', *Nyasa Times*, 1 May <www.nyasatimes.com/national/malawi-reacts-to-intentions-of-banning-polygamy.html>, accessed 24 June 2011.

(2010b) 'Should police suspects reveal their HIV statuses when arrested?', *Nyasa Times*, 22 June <www.nyasatimes.com/features/should-police-suspects-reveal-their-hiv-statuses-when-arrested.html>, accessed 4 January 2011.

(2010c) 'UDF condemns plans to outlaw polygamy', *Nyasa Times*, 18 May <www.nyasatimes.com/national/udf-condemns-plans-to-outlaw-polygamy.html>, accessed 24 June 2011.

(2011a) 'Chaponda tables Local Courts Bill', *Nyasa Times*, 8 February <www.nyasatimes.com/national/chaponda-tables-local-courts-bill.html>, accessed 16 June 2011.

(2011b) 'Parliament passes Local Courts Bill', *Nyasa Times*, 10 February <www.nyasatimes.com/national/parliament-passes-local-courts-bill.html/comment-page-1-comments>, accessed 17 June 2011.

(2015) 'Malawi Marriage, Divorce, and Family Relations Bill passed by parliament', *Nyasa Times*, 17 February <www.nyasatimes.com/2015/02/17/malawi-marriage-divorce-and-family-relations-bill-passed-by-parliament/>, accessed 19 March 2015.

Nyondo, E. (2012) 'When a woman knows', *The Nation*, 4 June <www.mwnation.com/features-the-nation/development/6259-when-a-woman-knows>, accessed 13 June 2012.

Nzegwu, N. U. (2006) *Family Matters: feminist concepts in African philosophy of culture*. Albany NY: State University of New York Press.

Okome, M. O. (2003) 'What women, whose development? A critical analysis of reformist feminist evangelism on African women' in O. Oyěwùmí (ed.), *African Women and Feminism: reflecting on the politics of sisterhood*. Trenton NJ: Africa World Books.

Okonjo, K. (1976) 'The dual-sex political system: Igbo women and community politics in midwestern Nigeria' in N. J. Hafkin and E. G. Bay (eds), *Women in Africa: studies in social and economic change*. Stanford CA: Stanford University Press.

Oppong, C. (1974) *Marriage among a Matrilineal Elite: a family study of Ghanaian senior civil servants*. Cambridge: Cambridge University Press.

(ed.) (1983) *Female and Male in West Africa*. London: George Allen & Unwin.

Oyěwùmí, O. (1997) *The Invention of Women: making an African sense of Western gender discourses*. Minneapolis MN: University of Minnesota Press.

(2002) 'Conceptualizing gender: the Eurocentric foundations of feminist concepts and the challenge of African epistemologies', *JENdA: a Journal of Culture and African Women's Studies* 2 (1) [online] <www.africaknowledgeproject.org/index.php/jenda/article/view/68>, accessed 9 November 2012.

(2003a) *African Women and Feminism: reflecting on the politics of sisterhood*. Trenton NJ: Africa World Press.

(2003b) 'The white woman's burden: African women in Western feminist discourse' in O. Oyěwùmí (ed.), *African Women and Feminism: reflecting on the politics of sisterhood*. Trenton NJ: Africa World Press.

Paas, S. (2009) *Dictionary Mtanthauziramawu: Chichewa/Chinyanja – English, English – Chichewa/Chinyanja*. First edition. Zomba, Malawi: Kachere Series.

Paliani, P. (2000) 'Woman survives serial killer', *Daily Times*, 30 March.

Peters, P. E. (1983) 'Gender, developmental cycles and historical process: a critique of recent research on women in Botswana', *Journal of Southern African Studies* 10 (1): 100–22.

(1997a) 'Against the odds: matriliny, land and gender in the Shire Highlands of Malawi', *Critique of Anthropology* 17 (2): 189–210.

(1997b) 'Introduction: revisiting the puzzle of matriliny in South-Central Africa', *Critique of Anthropology* 17 (2): 125–46.

(2002) 'Bewitching land: the role of land disputes in converting kin to strangers and in class formation in Malawi', *Journal of Southern African Studies* 28 (1): 155–78.

(2006) 'Rural income and poverty in a time of radical change in Malawi', *Journal of Development Studies* 42 (2): 322–45.

(2010) '"Our daughters inherit our land, but our sons use their wives' fields": matrilineal-matrilocal land tenure and the New Land Policy in Malawi', *Journal of Eastern African Studies* 4 (1): 179–99.

Peters, P. E. and D. Kambewa (2007) 'Whose security? Deepening social conflict over "customary" land in the shadow of land tenure reform in Malawi', *Journal of Modern African Studies* 45 (3): 447–72.

Peters, P. E., D. Kambewa, and P. Walker (2008) *The Effects of Increasing Rates of HIV/AIDS Related Illness and Death on Rural Families in Zomba District, Malawi: a longitudinal study*. Washington DC: International Food Policy Research Institute (IFPRI) <http://ebrary.ifpri.org/cdm/compoundobject/collection/p15738coll2/id/30738/rec/17>, accessed 18 July 2017.

Peters, P. E., D. Kambewa, and P. A. Walker (2010) 'Contestations over "tradition" and "culture" in a time of AIDS', *Medical Anthropology* 29 (3): 278–302.

Peters, P. E., P. A. Walker, and D. Kambewa (2008) 'Striving for normality in a time of AIDS in Malawi', *Journal of Modern African Studies* 46 (4): 659–87.

Phiri, K. (1983) 'Some changes in the matrilineal family system among the Chewa of Malawi since the nineteenth century', *Journal of African History* 24 (2): 257–74.

Piot, C. (1999) *Remotely Global: village modernity in West Africa*. Chicago IL: University of Chicago Press.

Poewe, K. O. (1981) *Matrilineal Ideology: male–female dynamics in Luapula, Zambia*. London: Academic Press.

Poulin, M. (2007) 'Sex, money, and premarital partnerships in southern Malawi', *Social Science and Medicine* 65 (11): 2383–93.

Power, J. (1995) '"Eating the property": gender roles and economic change in urban Malawi, Blantyre-Limbe, 1907–1953', *Canadian Journal of African Studies* 29 (1): 79–107.

(2010) *Political Culture and Nationalism in Malawi: building kwacha*. Rochester NY: University of Rochester Press.

Prince, R. (2012) 'HIV and the moral economy of survival in an East African city', *Medical Anthropology Quarterly* 26 (4): 534–56.

Probst, P. (1999) '"*Mchape*" '95, or, the sudden fame of Billy Goodson Chisupe: healing, social memory and the enigma of the public sphere in post-Banda Malawi', *Africa* 69 (1): 108–37.

Ralph, M. (2008) 'Killing time', *Social Text* 26 (4): 1–29.

Rankin, W., S. Brennan, E. Schell, J. Laviwa, and S. Rankin (2005) 'The stigma of being HIV-positive in Africa', *PLoS Medicine* 2 (8): 702–4.

Read, M. (1942) 'Migrant labour in Africa and its effects on tribal life', *International Labour Review* 45 (6): 605–31.

Reniers, G. (2003) 'Divorce and remarriage in rural Malawi', *Demographic Research* S1: 175–206.

Rhine, K. (2009) 'Support groups, marriage, and the management of ambiguity among HIV-positive women in northern Nigeria', *Anthropological Quarterly* 82 (2): 369–400.

Ribohn, U. (2002) '"Human rights and the multiparty system have swallowed our traditions": conceiving women and culture in the new Malawi' in H. Englund (ed.), *A Democracy of Chameleons: politics and culture in the new Malawi*. Uppsala: Nordiska Afrikainstitutet.

Richards, A. I. (1934) 'Mother-right among the central Bantu' in E. E. Evans-Pritchard, R. Firth, B. Malinowski, and I. Schapera (eds), *Essays Presented to C. G. Seligman*. London: Kegan Paul, Trench, Trubner & Co.

(1939) *Land, Labour and Diet in Northern Rhodesia: an economic study of the Bemba tribe*. Oxford: Oxford University Press.

(1940) 'Bemba marriage and present economic conditions', *Rhodes Livingstone Institute Papers* 4: 1–123.

(1950) 'Some types of family structure amongst the central Bantu' in A. R. Radcliffe-Brown and D. Forde (eds), *African Systems of Kinship and Marriage*. London: Oxford University Press.

(1982 [1956]) *Chisungu: a girl's initiation ceremony among the Bemba of Zambia*. London: Routledge.

Rifkin, J. (1980) 'Toward a theory of law and patriarchy', *Harvard Women's Law Journal* 3: 83–95.

Rosaldo, M. Z. and L. Lamphere (eds) (1974) *Woman, Culture, and Society*. Stanford CA: Stanford University Press.

Rossi, B. (2016) 'Dependence, unfreedom and slavery in Africa: towards an integrated analysis', *Africa* 86 (3): 571–90.

Rowley, H. (1867) *The Story of the Universities Mission to Central Africa*. New York NY: Negro Universities Press.

Rubin, G. (2006 [1975]) 'The traffic in women: notes on the "political economy" of sex' in E. Lewin (ed.), *Feminist Anthropology: a reader* Oxford: Blackwell Publishing.

Rupp, L. J. (2008) 'Revisiting patriarchy', *Journal of Women's History* 20 (2): 136–40.

Saradamoni, K. (1999) *Matriliny Transformed: family, law and ideology in twentieth century Travancore.* London: Sage Publications and Alta Mira Press.

Saur, M., L. Semu, and S. H. Ndau (2005) *Nkhanza: listening to people's voices: a study of gender-based violence nkhanza in three districts of Malawi.* Zomba: Kachere Series.

Schärf, W., C. Banda, R. Rontsch, D. Kaunda, and R. Shapiro (2002) *Access to Justice for the Poor of Malawi? An appraisal of access to justice provided to the poor of Malawi by the lower subordinate courts and the customary justice forums.* Birmingham: Governance and Social Development Resource Centre for Department for International Development <www.gsdrc.org/go/display&type=Document&id=1249>, accessed 19 May 2011.

Schmidt, E. (1990) 'Negotiated spaces and contested terrain: men, women, and the law in colonial Zimbabwe, 1890–1939', *Journal of Southern African Studies* 16 (4): 622–48.

(1992) *Peasants, Traders, and Wives: Shona women in the history of Zimbabwe, 1870–1939.* London: James Currey.

Schneider, D. M. (1961) 'Introduction: the distinctive features of matrilineal descent groups' in D. M. Schneider and K. Gough (eds), *Matrilineal Kinship.* Berkeley CA: University of California Press.

Schneider, D. M. and K. Gough (eds) (1961) *Matrilineal Kinship.* Berkeley CA: University of California Press.

Schuster, I. M. G. (1979) *New Women of Lusaka.* Palo Alto CA: Mayfield Publishing.

Scott, D. C. (1892) *A Cyclopaedic Dictionary of the Mang'anja Language: spoken in British Central Africa.* Edinburgh: Printed for the Foreign Mission Committee of the Church of Scotland.

Scottish Government (2012) 'Aid effort to tackle female poverty'. Press release, 13 May. Edinburgh: Scottish Government <www.scotland.gov.uk/News/Releases/2012/05/Malawi-funding13052012>, accessed 13 June 2012.

Scully, P. (2011) 'Gender, history, and human rights' in D. L. Hodgson (ed.), *Gender and Culture at the Limit of Rights.* Philadelphia PA: University of Pennsylvania Press.

Sekeleza, C. (2009) '"My husband mutilated my genitals"', *The Nation,* 17 July.

Semu, P. (2000) 'Mad man said behind Chiradzulu murders', *The Nation,* 13 March.

Shadle, B. L. (1999) '"Changing traditions to meet current altering conditions": customary law, African courts and the rejection of codification in Kenya, 1930–60', *Journal of African History* 40 (3): 411–31.

(2003) 'Bridewealth and female consent: marriage disputes in African courts, Gusiiland, Kenya', *Journal of African History* 44 (2): 241–62.

Simpson, A. (2009) *Boys to Men in the Shadow of AIDS: masculinities and HIV risk in Zambia.* Basingstoke: Palgrave Macmillan.

Singerman, D. (2007) 'The economic imperatives of marriage: emerging practices and identities among youth in the Middle East'. Middle East Youth Initiative Working Paper. Washington DC: Wolfensohn Center for Development and Dubai School of Government.

Smith, D. J. (2009) 'Managing men, marriage, and modern love: women's perspectives on intimacy and male infidelity in southeastern Nigeria' in J. Cole and L. M. Thomas (eds), *Love in Africa.* Chicago IL: University of Chicago Press.

Smith, P. (2010) 'Feminist jurisprudence' in D. Patterson (ed.), *A Companion to Philosophy of Law and Legal Theory*. Oxford: Wiley-Blackwell.

Sommers, M. (2012) *Stuck: Rwandan youth and the struggle for adulthood*. Athens GA: University of Georgia Press.

Sonani, B. (2010) 'Muslims cautions Malawi on polygamy', *The Nation*, 30 May <www.mwnation.com/index.php?option=com_content&view=article&id=137:muslims-cautions-malawi-on-polygamy&catid=119:national-news&Itemid=125>, accessed 24 June 2011.

(2011) 'Govt to create local courts', *The Nation*, 20 January <www.nationmw.net/index.php?option=com_content&view=article&id=13065:govt-to-create-local-courts&catid=1:national-news&Itemid=3>, accessed 17 June 2011.

Spivak, G. C. (1993 [1988]) 'Can the subaltern speak?' in P. Williams and L. Chrisman (eds), *Colonial Discourse and Post-colonial Theory: a reader*. Hemel Hempstead: Harvester Wheatsheaf.

Strathern, M. (1987) 'An awkward relationship: the case of feminism and anthropology', *Signs* 12 (2): 276–92.

(2004) 'Losing (out on) intellectual resources' in A. Pottage and M. Mundy (eds), *Law, Anthropology, and the Constitution of the Social: making persons and things*. Cambridge: Cambridge University Press.

(2005) 'Resistance, refusal and global moralities', *Australian Feminist Studies* 20 (47): 181–93.

(2016) *Before and After Gender: sexual mythologies of everyday life*. Chicago IL: Hau Books.

Sudarkasa, N. (2005 [1986]) 'The "status of women" in indigenous African societies' in A. Cornwall (ed.), *Readings in Gender in Africa*. Oxford: James Currey.

Talle, A. (1998) 'Sex for leisure: modernity among female bar workers in Tanzania' in S. Abram and J. Waldren (eds), *Anthropological Perspectives on Local Development: knowledge and sentiment in conflict*. London: Routledge.

Tamale, S. (2005) 'Eroticism, sensuality and "women's secrets" among the Baganda: a critical analysis', *Feminist Africa* 5: 9–36.

(2008) 'The right to culture and the culture of rights: a critical perspective on women's sexual rights in Africa', *Feminist Legal Studies* 16: 47–69.

(ed.) (2011) *African Sexualities: a reader*. Oxford: Pambazuka Press.

Tamanaha, B. Z. (1993) 'The folly of the "social scientific" concept of legal pluralism', *Journal of Law and Society* 20 (2): 192–217.

(2008) 'Understanding legal pluralism: past to present, local to global', *Sydney Law Review* 30: 375–411.

Tayanjah-Phiri, F. (2009) 'Man burns wife', *Daily Times*, 22 July.

The Global Fund (2011) 'Country grant portfolio, Malawi'. Geneva: The Global Fund to Fight AIDS, Tuberculosis and Malaria <http://portfolio.theglobalfund.org/Country/Index/MLW?lang=en>, accessed 17 January 2011.

Thomas, L. M. and J. Cole (2009) 'Introduction: thinking through love in Africa' in J. Cole and L. M. Thomas (eds), *Love in Africa*. Chicago IL: University of Chicago Press.

Thornberry, E. (2010) 'Sex, violence, and family in South Africa's Eastern Cape' in E. Burrill, R. Roberts, and E. Thornberry (eds), *Domestic Violence and the Law in Colonial and Postcolonial Africa*. Athens OH: Ohio University Press.

UNDP (2014) 'Human development statistical tables'. New York NY: United Nations Development Programme (UNDP) <http://hdr.undp.org/sites/default/files/hdr14_statisticaltables.xls>, accessed 10 October 2014.

UNICEF (n.d.a) 'Photo essay: victim support units'. New York NY: UNICEF <www.unicef.org/malawi/7044.html>, accessed 13 June 2012.

(n.d.b) 'The situation of women and children'. New York NY: UNICEF <www.unicef.org/malawi/children.html>, accessed 13 June 2012.

United Nations (2010) *Rethinking Poverty: report on the world social situation 2010*. New York NY: United Nations <www.un.org/esa/socdev/rwss/docs/2010/fullreport.pdf>, accessed 4 December 2014.

Vail, L. (1975) 'The making of an imperial slum: Nyasaland and its railways, 1895–1935', *Journal of African History* 16 (1): 89–112.

(1984) 'Peasants migrants and plantations: a study of the growth of Malawi's economy', *Journal of Social Science (University of Malawi)* 11: 1–36.

Vail, L. and L. White (1991) 'Tribalism in the political history of Malawi' in L. White (ed.), *The Creation of Tribalism in Southern Africa*. Berkeley CA: University of California Press.

van Dijk, R. (2014) 'Diasporic romance: marriage, consumerism and Ghanaian experiences in Botswana'. Seminar, Centre of African Studies, University of Cambridge.

Vaughan, M. (1983) 'Which family? Problems in the reconstruction of the history of the family as an economic and cultural unit', *Journal of African History* 24 (2): 275–83.

(1985) 'Household units and historical process in southern Malawi', *Review of African Political Economy* 34: 35–45.

(1987) *The Story of an African Famine: gender and famine in twentieth-century Malawi*. Cambridge: Cambridge University Press.

Venkatesan, S., J. Edwards, R. Willerslev, E. Povinelli, and P. Mody (2011) 'The anthropological fixation with reciprocity leaves no room for love: 2009 meeting of the Group for Debates in Anthropological Theory', *Critique of Anthropology* 31 (3): 210–50.

Walker, C. (1991) 'Women and gender in Southern Africa to 1945: an overview' in C. Walker (ed.), *Women and Gender in Southern Africa to 1945*. Oxford: James Currey.

Werbner, P. (2014) '"The duty to act fairly": ethics, legal anthropology, and labor justice in the Manual Workers Union of Botswana', *Comparative Studies in Society and History* 56 (2): 479–507.

White, L. (1987) *Magomero: portrait of an African village*. Cambridge: Cambridge University Press.

Whyte, S. R. (2005) 'Going home? Belonging and burial in the era of AIDS', *Africa* 75 (2): 154–72.

Wilson, R. A. (2000) 'Reconciliation and revenge in post-apartheid South Africa: rethinking legal pluralism and human rights', *Current Anthropology* 41 (1): 75–98.

(2001) *The Politics of Truth and Reconciliation in South Africa: legitimizing the post-apartheid state*. Cambridge: Cambridge University Press.

(2007) 'Tyrannosaurus lex: the anthropology of human rights and transnational law' in M. Goodale and S. E. Merry (eds), *The Practice of Human Rights: tracking law between the global and the local*. Cambridge: Cambridge University Press.

Winchester, M. S., J. W. McGrath, D. Kaawa-Mafigiri, F. Namutiibwa, G. Ssendegye, A. Nalwoga, E. Kyarikunda, J. Birungi, S. Kisakye, N. Ayebazibwe, E. J. Walakira, and C. Rwabukwali (2016) 'Routines, hope, and antiretroviral treatment among men and women in Uganda', *Medical Anthropology Quarterly* 31 (2): 237–56.

WLSA (2000) *In Search of Justice: women and the administration of justice in Malawi*. Blantyre: Dzuka Publishing Company for Women and Law in Southern Africa Research and Educational Trust (WLSA) Malawi.

World Bank (2007) *Malawi. Poverty and vulnerability assessment: investing in our future: full report*. Washington DC: World Bank <http://documents .worldbank.org/curated/en/645221468272375497/Full-Report>, accessed 4 December 2014.

    (2014) 'World development indicators: poverty rates at international poverty lines'. Washington DC: World Bank <http://wdi.worldbank.org/table/2.8>, accessed 3 December 2014.

Yang, L., A. Kleinman, B. Link, J. Phelan, S. Lee, and B. Good. (2007) 'Culture and stigma: adding moral experience to stigma theory', *Social Science and Medicine* 64 (7): 1524–35.

Yngvesson, B. (1988) 'Making law at the doorway: the clerk, the court, and the construction of community in a New England town', *Law and Society Review* 22 (3): 409–48.

Young, A. E. (2010) 'Irreconcilable differences? Shari'ah, human rights, and family code reform in contemporary Morocco' in K. M. Clarke and M. Goodale (eds), *Mirrors of Justice: law and power in the post-Cold War era*. Cambridge: Cambridge University Press.

Zelizer, V. A. (2005) *The Purchase of Intimacy*. Princeton NJ: Princeton University Press.

Zigon, J. (2007) 'Moral breakdown and the ethical demand: a theoretical framework for an anthropology of moralities', *Anthropological Theory* 7 (2): 131–50.

    (2013) 'On love: remaking moral subjectivity in postrehabilitation Russia', *American Ethnologist* 40 (1): 201–15.

Zulu, E. M. (1996) 'Social and cultural factors affecting reproductive behavior in Malawi'. PhD thesis, University of Pennsylvania.

Index

Titles in the series